THE
WINNING
KEYS

Unlocking Kingdom Results from the Inside-Out

GARETH MORGAN

THE
WINNiNG
KEYS

Unlocking Kingdom Results from the Inside-Out

The Christians guide to *The Winning Conversation*

All bible references are NIV unless otherwise stated:

NIV New International Version (NIV)
Holy Bible, New International Version®, NIV® Copyright ©1973, 1978, 1984, 2011 by Biblica, Inc.®

AMP Amplified Bible (AMP)
Copyright © 2015 by The Lockman Foundation, La Habra, CA 90631.

NLT New Living Translation (NLT)
Holy Bible. New Living Translation copyright© 1996, 2004, 2007, 2013 by Tyndale House Foundation. Carol Stream, Illinois 60188.

NKJV New King James Version (NKJV)
Scriptures taken from the New King James Version®. Copyright © 1982 by Thomas Nelson.

KJV King James Version (KJV)
by Public Domain

ESV English Standard Version (ESV)
The Holy Bible, English Standard Version Copyright © 2001 by Crossway Bibles, a publishing ministry of Good News Publishers.

MESSAGE The Message (MSG)
Copyright © 1993, 1994, 1995, 1996, 2000, 2001, 2002 by Eugene H. Peterson

NASB New American Standard Bible (NASB)
Copyright © 1960, 1962, 1963, 1968, 1971, 1972, 1973, 1975, 1977, 1995 by The Lockman Foundation

Living Bible (TLB)
The Living Bible copyright © 1971 by Tyndale House Foundation. Tyndale House Publishers Inc., Carol Stream, Illinois 60188.

The Winning Keys
Unlocking Kingdom Results from the Inside-Out
The Christian's guide to The Winning Conversation

Copyright © 2016 Gareth Morgan / Personal Revolution Ltd.

Published using KWS services: www.kingdomwritingsolutions.org

No part of this book shall be reproduced or transmitted in any form or by any means, electronic or mechanical, including photocopying, recording, or by any information retrieval system without written permission from the publisher. All photographs are from the authors private collection.

ISBN: 978-1530230440

Contents

Introduction to the guide 09
A Parable...15

Day 1: The Winning Order 45
Day 2: The Winning Circles 47
Day 3: The Winning You 50

Section 1: The Winning Purpose—I value my purpose........55
Understanding how to unlock your winning purpose

Day 4: The Winning Legacy..55
Day 5: The Winning Goal 58

Section 2: The Winning Conversation—I value my self.......63
Understanding how to unlock your winning self

Day 6: The Winning Conversation...63
Day 7: The Winning Voices in the Boardroom 65
Day 8: The Conversation that Shapes my Identity 68
Day 9: The Winning Mood on the Office Floor 72
Day 10: Awareness of the Script that Forms the Conversation 76
Day 11: The Winning Language 81
Day 12: The Winning Mindsets in the Meeting Room 85
Day 13: The Winning Determination....................................89
Day 14: The Winning Behaviour in the Assembly Room 94

Section 3: The Winning Team—I value people 101
Understanding how to unlock your winning relationships

Day 15: The Winning People in my Life 101
Day 16: The Winning People around my Purpose 105
Day 17: The Winning Evaluation 110
Day 18: The Winning Accountability................................... 117

The Conversation that makes you MORE

Section 4: MORE Prominent 123

Day 19: The Winning Conversation makes you MORE Prominent 123
Day 20: The Winning Voice of Devotion 128
Day 21: The Winning Mood of Expectation... 135
Day 22: The Winning Mindset of Determination................................ 138
Day 23: The Winning Behaviour of Commitment 144
Day 24: The Winning Evaluation 151
Day 25: The Winning Accountability—*Ace Life*................................. 156

Section 5: MORE Resilient.. 161

Day 26: The Winning Conversation makes you MORE Resilient...... 161
Day 27: The Winning Voice of Passion 165
Day 28: The Winning Mood of Optimism 173
Day 29: The Winning Mindset of Perseverance................................... 177
Day 30: The Winning Behaviour to Complete 184
Day 31: The Winning Evaluation 189
Day 32: The Winning Accountability—*Stir Life*................................. 194

Section 6: MORE Memorable 199

Day 33: The Winning Conversation makes you MORE Memorable... 199
Day 34: The Winning Voice of Relevance... 204
Day 35: The Winning Mood of Helpfulness... 211
Day 36: The Winning Mindset of Sincerity 215
Day 37: The Winning Behaviour to Contribute 221
Day 38: The Winning Evaluation 226
Day 39: The Winning Accountability—*Build your Platform*............. 231

Section 7: MORE Influential... 235

Day 40: The Winning Conversation makes you MORE influential 235
Day 41: The Winning Voice of Inclusiveness....................................... 239
Day 42: The Winning Mood of Curiosity 247
Day 43: The Winning Mindset of Confidence..................................... 250
Day 44: The Winning Behaviour to Connect 257
Day 45: The Winning Evaluation 260

Day 46: The Winning Accountability—*Become an Answer*.................266

Section 8: MORE Expansive...271

Day 47: The Winning Conversation makes you MORE Expansive... 271
Day 48: The Winning Voice of Creativity 276
Day 49: The Winning Mood of Enthusiasm 286
Day 50: The Winning Mindset of Progress..290
Day 51: The Winning Behaviour to Construct......................................298
Day 52: The Winning Evaluation 303
Day 53: The Winning Accountability—*Multiply Results*.....................308

Section 9: MORE Valuable 313

Day 54: The Winning Conversation makes you MORE Valuable 313
Day 55: The Winning Voice of Excellence 318
Day 56: The Winning Mood of Gratitude..327
Day 57: The Winning Mindset of Diligence 332
Day 58: The Winning Choices to Compete 339
Day 59: The Winning Evaluation 343
Day 60: The Winning Accountability—*Uncommon Care*...................347

Section 10: The Winning Momentum..353

Day 61: The Winning Gears 1..353
Day 62: The Winning Gears 2..357
Day 63: The Winning Awareness 1 363
Day 64: The Winning Awareness 2 365
Day 65: Momentum Killers and Builders 368
Day 66: The Enjoyment of Winning...377

Introduction

Do you have an ache inside – a deep longing that there must be MORE to your life than what you are experiencing right now? Do you hit those moments of frustration when your actions fall short of your best intentions and wonder if you can ever get past the point to which you keep returning? This is a very common experience yet so many people feel as if they cannot talk about or even admit to having such feelings. As a Christian I knew that I had been made a new creation and yet my experience felt old and predictable. I was frustrated because my life felt at odds with the new life I believed I should be experiencing in Christ Jesus. I decided to take this frustration and focus it on finding the key to unlock the new life Christ had for me and this book is a result of this ongoing process.

As believers we suppress these feelings for fear of how other Christians will perceive us. Religion can create a pressure to hide our failings and present ourselves as doing better than we really are. We project an 'all togetherness' that not only avoids the key questions and issues but also makes our lives and the Church highly irrelevant to the world around us.

We believe the lie that it is a weakness to be open about these struggles because vulnerability could be interpreted as failure, or worse still unbelief. Our churches unknowingly create a success ladder that promotes those who appear to have it 'all together' and avoids talking about the real issues that build a strong life. Thus we feel we have to perpetuate living a lie, especially if we want to be seen worthy of increased responsibility.

So how do we break the cycle of frustration? Jesus has already given us the winning key. It's called *discipleship*.

The distinct lack of discipleship is the missing key designed to unlock the potential inside us.

The way to unlock your potential and your purpose is to be discipled by someone and to disciple others.

I believe the best 21st century term to describe discipleship is coaching.

In this book I want us to face and pinpoint this problem together but I also want us to see the potential that lies behind the problem.

I believe that inside every person there is a God-given desire to win in life - a longing to make MORE of life and to connect with something bigger than ourselves. The key to unlocking the MORE is what I call a *discipleship conversation*.

There is treasure deep within us but this is only accessed when we are coached into hosting the right kind of conversations.

So, I want to start a conversation with you:

A conversation designed to heighten your awareness of the conversation you have with yourself and how our conversation with God needs to shape this.

A conversation that acts as a catalyst to help you have life-changing conversations with other people.

There is a proverb in the Bible that has become the driving force for everything I do: *The purposes of a man's heart are like deep waters, but a man of understanding draws them out* (Proverbs 20:5).

In the pages that follow I want to dive with you into the deep waters of your created 'being' to discover the purposes and potential that should be shaping your 'doing.' As we explore the deep ocean trenches of your life we will not only discover the astonishing possibilities that are tied into your potential but also some of the toxic dump from your negative life experiences that are poisoning the waters and preventing your desires from growing into realities.

INTRODUCTION

I pray that as I direct a strong beam of light onto your life that alongside the guidance of the chief coach, the Holy Spirit, you can take a good honest look at what is really happening in you.

I want to connect to the God-inspired aspiration inside you that wants to win in life (Phil 3:14). That aspiration may be like a strong flame that just needs more fuel or it may be a dying ember that needs fanning into life. Whatever the case, this conversation will challenge you to remove the beliefs that are extinguishing the fire within and reinforce the beliefs that fuel an inner inferno (2 Timothy 1:6).

Ephesians 3:20 says: *He is able to do immeasurably more than all we can ask or imagine according to His Spirit that is at work in me.*

When you make Jesus the leader of your life, He makes His home in you and you become part of His Kingdom strategy for heaven to impact earth (Matthew 6:10). He has a specific assignment for your life; it is the reason He put you on this planet today, not a 100 years earlier, or later.

My task is to be a coach that asks the questions that will lead to clarity on the WHY of your life. My task is to help you take control of the winning keys that will unlock the Kingdom results that God has lined up for you.

What are the winning keys?

In Matthew 16:19 Jesus said to Peter, *I will give you the keys of the Kingdom of heaven; whatever you bind on earth will be bound in heaven, and whatever you loose on earth will be loosed in heaven.*

It is my belief that these keys speak of authority - an authority Peter would demonstrate on the Day of Pentecost (Acts 2.)

Today we have winning keys as well. These keys are the principles in God's Word alongside the power of the Holy Spirit who works and partners with us. Together these make up our authority.

To build a strong 'rock like' life as described by Jesus in Matthew 16:18, we need to know and use these keys.

The Winning Keys is a Christian's guide to my first book *The Winning Conversation.* The Winning Conversation is a book designed for the mainstream, designed to coach the potential out of all people, whether Christian or not. *The Winning Keys* provides the Biblical source for what I wrote there.

While *The Winning Keys* can be read on its own, reading it alongside T*he Winning Conversation* helps us to understand how the principles of the Bible can be communicated in a day-to-day coaching context in today's world. I believe the future of the Church lies in the untapped potential of a 21st century understanding of discipleship.

If a disciple is a coach and we are all called to make disciples, then we should all be asking the question 'What coaching opportunities are there for me to outwork my calling to coach for Christ?'

The Winning Keys follows the same framework as *The Winning Conversation.* It will challenge you to keep your conversation going with a community of like-minded believers who will cheer you on towards the life God has for you.

To do this, I will help you to establish three building blocks in your life:

i) The Winning Conversation

This is about creating self-awareness through prayer and building an impenetrable self-belief through the principles of the Bible.

ii) The Winning Goal

This will be your life map designed to help you establish clear personal goals and a means to staying on course.

iii) The Winning Team

This is the group of like-minded believers to which you need to be accountable if you are going to remain committed to your goals.

So then, how should you read this book?

This book works best when read as part of our daily devotions

INTRODUCTION

with God. Each chapter is designed to take approximately 20 minutes each day over the course of 66 days. Each chapter will heighten your awareness of the Bible's power to shape the internal conversation that is shaping your life.

As you read I am going to encourage you to create your own immersive experience - one essential for bringing lasting change.

You can also connect into our online conversation taking place throughout social media. Head to www.garethmorgan.tv and get involved.

This book will revolutionise your discipleship/coaching journey. It will lead to unprecedented opportunity and conversations with people.

I will begin with a parable that will introduce you to the framework of our conversation…

A Parable

LIFE Incorporated is a long established business running in New York. For over 25 years they have been a market leader in producing lifestyle goods that encourage people to live life in a positive and motivated way. They produce clothing, household items and even games that inspire people to look at their lives in a different way. They have steadily grown to the point where they now employ over 150 staff members. The owner, Jim Burns, has been the life and soul of the company and an ever-present figure. Five years ago, however, he decided to take more of a back seat.

Jim had a very clear goal for *LIFE Inc*. He wanted to produce products that inspired people to become MORE in their world: MORE

i) Valuable
ii) Prominent
iii) Resilient
iv) Influential
v) Memorable
vi) Expansive

He empowered six directors to be his voice and manage the business.

However, since Jim withdrew, the life that had once run through the company had slowly ebbed away. The business had fallen into the habitual pattern of simply creating what they knew worked. There was no proactive consideration for changes in the market or future events. The directors lacked the stimulus to rethink their approach or reflect how they could do things differently. There was a mood of complacency.

Jim knew that the business had the potential to do far more than it is was accomplishing but without much challenge from competitors and with the company still producing a healthy profit he put off doing anything. While they were still leading competitors in the lifestyle market there was no sense of urgency. It would take a crisis to create any need for a change.

The Crisis

A day finally came when the business had to sit up and take notice. This was not an internal but an external crisis. The American economy had taken a catastrophic hit. Being in the non-essential goods market, the lifestyle sector was severely affected as people stopped spending on what they really did not need. Sales dropped. Demand from wholesalers for lower prices increased. The Eastern markets became a real threat; they were producing similar products in quantities and at prices with which *LIFE Inc* could not compete.

Jim Burns relinquished his back seat to get to grips with the company that had been the love of his life. The more Jim focussed on the financial situation through dialogue with the directors the more he became frustrated. Jim knew that his current conversation with the directors was not producing any way forward so he looked outside the company for new input.

He came across a consultancy firm called *Quick Fix Solutions Inc* (QF). They were specialists at going into challenging work environments and quickly identifying WHAT the owner/leaders could do to rectify the situation. Jim called QF and arranged for a meeting. QF was in great demand as innumerable businesses were being negatively influenced by the downturn. QF seemed to be one of the few companies experiencing real growth at this challenging time.

Jim met with a consultant called Max Whyte. Max was a hugely positive character who immediately impressed him. His charisma and ability to put Jim at ease gave Jim a strong feeling that he had made the right call.

Max was shown around *LIFE Inc* and given access to the

company for a week to look into HOW it was working with its systems and methods, and into WHAT they were producing for the current market.

Max Whyte unpacked his findings in the boardroom:

'Jim, I've got some good news and some not so good news.' Max leaned forward in his chair. 'The good news is that I think you have the ingredients to get out of this hole. Taking the existing strengths but introducing new approaches and products I think in a short period of time we can get this ship turned around. The not so good news is that you are going to have to throw some significant money at new systems and approaches in order to reduce the time it takes to produce your goods. We need to develop additional product lines so that you can appeal to more people. If you can create a new way in HOW you approach the production line and WHAT it is that you produce then I really feel you can survive this storm and position yourself for a greater future.'

Jim sighed with relief. 'That doesn't seem so desperate to me. In fact it makes perfect sense. After all it's the speed of our competitors and their greater range of goods that is making us a poor competitor in the current market. How long do you think it will take before we see different results?'

'I would say three months from the moment the investment is actioned. I will have my team pull together my report and suggested options to bring a quick fix to this great company.'

Jim's reply was filled with a renewed sense of belief. 'I'll get the directors together and we'll implement your suggestions.'

Jim thanked Max and had his PA arrange an emergency director's meeting.

The Changes

Jim sat down with the six directors and went through the report. Each of the directors had an area to focus on and a budget to throw at the problems identified by QF. They agreed to meet weekly during the three months that Max estimated would be needed to get the company back to its former glory days. The directors were invigorated by the proposals as they loved systems and processes. The freshness that came with the new product lines captured everyone's imagination. They were ready to focus intensely on HOW and WHAT they were doing in order to produce different results.

Three months later a two-day review was held and each of the directors gave a report.

The facts and feedback were not what the group had been expecting. They certainly weren't what Jim had been hoping for. The reports contained feedback based on financials and market research. Some of the conclusions were devastating:

'The market no longer understands the identity of *LIFE Inc* and therefore the positioning of the brand is suffering.'

'The new products have had minimal exposure on the shelf and have failed to be noticed. Promotional products have failed to become memorable to the users and so failed to create brand loyalty.'

'The quality of the products has suffered with the increase in production. MORE busyness in the factory has created a fragile product.'

'The financials show a sharp drop in overall sales along with poor performance of new products. The company is diminishing.'

The accountant concluded that the overall worth of the company had now reduced and was in fact significantly in debt as it had tried to change its future by changing HOW it operated and WHAT it produced.

Jim had started the first day of the meetings with renewed hope but as the day of reporting and discussion came to a close he sat alone in the empty boardroom. With deep sadness he realised that what had once been a vibrant organisation was now on a life-support machine. With little remaining in the bank the situation seemed hopeless.

That night Jim had the worst night's sleep he could remember. His mind was full of decisions he had made being replayed over and over again. He spent much of the night pacing up and down the floorboards of his home while his wife lay asleep. He had come to the conclusion that if he could not come up with a solution on day two then there was only one option—to close down the company.

The Conversation

On day two the 150 staff members at *LIFE Inc* were blissfully unaware of the desperate state of the company. Some had been with the company since the very beginning. Others had come in at the junior apprentice level as part of their college course in order to acquire industry experience. The company had been committed to bringing younger people in, largely because they were a cost-efficient way of getting some of the more menial jobs done. Some of these had become key members of staff over the years.

One of them was a young man in his early 20's called Jo Styles. Jo had been taken on in a full-time capacity after he completed his college course. He had started to take on more responsibility once he had a fuller understanding of how the company operated. He was full of life and had aspirations to see *LIFE Inc* become all it could be. However, he had also recently become very frustrated as he realised that not everyone carried that same desire to grow and excel. He was committed to the future of the company so he hung in.

It was 10:30am on day two of the director's review meeting and along with his normal daily duties Jo was to be on hand that day to make sure the boardroom had food, drinks and a clean environment.

Jo went up to the door of the boardroom and listened in to see if now would be an appropriate time to go in. He knocked.

'Come in,' Jim said.

Jo walked into a very depressed atmosphere.

'Excuse me, gentlemen,' Jim said as he made his way to use the washroom.

As Jo was clearing away he could not help catch the various conversations at the boardroom table. He realised that something serious was happening. He heard two directors speak negatively about Jim. One of the directors just sat despondently, looking at his mobile phone. The other three seemed to be reeling off a list of excuses why they the company was performing badly. He heard them question the integrity of the managers, the commitment of the staff members, the methods implemented by the product teams and even the president of the US and his policies. Those at the helm of the company were consumed by negativity, blame and excuses.

Jo cleared up and started to make his way out, just as Jim came back in.

'Thank you...' Jim stuttered as he looked for Jo's ID on his lanyard.

'Jo, sir. My name is Jo Styles. It's a pleasure to meet you.' Jo shook Jim's hand.

'Well thank you, Jo.'

Jo suddenly realised he was staring so he closed the door. He then continued to sort out his trolley and as he did listen to Jim's voice through the keyhole.

'Well, gentlemen, all I have heard today and yesterday is tremendously disappointing. It really is. I was awake most of the night. This is a very dark situation for us as a company.'

Jo was leaning in heavily now.

'Time is of the essence and I am proposing that we call it a day. We only have two months worth of operating costs left and I think we need to action a process of winding this company up.'

Jo quickly pulled away in shock. As he returned the trolley to the kitchens his mind was awash with fear and a strange excitement. Jo was afraid that the company was about to be closed but excited about the dreams he had for change.

A PARABLE

At lunchtime Jo was pacing around the factory floor when he saw Jim Burns over at the vending machine fetching a bottle of cola.

'Sir, could I have a minute?'

Jim turned round. 'Ah, John isn't it?'

'No it's Jo, sir … Jo Styles.'

'Ah yes, Jo. What can I do for you?'

'I hope you don't mind but when I came in to clear up earlier I could sense that it was a difficult meeting you were having and well… to be totally honest I overheard that the company is on the brink of closure.'

Jim frowned.

Jo continued. 'I was wondering if I could make one observation before you decide to close the company or not.'

Jim looked quizzically at Jo before smiling. 'Come with me, Jo. You have two minutes before I have to go back.'

The two of them stepped into a vacant office.

'I'm all ears.'

Jo cleared his throat. 'I have been in the company for five years, I came through the graduate scheme and I have gotten to understand how things are around here. When I was in the boardroom this morning it was a light bulb moment. I understood what the source of the challenge is and therefore I believe we have the potential to find a solution.'

Jo took a deep breath. 'It is going to sound so simple but it's one word—'conversation'. The conversations in that boardroom are the problem. And if you, like me, want to see this company turned around then the conversations need to change. When you walked out of the room I could hear the comments. They were from people who did not have the right beliefs to produce the LIFE that this company needs. Those conversations set the environment for the factory floor, the managers, the team members and every member of staff. Those conversations are setting the culture and atmosphere. They are the unseen driving force behind the visible results. It is those conversations first of all that need to change if we are to be good enough for the market we are serving in the current economic climate.'

Jim stood in silence as Jo finished.

'Jo, I want you to meet me at 5pm in the boardroom,' he said after a pause. 'I think you and me need to carry on this conversation.'

Jo went to the board room at 5pm just as the other directors were leaving. He received strange looks from the men as they walked past him.

'Come in Jo,' Jim called out. 'Take a seat. Those were some pretty bold words you gave me earlier. It must have taken some courage.'

'I care about this company and my job,' Jo replied. 'I felt a personal responsibility to do something.'

'I could tell that. You are the first person to actually take responsibility for the situation. I am sick and tired of excuses. You stood out today because even though you don't have the position to do so, you spoke because you care. I was going to make the call to close the company today but your words have pulled me back from the brink for now.'

'I certainly would be willing to do whatever it takes,' Jo said.

'Good. Be here tomorrow at 10am and we will carry this on.'

The Coach

The next day Jo was at the boardroom for 10:00AM on the dot. He knocked on the door and entered. Jim was sat with a lady Jo did not recognise.

'Jo, let me introduce you to Creatia. Creatia is going to help us fully understand your observations.'

'Hi Jo, it's a pleasure to meet you,' said the very smart and efficient looking woman.

'I met Creatia last year,' Jim said. 'She has a great gift for helping to present peoples' ideas in a creative and meaningful way. I thought she would be the perfect person to help you over the next seven days to unpack your thoughts ready to present to me a week tomorrow. I do not want to put pressure on you, Jo, as this is a wild punt, a last gasp attempt to change what I fear may be an unchangeable and inevitable situation. But even at very least if it develops you and helps me to know we have exhausted all opportunities then it will be worth the time. I'll leave you to get on.'

With that Jim left the room.

Jo smiled. 'I can't quite believe I'm here to be honest.'

'Well Jo', said Creatia. 'Jim saw something in you yesterday. I am here to simply ask the right questions to unpack your thoughts.'

'Great,' said Jo. 'I'll be here at 9am to get started!'

The next day Jo was in the boardroom at ten to nine and in walked Creatia.

'Are you ready then?' she asked.

'Oh yes!'

'Well, the best place to start is by asking what we want the end goal to be,' Creatia said.

Jo took a deep breath. 'Jim wants to see us produce goods that are:

i) Valuable in the eyes of the customer
ii) Prominent in the market place
iii) Resilient in durability
iv) Influential in their reach within the world
v) Memorable to the user
vi) Expansive in terms of how they can develop and grow

In order to achieve this, the people in this factory need to have these same qualities. The more they display these qualities the more the products will carry the same level of distinction. I don't believe you can separate the product from the person. The fruit a tree produces comes from the root of the tree.'

'That makes sense,' Creatia said. 'How do you propose to do this?'

'I've been thinking about this and what is obvious to me and what that I do not think is necessarily obvious to everyone else is the tone and content of the conversations between company employees. The challenging economic climate has created a negative conversation in the workplace which has created a negative conversation in the employees. *LIFE Inc* may be our badge but Death Inc is what we have become. The company drains life rather than produces it! We need to create employees who hold positive and energising conversations that instil a winning mood in the workplace and then create a winning product and winning results for the company. If *LIFE Inc* works hard on producing winning employees then they will produce winning products.'

'I have heard it said,' Creatia interjected, 'that a person's output will never surpass their personal investment. So if we invest in the people, the products will increase in quality and quantity. This means we are looking for a change from employees working according to an OUTSIDE-IN conversation, defined by the environment, to an INSIDE-OUT one in which beliefs drive actions.'

'You've got it!' Jo exclaimed.

'We will pick this up tomorrow,' Creatia said. 'I'll leave you to use the rest of today to think this through.'

Creatia packed her belongings away and left while Jo sat down with blocks of sticky notes and began to jot down his ideas.

The Custodians

'Good morning, Jo,' Creatia said as she walked into the boardroom the next day.

'It is a good morning, isn't it?' Jo said, looking up from his notes.

Cretia looked surprised. 'It's good to hear that you are so positive. Do you have a breakthrough?'

'I believe I have. When I talked with Jim I said that the problem came down to the conversations taking place in this boardroom between the directors. They were negative and destructive. I realised that what was in them had filtered through the entire company. If we want to turn this company round the people we have directing from now on have to embody the qualities of the products. The people Jim brings in as directors going forwards have to be custodians of the qualities.'

'If they are going to produce winning results,' Creatia added, 'they will have to hold to winning beliefs!'

'Yes, that's right.'

With that Jo and Creatia began to discuss and write out the six values that were represented by the current board and then the six opposing values that that would unlock the winning results in the employees.

After hours researching and discussing they settled on the six that would create the right belief system in the boardroom, as well as the six that Jo had witnessed in what he now refers to as the 'losing conversation.'

LOSING Voices behind a LOSING conversation	WINNING Voices behind a WINNING conversation
Lethargy	Passion
Irrelevant	Relevant
Exclusive	Inclusive
Predictable	Creative
Mediocre	Excellent
Apathetic	Devotion

'If a winning conversation is to be developed in this company, then these are the voices that need to be heard in the boardroom,' Jo concluded.

'I like it!' Creatia smiled. 'I like it a lot! People can remember that and we could even put up pictures in the boardroom of the six voices that speak of WHO we are.'

Both left the boardroom on day two buzzing about what they called 'the winning conversation.'

The Clarity

Jo worked into the night. He jotted down some thoughts about the colleagues he had seen move on from *LIFE Inc.*

'WHY HAVE PEOPLE LEFT?

These were good people who never wanted to leave. However what was in them seemed to have become incompatible and at odds with what the company started to represent.

They were strong in self-belief and high in aspiration, focus and commitment. These attributes stood in stark contrast to those I encountered that day in the boardroom. The directors were low in self-belief, aspiration, focus and commitment. The directors have become consumed by a losing conversation that in turn was responsible for the results of the company.'

The next morning Creatia opened. 'Having a winning conversation in the boardroom of belief is one thing but this is just one room hidden in the centre of this building. How do we get the conversation to spread throughout the floors of the factory? We know that people often view their job as a means to an end and so will not have the same awareness and ownership the directors have. How do we get that awareness and ownership throughout the rest of the workforce in order for the winning conversation to really take effect?'

'That's a good point. As someone who has spent much of the last few years across most of the floors it always amazed me how much the mood of the people affects what we do and what we produce. Great mood equals great results. Negative mood equals negative results. We need to create a winning mood, a winning feeling.'

'I know what you mean,' said Creatia. 'It's like we all have these appetites that need feeding and when they are starved we cannot function effectively.'

'That is a great way of putting it. My Mum used to always say, "Jo, don't go out on an empty stomach" in the mornings. I would love to see managers bringing their teams together every morning or at the start of each shift and for a few minutes set the tone of the conversation.'

'For this to work,' Creatia interrupted, 'It is vital that the leaders in the boardroom spend time with the managers. In fact for the sake of our diagram let's call it the 'office floor of feelings.' The managers are first and foremost 'mood managers'. Each manager needs to actively cultivate a particular 'feeling.' So we need to identify and list these feelings and identify the role of the director/leader in the conversation.'

Creatia stepped up to the white board to act as scribe.

'Well,' Jo replied. 'During the remainder of yesterday I got the go ahead from Jim to observe the workforce and I listened closely to the conversation and observed the mood of the place. In those producing a good mood in the workplace I could see that their internal needs were being met. For instance those who felt like they had a voice in what was taking place carried a sense of ownership and they became more helpful to the managers and leaders. Likewise, those who felt unappreciated produced less than satisfactory results.'

'So the managers who created the right mood were those who understood the needs of the workers and worked hard to feed their internal appetites,' Creatia said.

'That's right. It's like when you are physically hungry you are more likely to be in a bad mood which in turn affects your results. And the same is true for our soul appetites. We need to discern what these appetites are.'

The two now worked out what appetites needed to be fed in order for the right mood to be created. They also identified the results of these appetites not being fed and the subsequent moods that would ensue.

THE WINNING KEYS

WINNING CONVERSATION	EXPANSIVE CONVERSATION	INFLUENTIAL CONVERSATION	VALUABLE CONVERSATION	RESILIENT CONVERSATION	MEMORABLE CONVERSATION	PROMINENT CONVERSATION
VALUE (Director)	Creative	Inclusive	Excellent	Passionate	Relevant	Devoted
APPETITE	Achievement	Acceptance	Appreciation	Assurance	Authority	Affection
MOOD (Manager)	Enthusiastic	Curious	Grateful	Optimistic	Helpful	Expectant

LOSING CONVERSATION	DIMINISHING CONVERSATION	INFERIOR CONVERSATION	WORTHLESS CONVERSATION	FRAGILE CONVERSATION	FORGETTABLE CONVERSATION	UNNOTICED CONVERSATION
VALUE (Director)	Predictable	Exclusive	Mediocre	Lethargic	Irrelevant	Apathetic
APPETITE	Underachieved	Un-Accepted	Unappreciated	Unassured	Unauthorised	Undervalued
MOOD (Manager)	Unenthusiastic	Uninterested	Ungrateful	Pessimistic	Unhelpful	Unexpectant

The next day Creatia was in the boardroom getting ready for the day ahead and looked at the clock. Jo was late.

A few minutes later Jo rushed in through the door. 'I'm so sorry, Creatia. I hate being late but something caught my attention at reception. I think it's going to help us.'

'What is it?'

'Last night I was unable to sleep because I was aware we needed a framework to communicate what we are unpacking. I remembered that at reception we have this large plan of this building containing instructions how people are to evacuate the building in case of a fire. The factory building is effectively made up of four oval layers. When I drew it on my notepad I realised we could communicate our findings in the form of the building layout.'

Jo proceeded to draw four concentric circles.

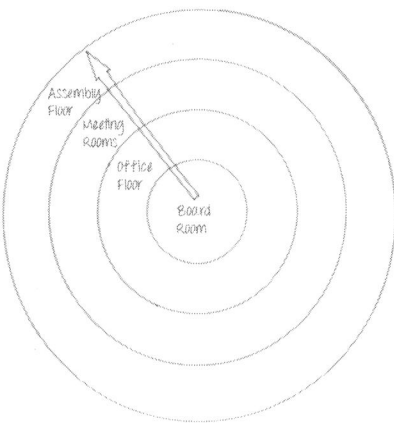

'The boardroom sits at the centre. We have agreed this is where the BELIEFS, VALUES, IDENTITY and the HEART of the company are. Then we have the next layer, the office floors of management which is where the FEELINGS, DESIRE, DRIVE and SOUL of the company are. I then saw a pattern forming. The next layer in the building is the meeting rooms where the managers meet team leaders to formulate plans and rotas—they are the MIND of operations. Anything that gets actioned is decided here. It's where the THOUGHTS are determined and from where the PRACTICE and the MIND of the company operate. Finally, you have the assembly floor where the products are made and leave the factory to go out to the customer.'

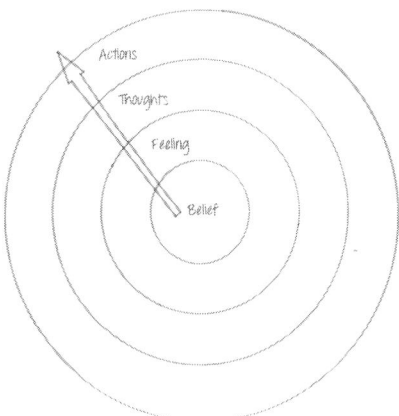

Jo put the pen down and turned to Creatia.

'So far we have looked at the winning beliefs from the boardroom and the winning mood on the office floors but now we have to understand how the conversation moves into the meeting rooms where the mindsets are established and the plans for action are in place. This is the HOW of the factory.'

'I can see the pattern,' Creatia commented. 'The problem is that because of weak leadership in the boardroom the external and poor results ultimately defined the belief of the company. The actions, thoughts, feelings and ultimately beliefs have been shaped from the OUTSIDE-IN.'

'Yes!' Jo cried. 'That is right, exactly right.'

'So how do we keep the conversation flowing through all layers of the building?' asked Creatia. 'What does the conversation need to sound like?'

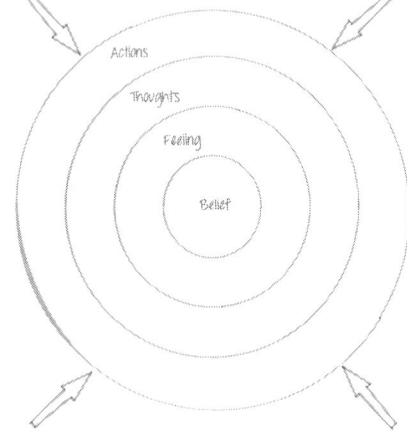

'The relationship between the manager's team room and the assembly floor is essential. The manager's team can come up with all the plans they want but if there's a disconnect in relationship between them and the assembly floor then the plans are useless, just as intention without action is meaningless. What use is a plan in the team room if it does not make it onto the assembly floor? The THINKING and FOCUS of the team room need to inform the CHOICES and COMMITMENT of the assembly room to activate the RESULTS we want to see.'

Jo quickly drew on the board the flow of conversation that needed to happen:

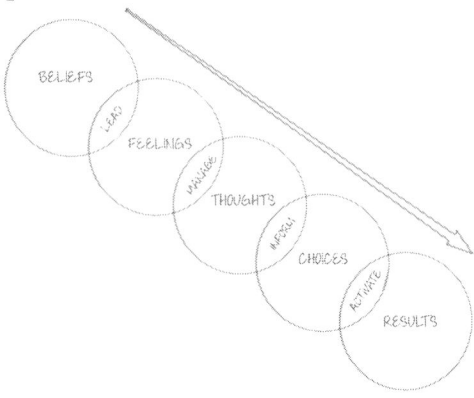

A PARABLE

'You can see from this diagram that if the directors effectively outline and embody the values and beliefs of the company working closely with the managers who will set the mood of the floor it is then down to the team leaders to develop 'a winning mindset' that becomes the mentality of the company. Each manager has a team leader and they come together in the meeting rooms to help them manage their area and key team members. Here they train their workers with the action plans for their area of the production process.

A mindset as you know is an accepted attitude. Our attitude influences our approach to everything we do; it informs our choices. We need six THOUGHTS and ATTITUDES that form the MINDSETS in order to progress a consistent conversation from the leader to the manager and from the manager to the team leader.'

'That looks like our job for today then,' said Creatia.

Both Creatia and Jo got to work for the rest of the day. They made a list of the mindsets that naturally flow from the winning conversation and then identified the losing mindsets of the losing conversation. By the end of the day they had clarity on their findings.

LOSING CONVERSATION	DIMINISHING CONVERSATION	INFERIOR CONVERSATION	WORTHLESS CONVERSATION	FRAGILE CONVERSATION	FORGETTABLE CONVERSATION	UNNOTICED CONVERSATION
BELIEF	Predictable	Exclusive	Mediocre	Lethargic	Irrelevant	Apathy
MOOD	Unenthusiastic	Uninterested	Ungrateful	Pessimistic	Unhelpful	Unexpectant
MINDSET	Maintenance	Unconfident	Careless	Unwilling	Insincere	Undetermined

WINNING CONVERSATION	EXPANSIVE CONVERSATION	INFLUENTIAL CONVERSATION	VALUABLE CONVERSATION	RESILIENT CONVERSATION	MEMORABLE CONVERSATION	PROMINENT CONVERSATION
BELIEF	Creativity	Inclusive	Excellence	Passion	Relevant	Devotion
MOOD	Enthusiastic	Curious	Grateful	Otimistic	Helpful	Expectant
MINDSET	Progressive	Confident	Diligent	Perseverance	Sincerity	Determinined

The Cause

The next morning Creatia was going to be late into the factory and this gave Jo some time to think through how the winning conversation was going to work its way from the team room of thoughts onto the assembly floor of action.

Jo often found it useful to journal his thoughts and ideas so he took out his computer and began to talk with himself.

'In my experience this has always been a real weakness in the factory. A real division has existed between the MEETING ROOM of team leaders and the ASSEMBLY FLOOR. Because of this many of the plans in the team room were never actioned. Sometimes you will get a team who are CAN DO people but then assembly workers who won't action the plan. This is like the MINDSET having a clear and positive intention but the BODY not putting the intention into action. What use is a positive mindset with no action? Therefore the only way to get these two to work together is to have a clear goal that is burning inside of them that produces the results we are looking for. I suggest goal setting, and accountability to those goals, should become part of the working relationship between these two areas. If there is agreement between them and shared ownership of the goal then the goal will be the unifying driver. The more I think about this the more I realise that this is same for my life. Many of my intentions have never made it through to action which has left me feeling frustrated because the belief, the feeling and thoughts have been there but for some reason the process breaks down more than it works.'

Time had flown by when Creatia came into the boardroom.

'Hey Jo, are you winning?'

'At first I wasn't but I am now.' Jo went on to explain what he had been journaling.

'That is so true in business and life,' said Creatia. 'Goal setting is powerful and when it is not present a team lacks passion. So what picture do you think could generate the life back into this company again?'

'We have to create conversations in our team meetings that encourage individuals to share their personal goals. We then have to find the link between the personal goal and the goal of the company. Our people need to see that this is more than a job; it is about their development as people and the unlocking of their potential.

This will influence every area of their lives!' Jo concluded. 'When we get a unified vision then this pulls us past any disagreement or disconnect that may exist because the CAUSE is bigger than a personality.'

'So if you can get agreement on a goal,' Creatia added, 'this galvanises each layer of *Life Inc* to cultivate the conversation that will lead to results in both the business and the employee's lives. So let's come up with the six behaviours that reveal a person hosting the winning conversation!'

The two now set out to list six actions for each corresponding conversation:

LOSING CONVERSATION	DIMINISHING CONVERSATION	INFERIOR CONVERSATION	WORTHLESS CONVERSATION	FRAGILE CONVERSATION	FORGETTABLE CONVERSATION	UNNOTICED CONVERSATION
BELIEF I AM	Predictable	Exclusive	Mediocre	Lethargic	Irrelevant	Apathy
MOOD I AM IN	Unenthusiastic	Uninterested	Ungrateful	Pessimistic	Unhelpful	Unexpectant
MINDSET I HAVE	Maintenance	Uncertain	Careless	Unwilling	Insincere	Undetermined
ACTION I WILL	Duplicate	Disconnect	Disregard	Drop out	Distance	Disengage

WINNING CONVERSATION	EXPANSIVE CONVERSATION	INFLUENTIAL CONVERSATION	VALUABLE CONVERSATION	RESILIENT CONVERSATION	MEMORABLE CONVERSATION	PROMINENT CONVERSATION
BELIEF I AM	Creative	Inclusive	Excellent	Passionate	Relevant	Devoted
MOOD I AM IN	Enthusiastic	Curious	Grateful	Optimistic	Helpful	Expectant
MINDSET I HAVE	Progressive	Confident	Diligent	Perseverance	Sincerity	Determined
ACTION I WILL	Construct	Connect	Compete	Complete	Contribute	Commit

The Convergence

There was one more part of the pattern that needed to be discovered. How was Jo going to present the conversations so that the results could be tracked and measured?

He then remembered something Creatia had said in conversation about the workers actually being the products that they are selling. It felt like an 'Aha' moment. Here they were making and distributing LIFE products but most did not have any interaction with the products or principles they were selling. They were selling a message they weren't embodying. What if Jo could create a programme through which the workers could use the products, learn the principles and relate the winning conversation of the factory to their own lives?

'Creatia, I've got something to show you.'

'Sounds intriguing,' replied Creatia. Jo explained the idea of the employees using the products they were creating.

'What if each employee at *Life Inc* developed a LIFE map? It would be based around goals they have for their lives beyond their employment. If we showed we were committed to their personal development, to the whole person, I know that the productivity levels in this place would more than double in due course.'

'So what does a LIFE map look like? And how would the worker interact with it?'

'I have something that I use to help me,' said Jo as he pulled out his journal. 'I start with the most important conversations I will have with people at the end of my life. I allow the ultimate conversations of my life to shape my immediate conversations. Then I ask myself what is the legacy that I want to leave, the one thing that I feel my life is about and I create different plot points and set goals.'

'That is really good,' said Creatia. 'I am guessing that is why you are in the position you are right now. You have worked on your personal development in every area and it has prepared you for promotion.'

'Maybe,' Jo blushed. 'But what excites me is the potential of every person in *Life Inc* to contribute to the success of the company by the company focussing on the success of the individual. In most areas of life people are looking to consume what others bring.'

'Which is outside-in,' added Creatia.

'Exactly, but what if we flipped that and said we were about unlocking the potential of our people first? I believe the results will be unrecognisable. Stress levels would be down, absenteeism reduced, job satisfaction up, targets smashed and this workplace would become the place where people want to work. I even think we would get people offering themselves as volunteers just to get in the door!'

'I am beginning to feel like I want to work for the company,' Creatia laughed.

Jo spent the rest of the day walking the pattern through with Creatia and they came up with the finished matrix for what *Life Inc* should look like and also a very clear picture of what Death Inc looks like.

The Completion

It was the final day before Jo had to report back. Creatia and Jo sat down for the final time.

'What a week it has been Jo. I feel like I've been working with you forever!'

Jo smiled. 'I've loved it, Creatia, and I can't thank you enough for the partnership. Now we've just got to complete the pattern today!'

'I was thinking about that,' said Creatia. 'Do you think formal conversations are going to be the only environment where you keep the winning conversation going? You know supervisions, appraisals etc?'

'That's a great question. I think we can organise conversations through our formal lines of communication and this is important. However, for this to really take effect it ultimately has to be organic. People prioritise what they prefer to talk about rather than what is prescribed. So we have to connect what we want to see more of to what people are already passionate about. If we can list the things that people truly value and help them connect the results of these areas to the conversations then they are more likely to take up the conversations organically and therefore feed the culture we want at *Life Inc*.'

Creatia and Jo now set about listing a number of ways the

winning conversation would affect a person's life:

The Winning Conversation…changes how you feel…shapes your experiences…unleashes your passion…builds a strong family life…unlocks your ideas…defeats your fears.

Jo summed up. 'The more we connect the winning conversation to what people value in life the more I believe we will cultivate natural conversations. So I suggest we demonstrate this through powerful imagery around the factory. I've also come up with a very simple way of keeping it in front of people using a dice.'

'Dice?'

Jo went on to unpack his ideas as they put the finishing touches to the presentation.

The Culmination

Jo spent a lot of time over the weekend diligently polishing up on his presentation. He woke up Monday morning early and prepped himself before heading into the factory. He arrived at the boardroom—unchartered territory only a week ago—a place which in the past week he had spent more time in than his own home.

As he walked in expecting to find Jim and the directors, he saw Jim, Creatia and five new faces.

Jim spoke. 'Jo let me introduce to you my friends Reeva, Dev, Ince, Paz and Xavier.'

Jo gasped.

'You may be wondering why the other directors are not here. Well, on the back of what you said to me last week I realised that my confusion and inability to see a way past the problem was in large part down to the people surrounding me in my conversations. I had to shut those conversations down and so asked the directors to step down. Over the past five days Creatia has been keeping me up to date with how you have been getting on and while she has not disclosed anything of your presentation, she was hugely impressed. I have been having conversations with my business friends who are here today potentially interested in investing and therefore becoming the new directors along with Creatia ... should your presentation stimulate enough interest.'

Jim now handed proceedings over to Jo.

'Thank you, ladies and gentlemen, for giving me the opportunity to share my thoughts and findings with you. Since joining *Life Inc* I have come to understand that our goal and privilege was to serve the wider public with a life-inspiring message that would aim to unlock the potential inside every person who bought into our product. Our messages essentially communicate 'you are a winner'. They inspire and promote that champion spirit. Our vision is that when people put on our clothing, hang up that inspirational message or are given one of our gifts that they are reminded WHO they are and WHAT they can become.'

Jo took a sip of water. 'That vision requires there to be a resilience in this factory greater than the financial crisis happening right now. If we say you are a winner and yet cultivate a losing environment then our product does not match our practice. I also believe it shows that our practice does not match our potential.'

Several of the audience smiled.

'With so much running through my mind over the last number of days I was struggling to have a framework through which I could communicate to you exactly what I feel is the problem and therefore the solution. However it was late on the second day of working on this that I looked at the staff notice board with our fire procedure and an outline drawing of this building, highlighting the exit points. The more I looked at the drawing of the building the more I realised that right in front of me was the framework. As I looked at the four layers to the building and the activity that takes place in the different areas I realised there was a pattern.'

Jo then drew four concentric circles on the white board.

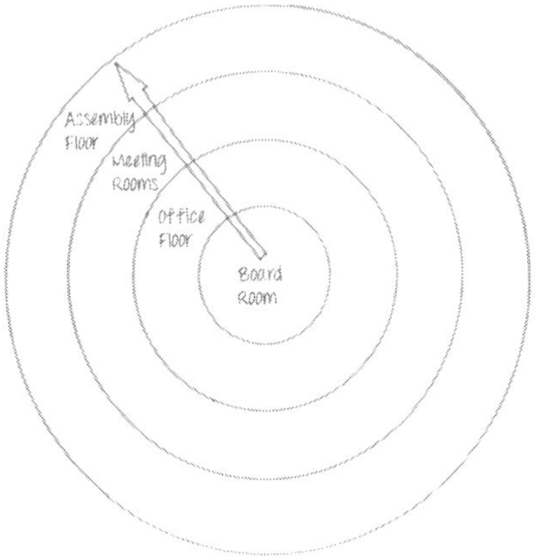
Assembly
Floor
Meeting
Rooms
Office
Floor
Board
Room

'Essentially the building is circular and has four areas of activity. There is the boardroom at the centre, the office floor, the managers' rooms and then assembly floor. Each of these spaces can be associated with a different action:

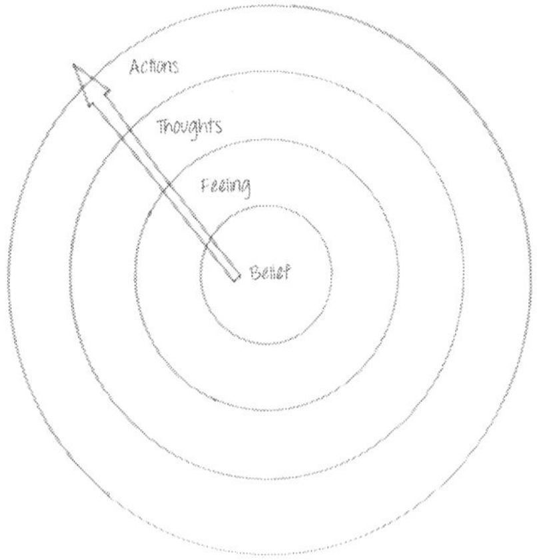
Actions
Thoughts
Feeling
Belief

Up to now it is my belief that the current climate has revealed that our current beliefs, drive, plans and actions are weaker than the external environment.

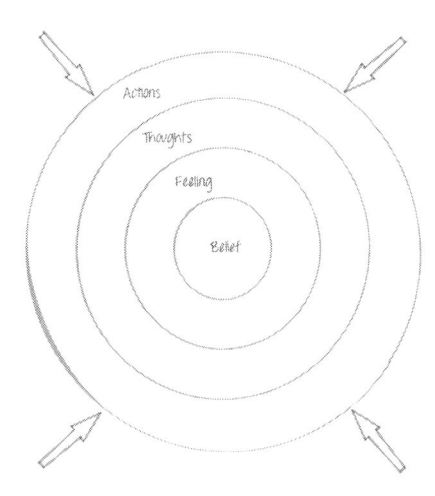

[Diagram: concentric circles labeled from outside to inside — Actions, Thoughts, Feeling, Belief — with arrows pointing inward from four corners.]

The conversations that have been voiced from this boardroom have indicated that this is essentially the case. Therefore the losing conversation we have been having has been the undercurrent to a winning life we are promoting. This duplicity has created an identity crisis. If we were called *Death Inc* it would better explain our reality.

Rather than creating products that are:

i) Valuable
ii) Prominent
iii) Resilient
iv) Influential
v) Memorable
vi) Expansive

Death Inc has created products that are:

i) Worthless
ii) Unnoticed
iii) Fragile
iv) Inferior
v) Forgettable
vi) Diminishing

While it was a natural reaction to bring in Quick Fix Solutions it was in fact the wrong decision.'

Jo had gone past the point of no return now.

'As a worker on the office floor during this three month period I witnessed time, energy and effort being poured into HOW we do things and WHAT we produced. However, this is like dealing with a dying tree by simply changing how it looks and the shape it takes. The source of the problem went deeper. It was in the WHO. This brings me to the boardroom. When you start from the boardroom you are starting with the root of the tree.'

Jo took another sip of water.

'As a worker who has experienced life on the various floors over the past five years I saw that I never had a direct conversation with any of the directors. My conversations were between me and my manager. I suddenly realised that the conversations quite literally flow from the central room that we are sat in now and make their way outward to the factory floor, then into the managers' development rooms. Conversations are POWERFUL! They shape our lives. The words we speak and the words we choose to listen to have impact.

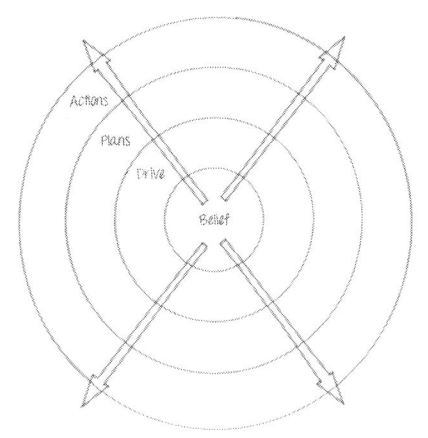

Therefore my presentation is based around the principle and framework that we do not want to be shaped by outside forces, what I would label an 'outside-in' pattern, but we want an 'inside-out' pattern. We want what is on the inside of this company to be the belief and driving force of our plans and actions. Therefore our product is not just WHAT we sell but it is a reflection of WHO we really are.

I want to present to you my plan called 'the winning conversation'.

Jo handed out notes and proceeded to tell the story of the seven day process of discovering and developing the WINNING CONVERSATION with Creatia.

'This concludes my presentation, ladies and gentlemen.'

The Consequences

There was a moment of silence. Then there was a round of applause led by Jim, who was smiling as he spoke.

'Jo, that was a profound presentation of what needs to happen in this organisation. As I explained to you earlier, I want and need the backing of these potential directors to turn this from what you have rightly called *Death Inc* back to *Life Inc*. While there's still lots of work to be done in applying what you have said I wonder if there are any questions from the group?'

Reeva put her hand up. 'Jo, what ideas do you have to start creating this 'winning conversation' as you call it?'

'The pattern of 'the winning conversation' is taught through creating an immersive experience. How did the previous regime, unintentionally, create the results they did? By hosting a constant conversation based upon beliefs that were self-focussed, self-serving and self-destructive. They immersed the culture of this company in that conversation. This led to people unconsciously behaving parallel to their beliefs. In order for us to establish a new culture there has to be a fresh immersion in the winning ethos through both organised and organic conversations.'

'Can you explain what those look like?' Reeva asked.

'I'll start with organized conversations. In every leader's and manager's team meeting I am encouraging them to use the 'winning dice.' Every game uses a dice and the dice is the key to winning. On each side of the dice there is a statement that communicates what we accept and what we reject, what we want to celebrate and what we will not tolerate. This helps to create a very clear distinction. It means that in every conversation there is a reference point that keeps a level of accountability amongst workers. Should you invest and become directors you will each own one of the conversations and in the manager you lead and the product development area you oversee you will guard and protect and proliferate that conversation.'

'And what about organic conversations?' Reeva asked.

'Creatia and I also discussed the importance of creating an immersive environment through ad hoc and unplanned conversations. We can celebrate winning stories of staff members who have made progress, sharing stories via our social media accounts.'

Jo started to show images on the projection screen in the boardroom.

'Images are powerful and if we can communicate that the winning conversation changes how you feel, shapes your experiences, unleashes your passion, builds a strong family life, unlocks your ideas and defeats your fears, this creates greater self-awareness and increases aspiration.'

'I like it, I really do,' Reeva said.

Jim turned to the group. 'There's lots to be done but what I want to know at this point is are you in? Will you invest the necessary time, effort and money to put *Life Inc* back on the map and release the potential of this company?'

A man called Ince raised his hand. 'I have been very happy with what I have heard but there is one condition to my investment?'

There was a pause.

'I will only invest if Jo accepts the job of becoming the CEO of *Life Inc.*'

All eyes moved to Jim and then swiftly to Jo.

Jim spoke first. 'I think that is absolutely the right call. Is everyone in agreement?'

Everyone except Jo nodded.

'Well Jo?'

'I am in!' Jo cried. 'If you as directors will accept your responsibility to guard the winning conversation then let's start having the right conversations and producing the right results.'

And with that a new era began.

Day 1: The Winning Order

Prize the Process:

Most people think of the word "process" as a season preparing them for some prize or other. In the Kingdom of God, however, the process is also the prize. This process involves gradually becoming more and more like Jesus. By making this our priority we unlock the desires of our hearts.

Jesus said in Matthew 6:33: *"Seek first His kingdom and His righteousness and all these things will be given to you as well."* The Kingdom of God calls us into a process in which Jesus comes to rule every aspect of our lives so that the glory of God can be released in and through us.

In his letters, the Apostle Paul is very honest about this internal process. He is one of the most influential figures in early Christianity and in the history of the Church. Without his letters, the New Testament would be far shorter and the Church far poorer. In Philippians 3:12-14 Paul outlines his priorities:

"Not that I have already obtained all this, or have already arrived at my goal, but I press on to take hold of that for which Christ Jesus took hold of me. Brothers and sisters, I do not consider myself yet to have taken hold of it. But one thing I do: Forgetting what is behind and straining toward what is ahead, I press on toward the goal to win the prize for which God has called me heavenward in Christ Jesus."

See how Paul prizes the <u>process</u>.

The prize Paul refers to is the process of becoming completely like Jesus. This is perfected when we pass from this life to heaven. However, the process actually starts the moment we choose to follow Jesus in this life. When we prize the eternal process that matters most, this process takes care of the earthly prizes that we need (Matthew 6:33).

The Losing Order:

When our lives are driven from the outside-in

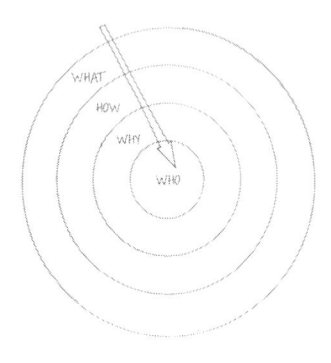

Outside-in living: *An individual's pursuit to prioritise making themselves feel good and look good by making the visible things of this world the source of satisfaction.*

When God created the earth He placed two trees at the centre (Genesis 2:9) - the Tree of the Knowledge of Good and Evil (Tree 1) and the Tree of Life (Tree 2). In verse 17 of Genesis 2 God warned Adam and Eve that to eat from Tree 1 would result in certain death. God's design was that they would have everything they needed to be prosperous in life if He were their source. Adam and Eve were drawn to the one thing they were not to have because it was pleasing to the eye (Genesis 3:6). Tree 1 - and by choosing to take from this tree they made a decision that God was not going to be their sole source. At this moment outside-in living was birthed; they began to try and satisfy an insatiable appetite from a source that could never fulfil them. This source looked good and made them feel good.

The Winning order:

When our lives are driven from the inside-out

Inside-out living: *An individual's pursuit to prioritise making God feel good and look good by making Him the source of our satisfaction.*

Unlocking our potential ultimately requires us to put Jesus Christ first in our lives. By centring our lives on Him, He becomes like the 'Tree of Life' (tree 2), a consistent source that feeds us from the inside-out. Jesus promises to meet our 'prize' needs when we position Him, 'the process', first and live our lives according to the correct order.

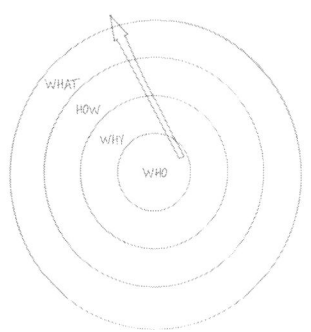

It is possible to have Jesus in our lives and yet put other people and things first. We might have all the right factors but in the wrong order.

Day 2: The Winning Circles

The Winning Circles:

The three winning circles are based upon the three elements from Matthew 22:37-40 where Jesus simplifies the whole of the Bible and God's will for our lives:

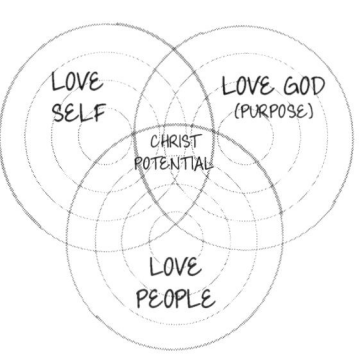

"*A teacher of the law asked Jesus which was the greatest commandment that had been given to them in the law. Jesus replied 'Love the Lord your God with all your heart and with all your soul and with all your mind.' This is the first and greatest commandment. And the second is like it: 'Love your neighbour as yourself. All the Law and the Prophets hang on these two commandments'* (Matthew 22 NIV)."

The three elements are:

i) Love God wholeheartedly
ii) Love people wholeheartedly
iii) Love people as you love yourself

Each of these is interlinked just like the three winning circles. For instance, our love for people is shaped by our ability to love ourselves. If our wholehearted love for God is genuine then this has to have an impact on the love we have for WHO we are.

i) Love God wholeheartedly

Firstly, our purpose is to love God. We love God by engaging our whole self in living a life that seeks to reflect Him, seeking to fulfil His plan for our lives. There is a reason He has put us on this planet at this time. Our love for God is directly linked to our pursuit of that purpose.

ii) Love people wholeheartedly

Secondly, Jesus commands us to

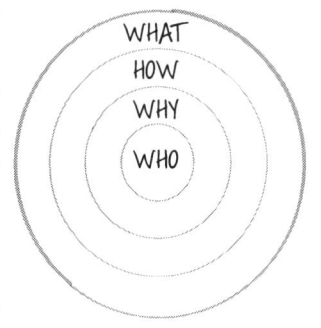

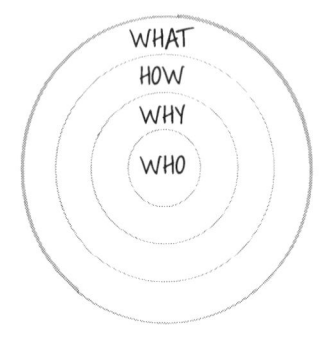

love others. While this is the second commandment Jesus gives it overlaps with the first. My love for God is demonstrated through my obedience to God which is connected to loving others as He loves them. God's original intention was to have a family with whom He could share his glory. He is still committed to that goal and therefore those who are obedient to him are part of outworking this intention.

iii) Love people as you love yourself

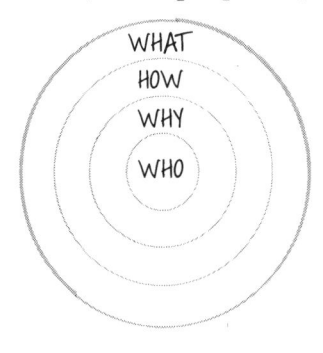

Thirdly, while there are only two commandments given we must not overlook the significance of the words that follow the second commandment: "Love your neighbour as *yourself*." When I do not love who I am I will struggle to love others. Therefore the third overlapping circle is 'self'. This is not about making the goal to love who I am. Rather, I love who I am so that I can love others.

From the Root to the Fruit

God's Word reveals our value. When we cultivate our belief system with the Word of God we create a rich environment to grow a significant life. The Word of God is His love letter to us and when we feed our beliefs on this we become like the tree mentioned by David in Psalm 1:1-3:

Blessed is the one...whose delight is in the law of the Lord, and who meditates on his law day and night. That person is like a tree planted by streams of water, which yields its fruit in season and whose leaf does not wither - whatever they do prospers.

When we ground our lives in the Word of God, we have a continual source of supply that feeds value to us so we can feed value to others.

The Concentric Circles

Jesus not only highlights what the greatest two commandments are but He also reveals how this involves the WHOLE person.

We are called to love God WHOLEheartedly, with all that we are. Jesus commanded His followers to love the Lord our God with all our heart, soul, mind and strength. This is a command to love from the inside-out.

Spirit - My Beliefs

Soul - My Feelings

Mind - My Thoughts

Body - My Actions

When our love is led by belief, we love from choice and not feeling.

Paul challenges us to love from the inside-out in Romans 12:9-10: *"Love from the centre of who you are; don't fake it"* (The Message).

If we try to love God, people or even ourselves from any other source than our spirit then our love will lack consistency. If we rely on a 'feeling', 'thought' or physical 'action' to stimulate our love then we will be inconsistent in showing it. However, God's love is based on His choice.

God is a principle-centred being. We know from John 3:16 that *"God so loved the world that He gave His one and only Son, that whoever believes in Him shall not perish but have eternal life."* This was not because we managed to create a 'feeling' in God, persuading Him through rational 'thought' that we deserved His love. Nor did we do anything through our 'actions' that could bring about such a response. It was a pure choice from WHO He is. He chose to love us and He chose to give everything with no guarantee that we would all respond to this act of self-sacrifice.

Conversation with God:

Father, I thank you that you chose to love out of WHO you are.

Today I pray that you will help me to do the same. Help me to love you wholeheartedly. Help me to love others selflessly. May I learn to love the person you have made me so that I may be a person of integrity, allowing my life to be a portal through which heaven comes to earth.

Day 3: The Winning You

My Results are my Responsibility

As Christians we believe that there are two key questions that will be asked of us when we stand before God on the Day of Judgment (2 Corinthians 5:10). Firstly, did we receive Jesus as our Lord and Saviour? Secondly, what did we do with what He entrusted to us? We will all one day have to give an account for what we have and the resources to which we have had access on earth (Romans 14:10-12; 1 Corinthians 3:11-15).

In the parable of the talents in Matthew 25:14-30, Jesus tells a story about a master who entrusts three servants with finances and instructs them to unlock the potential of it through investment. Two of them do so and double the return; they realise the potential of the money. However, the third gives excuses for his lack of activity and ultimately out of fear hides it in the ground. The potential is not realised and the master holds the servant to account for his lack of results.

When we are operating in the Kingdom of God we must avoid the blame-game and take responsibility for our choices and results.

Every Result Starts in an Unseen Place

We are spiritual beings first and foremost. God is Spirit and we are made in His image. We cannot see the spiritual dimension to life but we are aware that this drives everything that can be seen.

Hebrews 11:3: *"By faith we understand that the universe was formed at God's command, so that what is seen was not made out of what was visible."*

Faith is a belief that carries a command. Our belief shapes and creates our world. God's creative word was a command that brought what is seen out from the unseen. Any change that we seek to make in our world starts as faith and calls the seen from the unseen place.

The Creative Power of your Conversation

Our beliefs reside in our heart. Solomon who wrote Proverbs said, *"Above all else, guard your heart, for everything you do flows from it"* (Proverbs 4:23). The creative epicentre that drives our results is our belief system. Therefore any desire significantly to change the results that we see requires a deep excavation of our belief system. This is the reason for this book.

The Results of my Conversation

Jesus' first sermon about the Kingdom of God (the only full sermon we have of Jesus) is the Sermon on the Mount found in Matthew 5-7 and Luke 6.

He spoke this sermon to his disciples and followers. Both explicitly and implicitly we find the hallmarks of those who live the Kingdom life.

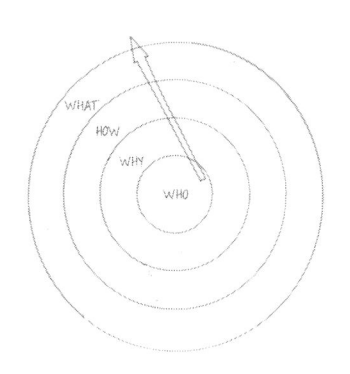

Kingdom people will become:

Valuable   - like salt (Matthew 5:13)
Prominent   - like a city on a hill (Matthew 5:14b)
Resilient   - like a house on a rock (Matthew 7:24)
Influential - like light to the world (Matthew 5:14a)
Memorable   - like good fruit (Luke 6:43-45)
Expansive   - like an unlimited potential/measure (Luke 6:38)

From Ordinary to Extraordinary

The apostle Paul helps us to understand one of the great paradoxes of the Kingdom of God - the way ordinary people can be the carriers of extraordinary riches. In 2 Corinthians 4:7-10 he writes:

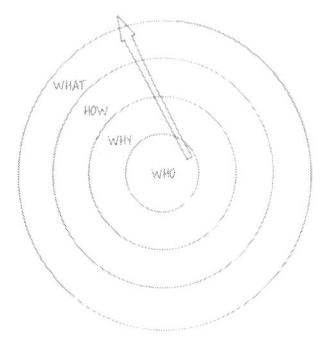

We have this treasure in jars of clay to show that this all-surpassing power is from God and not from us. We are hard pressed on every side, but not crushed; perplexed, but not in despair; persecuted, but not abandoned; struck down, but not destroyed. We always carry around in our body the death of Jesus, so that the life of Jesus may also be revealed in our body.

When a sculptor chips away at the stone this is the 'necessary pain' needed to unlock the beauty of the figure he imagines. So it is with us. God is actively chipping off my old identity in order for my new identity in Christ to shine through.

The Champion will be revealed in us when we endure the demands of a new expectation revealed by God's Word - the dream He has placed inside of us.

Revelation has great Internal Significance but very little Outward Significance … at First!

Jesus uses the analogy of mustard seed to speak about faith in Matthew 17:20: *"Truly I tell you, if you have faith as small as a mustard seed, you can say to this mountain, 'Move from here to there,' and it will move. Nothing will be impossible for you."*

The metaphor of the tiny seed highlights two things:

i) A belief is a thought that we drive deep inside us. It appears highly insignificant but shapes the landscape of the world in which we live.

ii) Like a seed, a belief needs to be watered over time in order for it to move from apparent 'insignificance' to being fully significant.

The most critical stage of transformation is the start because it can feel like nothing significant is ever going to come from our efforts. Take note of what the prophet Zechariah says in Zechariah 4:10: *"Who dares despise the day of small things?"*

Conversation with God:

Father, I thank you for the potential that you have invested in me. Help me to stay aware that your unseen power can shape the circumstances that I see. When I get impatient with my progress, help me to hold my faith in tension with patience. Help me to live as if the all-powerful creator God lives in me.

THE WINNING KEYS

Section 1: The Winning Purpose

Download your life map from 'thewinningconversation.com'

Day 4: The Winning Legacy

L.E.G.A.C.Y

Let Eternity Guide All the Choices You make

Our ultimate conversation with God should be shaping our immediate conversation with ourselves and others.

Am I building a life that is ultimately helping to point people to Him and to seeing them saved by Jesus Christ? Or am I building a self-serving life that is disguised as Christ-centred? Our ultimate conversation with God will reveal the truth so let that conversation shed light on our true motivations. That way we can shape up for eternity!

1 Corinthians 3:12-15 says:

"If anyone builds on this foundation using gold, silver, costly stones, wood, hay or straw, their work will be shown for what it is, because the Day will bring it to light. It will be revealed with fire, and the fire will test the quality of each person's work. If what has been built survives, the builder will receive a reward. If it is burned up, the builder will suffer loss but yet will be saved—even though only as one escaping through the flames."

Not only does my purpose involve fulfilling Christ's mission to see people connected back to the Father but it also serves to prepare us for life in eternity. In the Parable of the Talents (Matthew 25:14-30) the results achieved by the servants dictated the level of their promotion to greater responsibility. The eternal rewards God has for each of us differ and are correlated to how we deal with our earthly responsibilities. Start to build your eternal legacy now!

While we are to be fully present in the moment of opportunity, we are called to be big picture people who understand the WHY behind the choices that we make. This is why in 2 Corinthians 4 Paul says: *"We fix our eyes not on what is seen, but on what is unseen, since what is seen is temporary, but what is unseen is eternal."*

WHO - PEOPLE

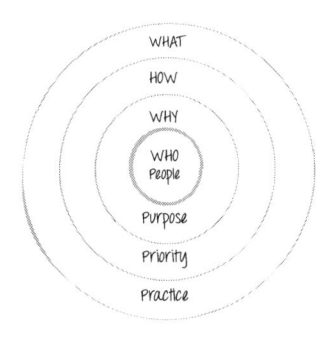

Our Kingdom mission is to make disciples of all nations (Matthew 28:19; Mark 16:15). God is not willing that any should perish. Our mission is therefore not about buildings, projects, businesses but people.

WHO are the people God has called us to reach? It starts first with our family, our friends and then the 'lost' people God puts on our hearts to reach. This is our cause. What kind of 'lost' person are we called to seek out and 'find'? (Luke 19:10)

Create Clarity through Tension

As people called to live by faith and not by sight (2 Corinthians 5:7), we must build our lives around a clear picture of what we want to see happen through our lives. Faith is the creative tension between what we see right now and the confidence and assurance of what cannot yet be seen. When this tension is taut we cause all our choices to follow our desired expectation.

Hebrews 11:1-2 says: *"Now faith is confidence in what we hope for and assurance about what we do not see. This is what the ancients were commended for."*

Our decisions need leading. The inside-out approach to decision-making comes from having clarity about the unseen so we can bring it into a 'seen' reality.

Without a Vision the Real You Dies

A vision of a preferred future establishes a much needed demand on our choices in the 'now'. Without this we do not have necessary restraints and we are in danger of making choices in the dark which will undoubtedly come back to bite us.

As Proverbs 29:18 says: *"Where there is no revelation, people cast off restraint; but blessed is the one who heeds wisdom's instruction."*

When our 'now' choices have no 'future' significance we are living in a 'hope'-less state. A human being without a daily hope is dying from the inside-out. Those who carry a burning hope for the future are growing from the inside-out regardless of what is happening to their physical state.

2 Corinthians 4:16 says: *"We do not lose heart. Though outwardly we are wasting away, yet inwardly we are being renewed day by day."*

View the Immediate through the Ultimate

WHY - PURPOSE

The writer to the Hebrews reveals that we are like every runner that has a race marked out for them - a race they are to complete and win. Every human being accordingly has a lane to run in.

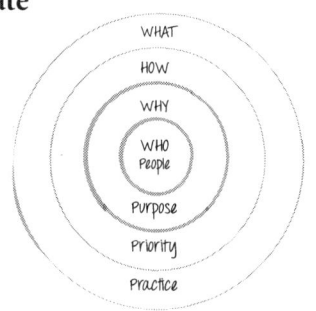

Hebrews 12:1 says: *"And let us run with perseverance the race marked out for us."*

The stories in the Bible help us to understand that our future purpose is directly linked to what we carry in the NOW.

When God revealed to Moses that he was to deliver the Israelites out of Egypt, Moses struggled to understand how he was to do this from his 'now' position. How did God get Moses over this obstacle?

In Exodus 4 God asks Moses, *'What is that in your hand?'* Here He establishes a principle: we have the seed of the future in our possession NOW. Answering the PLOT questions help us to discover 'what is in our hand?' (download the PLOT questions and your life map from www.thewinningconversation.com)

In an inspiring talk on TED, preacher Rick Warren speaks of how the staff represented Moses' income, influence and identity. The picture had a meaning. What is the picture that can start to bring clarity to our purpose?

Day 5: The Winning Goal
The ULTIMATE Priority - The NOT YET

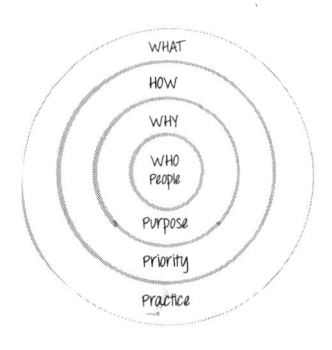

A definite plan creates the faith substance that pleases God and grants Him permission to unlock our future

As someone who lives inside-out, led by the Spirit, I choose to allow the NOT YET of what I believe God is ultimately going to do in and through me to determine my immediate priorities. While God is ultimately going to determine how our lives pan out, this does not mean we can or should abdicate the essential responsibility of good planning. Without such planning we will never unlock the Kingdom results in our lives. We know that God will do exceedingly above and beyond what we can ask or imagine (Ephesians 3:20). However, we still need to do the asking and utilise our imagination. Our plans and dreams become the faith substance that God works with in order to create our future.

Proverbs 21:5 says: *"The plans of the diligent lead to profit as surely as haste leads to poverty."*

Planning leads to a profitable future, whereas haste leads to making impulsive decisions, leading to a poor future. More than the plans coming to pass, it is what the process of planning is producing in us that will unlock our potential and in turn our future. Our plans are about us developing diligence.

Proverbs 16:9 says: *"In their hearts humans plan their course, but the Lord establishes their steps."*

Our plans are a platform from which God can work. God

certainly will not be hemmed in by our plans. We are called to plan diligently as this is the process by which we build the faith essential for us becoming more like Jesus. The only decisions that please God are those built on faith (Hebrews 11:6).

Conversation with God:

Father God, help me to make my daily decisions fall in line with the PLOT you have for my life. May even the smallest of decisions be full of faith for what you are going to do in and through me.

The IMMEDIATE Priority - Unlocking the glory of God ONE degree at a time!

The distinctiveness of God will be unlocked through distinctive decision-making.

There are times when God works instantaneously in our lives, where suddenly He responds to bring about an immediate result. However, more often than not He shows us that He is the God of process.

Paul reveals that our lives are part of a glorious process that is happening one degree at a time. This process is often not evident in the moment but God's glory can be seen as we look back and witness that He has been faithful when we are faithful to His process.

Do not lose heart by restricting your potential to a snapshot of how life currently appears. Make decisions based on what you have witnessed God do over longer periods of time.

2 Corinthians 3 says: "And we all, with unveiled face, beholding the glory of the Lord, are being transformed into the same image from one degree of glory to another. For this comes from the Lord who is the Spirit" (ESV).

The glory of God is the distinctive nature of God; it is heaven being unlocked and unleashed on earth in and through our lives, from the inside-out. This is a key part of the Lord's Prayer: *"Your Kingdom come, your will be done, on earth as it is in heaven"* (Matthew 6:9-13).

Have you ever wondered how Jesus would live your life if He were you?

It's a good question isn't it?

The Holy Spirit's role is to guide us in our daily decisions in order that we unlock the distinctiveness of God in our lives. Every decision can be infused with heaven when we follow a plan to unlock heaven's PLOT that is already inside of us.

PRACTICE - The Ultimate Picture driving our Immediate Choices

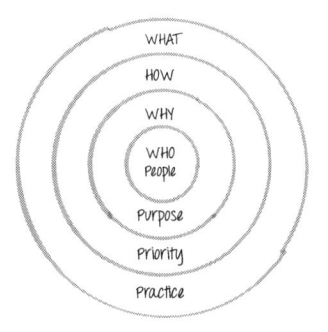

When our intentions fail to become actions we allow our internal disunity to create frustration.

James 1:4 (NIV) says: *"Let perseverance finish its work so that you may be mature and complete, not lacking anything."*

James calls for us to allow perseverance to finish its work in order to produce maturity and completeness. In other words we have to keep turning up and keep making the decisions until we see the change we desire to see. When our decisions are backed by God's principles we know that they will ultimately have an effect on the direction of our lives.

We need to embrace a process of following up our decisions to make sure we have followed through on our internal commitments.

"When you ask, you must believe and not doubt, because the one who doubts is like a wave of the sea, blown and tossed by the wind. That person should not expect to receive anything from the Lord. Such a person is double-minded and unstable in all they do" (James 1:6-7).

James suggests here that it is only definite intention that will result in definite action. A lack of action actually reveals a lack of true intention in our hearts. Testing our results helps to reveal what we truly believe. When we lack action, we can often identify double-mindedness, which is the disconnection between what I think I believe and what I truly believe. When we fail to deal with this we become unstable and frustrated with life. This can lead to discouragement and even depression.

While regular testing of our practice is not comfortable, it is the only way to avoid a double-minded state.

Conversation with God:

Father God, I thank you that you are at work in my life and you are changing me from one degree of glory to another. I am committed to being distinctive for you. I choose this day to make the ultimate goal of becoming like you to drive my immediate decisions.

THE WINNING KEYS

Section 2: The Winning Conversation— I value My Self

Understanding how to unlock your winning self

Day 6: The Winning Conversation

Every Conversation you have is Defined by the Internal Conversation

When we receive Jesus into our lives, our spirit is made alive in Christ (Romans 8:10). What does this mean? We were designed to live our lives fuelled by our conversation with God as a child in His family. When man sinned, this conversation ended because a Holy God could not and cannot be in relationship with a sinful man (Rom 3:23). Our connection was through our SPIRIT, the core of WHO we are (Rom 8:15).

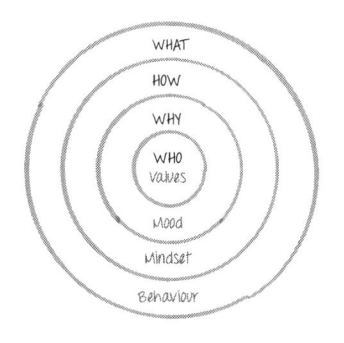

To illustrate, think about your mobile phone. An integral part of your phone is the SIM card. This is a chip is placed inside the handset so that it cannot be seen. It connects you to a network allowing you to have conversations. Without the SIM you have a phone but the ultimate reason for its existence cannot be fulfilled.

1 Corinthians 15:22: *For as in Adam all die, so in Christ all will be made alive.*

When Jesus Christ came to earth He died on the cross to take the punishment for my sin (Rom 5:8). In doing this He gave me the opportunity to be put back into relationship with God the Father. When Jesus was resurrected, defeating death, He made a way for my connection to a holy God to be re-established. When I ask God the Father to forgive me for my sin, when I receive Jesus as my LORD, I am made holy in God's sight (Colossians 1:22). I receive the Spirit of God. Paul says *Whoever is united with the Lord is one with Him in spirit* (1 Corinthians 6:17).

I now have a SIM [**S**pirit **I**n **M**e). My life is connected to heaven's network. This means that the conversation of heaven can be the key influence and shaper of my internal conversation.

Getting Past the Layers to the Core

The Word of God is able to cut through to the core of WHO I am which is essential for true life transformation.

Heb 4:12: *The word of God is alive and active. Sharper than any double-edged sword, it penetrates even to dividing soul and spirit, joints and marrow; it judges the thoughts and attitudes of the heart.*

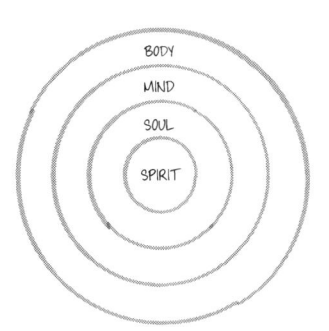

The writer to the Hebrews says that the Word of God can help us separate our SOUL script and our SPIRIT, our true beliefs. Without the light of truth being directed into the core of our lives we live based on how we feel. Our potential requires truth in order for us to fully uncover our WHY in life.

Opening the Lines of Communication

The words I allow to become present in my heart are what I allow to become manifest in my life. It is impossible for my external conversations not to be influenced by my internal conversations. Therefore if my PLOT in life is to impact the lives of other people in a powerful way I need to host a powerful internal conversation that deals with anything that is going to pull me off course.

As a follower of Christ it is vital that I choose to be led by the Spirit of God and the truth of His Word. This happens when I converse with God in prayer and through the reading of the Bible. Once again the unseen drives the seen.

The more I engage in a conversation with God, the more I uncover the winning conversation that will unlock my Kingdom potential. If I fail to engage in that conversation, I choose to walk in the fog of ambiguity created by an 'outside-in' conversation. Circumstances over time will erode the potential I have to make a real impact on this world for Christ.

The Results are Wanted but the Process Ignored

If I want to win in life then I need to be willing to allow my God conversation to create my internal script, my winning conversation. We have to lose our own *fear* script and embrace the *faith* script that Jesus Christ has for our lives. He is after all the author of our lives.

Heb 12:1b-2a: *Let us run with endurance the race that is set before us, looking unto Jesus, the <u>author</u> and <u>finisher</u> of our faith*

Jesus did not hold back from helping us see that losing is the first step to winning.

What I am willing to give up indicates what I am going to pick up.

Matthew 10:39: *'Whoever finds their life will lose it, and whoever loses their life for my sake will find it.'*

Conversation with God:

Father God, I choose to lose my internal script with all its pride, fear and insecurity and allow the script of my conversation to be led by your Spirit. I choose to keep my conversation going involving you in the daily decisions that are unlocking the glory of your plan in my life.

Day 7: The Winning Voices in the Boardroom
I value My Self

Understanding how to unlock your winning self

BEING A CHAMPION

The Right Leaders in your Boardroom

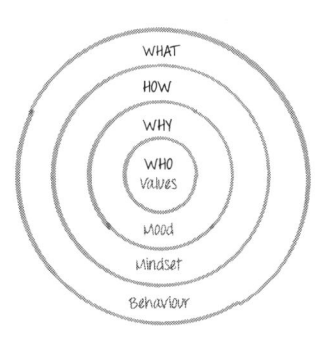

The six voices of the winning conversation are values that find their origin in God Himself. God created us in order that everything we would need as a source for success in life would start in Him. The world was created by the Word of God.

John 1:1: *In the beginning was the Word, and the Word was with God, and the Word was God. He was with God in the beginning. Through him all things were made; without him nothing was made that has been made.*

Whilst our potential has yet to be seen, it has been created. All potential comes from God, out of His being. He is the omnipotent one, the one who has limitless power, the God of ALL potential.

The way that we unlock this potential is through the voice of His word. God by His very nature (amongst other things) is DEVOTED, PASSIONATE, RELEVANT, INCLUSIVE, EXCELLENT and CREATIVE. The Kingdom of God is an extension of His nature made visible on earth. Therefore if God is PROMINENT, RESILIENT, MEMORABLE, INFLUENTIAL, VALUABLE and EXPANSIVE then when we allow His principles and values to be the voices hosting our internal conversation, the Kingdom results will follow.

The voices around the boardroom of belief are the words of God. While some people have claimed to have heard the audible voice of God, more often than not His voice is like the still small voice that Elijah experienced in 1 Kings 19:12. At this point in the Bible we find Elijah internalising a losing conversation. He went from the events of chapter 18, where he hosted an outward demonstration of the power of God, to being on the run in acute fear because he had heard that Queen Jezebel wanted him dead. He asked God to kill him in 1 Kings 19:4: 'I have had enough, Lord,' he said. 'Take my life; I am no better than my ancestors' (NIV).

The belief that he was alone and had no assurance of safety or provision caused Elijah to internalise a losing conversation which resulted in defeat getting into the core of his belief system. Elijah's story highlights how positive/successful events can sometimes turn into a source to meet our soul appetites.

The only way this depressive state was going to be reversed was for God to speak in order to help Elijah reverse his outside-in state to an inside-out state, drawing all he needed from God as his source.

God chose not to speak through spectacular external events, which is how so often we want Him to appear, so that it's obvious it is Him. He chose to speak through a whisper. While we do not know if this was an audible whisper or not, I believe that God speaks through the whisper of thoughts coming to mind while we wait on Him and allow His Word to speak to us. When we do that, thoughts come to mind that are His thoughts because we are hosting an open conversation with Him. God can take us from the most depressive state to a state of victory when we agree with what He whispers to us.

The Voice is a Principle

Heb 13:8: *Jesus Christ is the same yesterday and today and forever.*

God is unchanging and consistent by nature. Therefore when His voice leads our internal conversation the results will be seen in our lives. We see evidence of this in the Bible and throughout history. While the contexts of this world are in continuous transition and change (Rom 8:19), the Kingdom results will in essence continue to grow from strength to strength until God accomplishes His will here on earth (Matt 13:32).

The Voice is a Revelation

Jesus used parables as a means of communicating Kingdom principles. In the Gospels we find the Parable of the Sower. In the story the seed is a metaphor for the Word of God. In Mark's Gospel we read that the Kingdom seed (God's word) produces Kingdom results when a person will *hear the word* and *accept it*. What is accepted with certainty is what will 'produce a crop-thirty, sixty or even a hundred times what was sown' (Mark 4:20).

God's Word impacts our spoken words. The evidence of what we really believe is found in the words that we speak. Through

Christ (who is the Word, according to John's Gospel) I should see a difference in what I declare about WHO 'I am', WHY 'I will', HOW 'I can', and WHAT 'I have'.

The Voice is your Identity

The Word of God (His law) is the mirror of WHO I am. When I am reconnected with God the Father through the SIM (Spirit In Me) I am able to have an accurate understanding of WHO I am created to be.

James 1:25: *Whoever looks intently into the perfect law that gives freedom, and continues in it—not forgetting what they have heard, but doing it—they will be blessed in what they do.*

The Word of God is like the revelation brought to the eagle that he was not a barnyard chicken but an eagle (See the eagles story in the 'The Winning Conversation' day 7). The voice helped the eagle leave his old mistaken identity and soar into his designed identity. The more we listen to the voice of God through His Word and accept it, the more we will soar in life, seeing it from the heights from which we were designed to view it.

Conversation with God:

Father, I thank you that I have your Word (the Bible) as my mirror. I look into your mirror for my life and make my beliefs, feelings and thoughts follow what I see written there. I choose to leave behind all that does not match up with that as I move forward in the purpose you have for me. Forgive me for the times when I have given more authority to my own conclusions than to your conclusions for my life.

Day 8: The Conversation that Shapes my Identity

It all starts with WHO

The feeding source + root of the tree + the branches = the fruit

In his Gospel, John takes great care to include seven 'I AM' statements of Jesus. Jesus operated from the inside-out during His ministry years and in doing so revealed how we should live as Kingdom subjects in a world that is not our home but somewhere through which we are simply passing (John 17:16).

One of these seven statements is Jesus' self-declaration, 'I am the Vine.' This is an important analogy that Jesus uses to communicate His significance. It is also a picture of how we need to interact and intersect with Him in order to bear fruit, thereby unlocking Kingdom results.

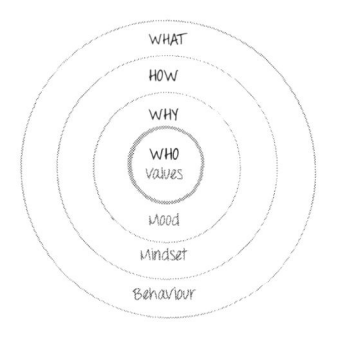

When we have the SIM (Spirit In Me) then we can allow the flow of conversation to be led from the root of the Father to the branches of our lives. The Spirit of God becomes our feeding source. In the analogy the branch is a person who connects into Christ, loses their isolation, trading it in for intimate community with Him and discovering a new identity in the process.

The branch is fed in order to feed the leaf in order to flourish. Jesus actually chose you in order to produce results, to bear fruit - not only for the NOW but also for the NOT YET.

John 15:16: *You did not choose me, but I chose you and appointed you to go and bear fruit - fruit that will last. Then the Father will give you whatever you ask in my name.*

The goal of us being connected to the Father through Jesus Christ is to produce results. Our potential is God-given and is not designed to remain inactive and fruitless. In fact there is a warning in Christ's analogy; any branch that does not activate its potential is cut off. This shows the serious approach God the Father takes to what He has invested in each person.

When we are <u>fed</u> to <u>feed</u> to <u>flourish</u> then the only limits that exist are those that we place on ourselves, as we read in verse 7:

If you remain in me and my words remain in you, ask <u>whatever</u> you wish, and it will be given you.

Living by design

It is only when I acknowledge that I am created by a master-designer that I can avoid the trap of being developed by the ideals of my world and the ideas of others.

Paul's instruction at the start of Romans 12 is critical for the life of every person who follows Christ. The only way we can unlock our Kingdom potential is if we daily learn to embrace the transformative process that we read in these verses.

I urge you, brothers and sisters, in view of God's mercy, to offer your bodies as a living sacrifice, holy and pleasing to God—this is your true and proper worship. Do not conform to the pattern of this world, but be transformed by the renewing of your mind. Then you will be able to test and approve what God's will is—His good, pleasing and perfect will.

WHO - *'In view of God's mercy.'*

The mercy of God refers to Christ's provision of forgiveness for sin that has been made possible through His death and resurrection. Now that I am a 'branch in the vine' I have been adopted into the family of God (Eph 1:4-5). This means that my identity has changed. This is not about adding to an established identity; this is about a total identity exchange. The old me was crucified at the cross and the new me was established through the resurrection (Gal 2:20). I have the new life of Christ in me (2 Cor 5:17).

When I choose to live every day from my new identity, my results are no longer based upon my old creation, I can truly experience Kingdom results.

WHY - *'...to offer your bodies as a living sacrifice, holy and pleasing to God—this is your true and proper worship.'*

I need to embrace what I call 'motivation salvation' everyday. In my new identity I live to make God 'look good and feel good'. My old identity is driven by a desire for me to 'look good and feel good.' This is no longer a priority for the true, new self.

The act of sacrifice in the Old Testament was an act that signified the prioritising of God's will in a person's life. In the New Testament the sacrificial system has been fulfilled through Christ's 'once and for all' sacrifice.' This means that I can position myself everyday as living first and foremost for the Kingdom of God rather than the Kingdom of Self. I can do many things in the name of God but if my WHY is really for the Kingdom of ME then it is invalid and will not unlock God's glory here on earth. Results will escape me!

HOW - *'Do not conform any longer to the pattern of this world. Be transformed by the renewing of your mind...'*

Upon me establishing the WHO and WHY I can now challenge the pattern of my thinking. The world around me is a powerful mind-moulder. The gateway of my heart, my mind (Prov 23:7), has to deal with millions of messages every day of which I am both consciously and subconsciously aware. When I live from DESIGN and not DEFAULT then I can choose to think differently. I can choose to allow the power of God's Word to shape me from the inside-out. I know that the WHO in me (Christ) is greater than the one who is attempting to use the world to shape me. I need the WHO of the Word of God to dominate and defeat the words that come at me from the world around me.

WHAT - *'Then you will be able to test and approve what God's will is — his good, pleasing and perfect will.'*

The opportunities God has for me do not need to be made up or manufactured; they have to be discerned. The opportunities exist; God has set you up for opportunity but you need to be operating in your new identity with the right motivation, the transformed mindset, and then you will receive clarity about what you should do. You need to be working on this circle of 'the winning conversation' while working on your 'winning purpose.'

The Voice is your Doorway to Tomorrow's Results

Who would have thought that an invisible conversation could have such an impact on our lives? Something that appears so insignificant has such a significant influence on our world and therefore the world around us.

The Kingdom of God is invisible because it starts with our internal conversation with God but when we unleash its power it is invincible. Through our behaviour and influence it invades everything we do.

Results are ready and waiting!

Jesus said mustard seed faith can move a mountain. The result of change that we want to see does not come by our strength or as a result of our striving. We simply have to follow the pattern we have been looking at and be amazed at the kingdom results that are on their way.

Conversation with God:

Father God, whilst I am aware of my strong defaults I thank you that through the power and strength of Jesus I can overcome them and live in the design of WHO you have called me to be. Increase my awareness today when I start to drift to my defaults. Lead me into your design through my choices today.

Day 9: The Winning Mood on the Office Floor
My Mood Moves Me

Mood is determined by the health of my soul

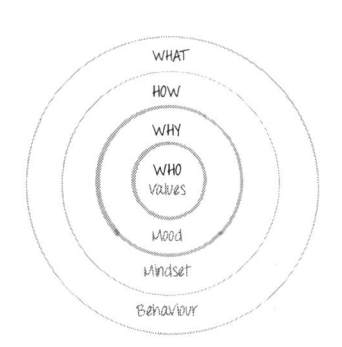

We are soul-led beings by default. What does this mean? It means that how we feel is the most powerful influence that affects our thoughts and therefore our choices. Our mood is a powerful force that we carry inside us and if we fail to make it our servant it will master our lives.

Paul helps us understand the power of the mood in Galatians 5:16-17: *So I say, walk by the Spirit, and you will not gratify the desires of the flesh. For the flesh desires what is contrary to the Spirit, and the Spirit what is contrary to the flesh. They are in conflict with each other, so that you are not to do whatever you want.*

What does Paul mean by the 'desires of the flesh?' Paul is referring to our internal desire to take what we see and make ourselves 'feel good and look good' by feeding from it as our soul source. This is the outside-in approach to life which forms the losing conversation. Our soul desires are based on a genuine need to feel satisfied. They are God-given needs. However, God Himself is supposed to be the consistent source for those needs. Only He can satisfy our soul desires; any substitute will result in us craving more and more of what cannot ultimately satisfy us. This can lead us down destructive paths.

Paul highlights that the Christ follower is to 'walk by the Spirit;' that is, inside-out. Remember, the Spirit is our SIM, our connection to the network of heaven which carries all the resources we need to feed our soul and have a healthy mood.

When we have a healthy mood we are ready for a winning mindset and winning behaviour. Without a healthy mood our thoughts and behaviour will be wrapped around pulling satisfaction into our soul from the outside-in. In the process we subtract from the environment around us.

SOUL APPETITES

Appetites Fed from the Inside-Out

If we rely upon our external environment our source will be irregular and ultimately no amount of supply will satisfy. Each of the appetites below - the appetite for affection, achievement, authority, acceptance, appreciation and assurance - has been readily supplied by heaven. We find in Jesus everything that we need. This is why Jesus said in John 6:35: *"I am the bread of life. Whoever comes to me will never go hungry, and whoever believes in me will never be thirsty."*

Our appetites are fed from WHO we are, from the inside-out. This means that

In Christ I am the Fathers AFFECTION - I matter to God

In Christ I have already ACHIEVED - I can add His value to

others and make progress for His Kingdom

In Christ I have AUTHORITY - I carry His voice and it will be heard through my story

In Christ I have ACCEPTANCE - I am seated in heavenly places and I am highly favoured by Him

In Christ I have APPRECIATION - I am Christ's workmanship, therefore I am priceless, beyond value

In Christ I have ASSURANCE - I am hidden with Christ and no one/nothing can touch me.

In the six conversations I will show you all the Bible verses that we can meditate on in order to be led by the Spirit and develop a healthy soul and powerful mood for Kingdom results.

Satisfy Appetites from Beliefs and not Results

Even as a Christian I can get drawn into gaining soul capital from external activity.

In Luke 10:40-42 Jesus was at the home of Mary and Martha. Martha was tearing around the house getting anxious about everything that had to be done and yet Mary was sat at Jesus' feet.

Martha was incensed and said to Jesus, *"Lord, don't you care that my sister has left me to do the work by myself? Tell her to help me!"*

"Martha, Martha," the Lord answered, *"you are worried and upset about many things, but few things are needed—or indeed only one. Mary has chosen what is better and it will not be taken away from her."*

What was Jesus saying? Jesus pointed out that Mary had centred her soul on Jesus rather than the completion of tasks. This was the source of her satisfaction in life. Jesus effectively said that the soul satisfaction Mary gained from centring herself on Him was a supply that would not run dry - in stark contrast to the temporal feelings that come with busyness or visible results.

Jesus was not against results. He taught us to bear fruit, after all (John 15). However HOW we go about getting results is the all important factor. Seeking first the Kingdom of God is about satisfying ourselves with Jesus the King and what we receive through that relationship. All the visible results we need will be taken care of by Him.

The Correct pilot

When we daily choose to centre our lives on Jesus Christ we invite the correct soul pilot to be in control.

Col 3:15:

Let the peace of Christ [the inner calm of one who walks daily with Him] be the controlling factor in your hearts [deciding and settling questions that arise]. To this peace indeed you were called as members in one body [of believers]. And be thankful [to God always] (AMP).

The controls of our soul reside in our heart and can only be correctly utilised if Jesus is our pilot. Then the flight is peaceful. Even if a storm rages on the outside, we can be serene and satisfied on the inside.

Find a Consistent Source of Supply

Jeremiah 17 provides the analogy of a tree by a river to help reinforce the design for our lives. Jeremiah starts with a warning for the one who makes other people (the external) the source of supply. The supply will run dry and therefore the Kingdom fruit/results will be limited:

"Cursed is the one who trusts in man, who draws strength from mere flesh and whose heart turns away from the Lord. That person will be like a bush in the wastelands; they will not see prosperity when it comes. They will dwell in the parched places of the desert, in a salt land where no one lives (v.6).

However, for the one who centres their life on WHO they are in Christ, Kingdom results are guaranteed regardless of the season:

"But blessed is the one who trusts in the Lord, whose confidence is in him. They will be like a tree planted by the water that sends out

its roots by the stream. It does not fear when heat comes; its leaves are always green. It has no worries in a year of drought and never fails to bear fruit" (7-8).

Feed to Feel to Focus to Function

There are Bible verses that can become the correct meditative 'food' to feed our souls, manage our thinking and inform our choices in order to unlock the relevant Kingdom results in our lives. When we meditate on these verses they create feelings which bring correct focus and productive function in our behaviour.

Conversation with God:

Father God, help me to make you my daily source. Help me to be aware when I am tempted to make external results my food. I want to feed on you as my daily bread. Help me meditate on your words and create in me a winning mood that can produce food that will bless others and in turn bring you glory (make you look good and feel good).

Day 10: Awareness of the Script that Forms the Conversation

<u>SOUL SCRIPT: The Manuscript of my Mood</u>

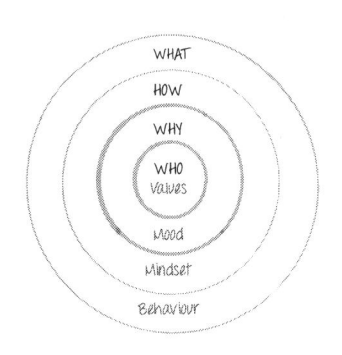

We learn early on in the Bible that God's laws and commands are powerful and that they are to become our focus if we want to feed on the right 'mood food'.

In Deuteronomy 11:18 God tells Moses: *'Fix these words of mine in your hearts and minds; tie them as symbols on your hands and bind them on your foreheads.'* Knowing that the internal script of a man's soul has an insatiable desire to feed from the outside-in, God instructs His people to keep His words tied to their heads as a symbolic action to signify that they are to meditate and fix their thoughts on His commands. Even to this day Orthodox

Jews tie phylacteries to their heads and/or arms during prayer.

Jeremiah foretold the coming of the Messiah Jesus and declared that this practice would be superseded by the internal work of the Holy Spirit when a person comes to receive Jesus as Lord and Saviour.

Jer 31:33: *"This is the covenant I will make with the people of Israel after that time," declares the Lord. "I will put my law in their minds and write it on their hearts. I will be their God, and they will be my people."*

Get your Hands on the Soul Script

The longer we are alive the more established the script of our soul becomes. Jesus said we would need to become like children to enter the Kingdom (Matt 18:3). I believe one of the reasons He said this was because a child's soul is like a blank canvas. There is plenty of canvas on which to write the Kingdom script that influences behaviour.

As followers of Christ we have to go through a process called 'sanctification'. Essentially this is the re-wiring of our beliefs and the re-writing of our soul script. The commands and words of God become engraved on our heart and these replace the self-destructive and self-glorifying scripts that we pick up from the pattern of the world around us.

The writer to the Hebrews reveals that the work of the Holy Spirit in our lives impresses the commands and laws of God on our heart at salvation. The rest of our lives as Christ followers is about those commands overthrowing our self-centred commands.

Heb 10:16: *"This is the covenant I will make with them after that time, says the Lord. I will put my laws in their hearts, and I will write them on their minds."*

Once the Holy Spirit has performed this in the life of the believer, there is no longer any need for the old practices of the law (Heb 8:13). An outside-in approach has been replaced by an inside-out one.

Change the Script to Change the Storyline

The Psalmist uses the analogy of the word of God being like a lamp that lights up our path.

Psalm 119:104-105: *Through your precepts I get understanding; therefore I hate every false way. Your word is a lamp to my feet and a light to my path.* ESV

It is my belief that God has mapped our future on our hearts. He has given us desires that can bring Him glory and in doing so will bring us incredible joy as we love Him and love people. The Word of God (the light) plus our desires (the path) create the storyline for our lives.

Your story can take an upward turn and soar to new heights but you have to be prepared to invest time in God's Word and allow the Holy Spirit to guide you, not your emotions. Emotions are not opposed to being led by the Spirit but healthy emotions are created as a result of being led by the Spirit.

There are many examples of how the storyline of peoples' lives have been changed by them <u>accepting</u> the Word of God. A favourite of mine is Gideon. Gideon was developed by his environment and therefore defined by his incorrect conclusions of WHO he was.

Judges 6:6-15: *The angel of the Lord came and sat down under the oak in Ophrah that belonged to Joash the Abiezrite, where his son Gideon was threshing wheat in a winepress to keep it from the Midianites. When the angel of the Lord appeared to Gideon, he said, "The Lord is with you, mighty warrior."*

"Pardon me, my lord," Gideon replied, "but if the Lord is with us, why has all this happened to us? Where are all his wonders that our ancestors told us about when they said, 'Did not the Lord bring us up out of Egypt?' But now the Lord has abandoned us and given us into the hand of Midian."

The Lord turned to him and said, "Go in the strength you have and save Israel out of Midian's hand. Am I not sending you?"

"Pardon me, my lord," Gideon replied, "but how can I save Israel?

My clan is the weakest in Manasseh, and I am the least in my family."

The word of the angel was in total contrast to Gideon's context. Here was a man hiding in a winepress from an enemy the angel said he would overcome. Gideon revealed the internal script for his fearful behaviour. The view he had of himself was a result of how he viewed his clan and his lowly position within in his own family. The commands of God were in stark contrast to his external context.

The winning conversation will require us overcoming established soul script. Gideon was told 'Go in the strength you have...' which reveals to us that the commands that he needed to unlock his potential existed inside of him already. If we build on the words and commands of God we will unlock the potential that God has placed inside us to overcome every opposition. We do not have to wait for something external to happen in order to bring about this change.

A Champion Needs to Identify the Final Word

There are crucial moments in the journey of a champion. Our ultimate example is Jesus. With the impending experience of the crucifixion, Jesus was in prayer and his soul was agonising at the thought of what he was about to go through. Not only was he about to face the most excruciating form of execution, but the weight of the world's sin was going to pulverise his very being. Luke records this moment:

Luke 22:42-43: *"Father, if you are willing, take this cup from me; yet not my will, but yours be done." An angel from heaven appeared to him and strengthened him.*

Jesus deals with the soul challenge by relegating the feeling of despair to a position below His Spirit choice. When Jesus did this heaven backed his choice and gave him strength.

We do not and cannot overcome our soul challenge on our own; we need to tap into the backing that comes from heaven. We get this when we choose to act upon our Spirit choice and not our soul feeling.

The Root to the Fruit

Focus is a critical part of unlocking the power of God's command in our lives. David records much of the battle between his soul and his spirit. In Psalm 63 David chooses his focus and his focus becomes his food which produces fruit.

His soul is thirsty and this causes his whole being to be crying out for spiritual food. Through praise and worship David declares *I will be fully satisfied as with the richest of foods; with singing lips my mouth will praise you* (v5).

In the moment you feel you are being led by emotion and not by the spirit stir up praise and worship and declare Christ as your source. He will not leave you wanting.

David learned through worship and meditation that the Word of God can be used to command our soul and therefore our experience.

Conversation with God:

Father, help me to grow in awareness of the script that is shaping my story. I want to live from your commands and to outwork the story you have for me.

SOUL FLOW: Sow what I Want to Grow

The river of God flows through the life of a believer (Ezekiel 47) but we are not to be reservoirs simply using it for our own satisfaction. We are designed to be a conduit and channel through which we can produce value that builds up the people around us.

The more we produce for others the greater the capacity we have to channel God's resource.

Luke 6:38: *"Give and it will be given to you. A good measure, pressed down, shaken together and running over, will be poured into your lap. For with the measure you use, it will be measured to you."*

When we stay in the position of consumers we reduce the supply for distributing the blessing of His kingdom. But humility unlocks a greater supply of Kingdom resource. The more the supply of God's resource becomes about others, the more He entrusts to us. If we become a reservoir instead of a free-flowing river, storing up resource for ourselves, then we are acting in pride and God opposes this and reduces the supply. Pride is when I elevate my needs and wants above those of others.

James 4:6: *But he gives us more grace. That is why Scripture says: "God opposes the proud but shows favour to the humble."*

Conversation with God:

Father God, I want to be a producer and not a consumer. I want to grow the supply I can carry for you. Help me to grow it by being generous in every way making others feel good and look good ahead of myself. I do this ultimately to make you look good and feel good.

Day 11: The Winning Language

KINGDOM KEYS

The Two Languages of my Soul Script

FAITH and FEAR

Our soul is like a distracted child. If you do not get the child to focus on what you want it to focus on then it will be in and out of anything it can get its hands on. In our house when our children are focussed then they are constructive and the house is in peace. However when they are unfocussed that is when they can find themselves occupying themselves in the wrong way and before long peace is a memory.

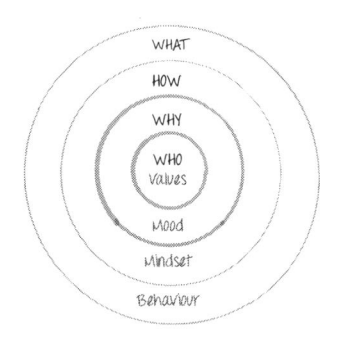

Faith is when the <u>parent</u> of my Spirit makes the <u>child</u> of my soul focus on Jesus Christ. Regardless of what is happening around me, peace rules the house and regardless of destructive circumstances, faith is busy constructing the unseen and yet very real future God has for me.

Fear is when the parent of my Spirit fails to focus the soul child on Jesus leaving the child to get taken up with anything that catches its attention. Satan is quick to distract the child leading it into all things unhealthy which rob the house of peace. Just as a child who loses its parent is filled with fear and dread, so the soul implodes when the appetite of assurance (along with the other appetites we have looked at) is not satisfied.

Paul says in Phil 4:6-7: *Do not be anxious about anything, but in every situation, by prayer and petition, with thanksgiving, present your requests to God. And the peace of God, which transcends all understanding, will guard your hearts and your minds in Christ Jesus.*

Prayer brings the parent of our Spirit back into position and disciplines the soul child creating a peaceful environment in which to build a strong life.

The Winning Interpretation

As people called to live by faith and not by sight (2 Cor 5:7) we have to manage the tension of not allowing our natural and more obvious methods of interpreting situations to lead us. For example our natural means of interpreting situations come through our physical senses of sight, taste, touch, sound and smell. We collect information through these senses and assimilate that information drawing very natural conclusions. Fear is often the language we use to interpret this information.

However, when your winning purpose is a faith goal and involves God's participation, we cannot interpret data the usual way. To put it simply, the language of the Kingdom is heaven's language of faith. Therefore carrying out any heavenly assignment requires us to do so using the language of heaven.

Abraham was given a heavenly assignment that needed a language of faith. He had every natural reason when looking at the elderly state of his wife Sarah and himself not to believe that they could have a child. Every time they felt the effects of age on their body, that feeling could have been interpreted as 'this dream is never going to come about.'

However Paul said Romans 4:19-20: *Without weakening in his faith, he faced the fact that his body was as good as dead—since he was about a hundred years old—and that Sarah's womb was also dead. Yet he did not waver through unbelief regarding the promise of God but was strengthened in his faith and gave glory to God...*

The parent of Abraham's spirit focussed the child of his soul and the result was constructive; he was strengthened. He believed a supernatural conclusion over a natural conclusion.

2 Cor 4:16-18: *Therefore we do not lose heart. Though outwardly we are wasting away, yet inwardly we are being renewed day by day. For our light and momentary troubles are achieving for us an eternal glory that far outweighs them all. So we fix our eyes not on what is seen but on what is unseen since what is seen is temporary, but what is unseen is eternal.*

This is the journey for the believer. While the external deteriorates, internally we are growing from strength to strength through the language of faith.

The Winning Disposition

It is important to realise that we all struggle with doubt. Doubt is the absence of faith while faith is deep confidence. We all lack deep confidence at times. Many of the well known characters in the Bible who did great things for God had to wrestle with doubt. However, what sets apart a champion is that they do not accept the conclusion doubt provides; they adopt a 'winning disposition' which is to ask for help in every moment of doubt.

In Mark 9:23-24 we see a father whose boy has been spiritually afflicted. The father comes to Jesus because the disciples could not heal his son. When asked if he could help, Jesus responds:

"'If you can'?" said Jesus. "Everything is possible for one who believes."

Immediately the boy's father exclaimed, "I do believe; help me overcome my unbelief!"

The miracle took place because the father asked for help in his unbelief. It was this that unlocked the miracle. The unseen faith of the boy's father released the Kingdom result.

When moments of doubt come, and they will, remember the kingdom disposition of building faith. When you need help to do so, call out to God, or ask another believer to pray with you to build faith. The Body of Christ (the church) is the community where we draw strength from others and give strength to others.

The conversation I want the most is the conversation I will host

Our conversation is our responsibility and we cannot attribute blame to anyone else for what we are allowing on the inside.

Gal 5:17 *For the desires of the flesh are against the Spirit, and the desires of the Spirit are against the flesh, for these are opposed to each other, to keep you from doing the things you want to do* (ESV).

We have a civil war taking place inside us between our soulful desires and the desires of God's Spirit in us. The one we back is the one that will win. How do I back the one I want to win? I choose to fix my focus on the right things.

Paul was under house arrest when he wrote Philippians 4:4-9. He could have allowed his soul to become bitter and his spirit to be broken but he chose to back the Spirit as his winner. He reveals in Phil 4 how we do this:

Rejoice in the Lord always. I will say it again: Rejoice! Let your gentleness be evident to all. The Lord is near. Do not be anxious about anything but in every situation, by prayer and petition, with thanksgiving, present your requests to God. And the peace of God, which transcends all understanding, will guard your hearts and your minds in Christ Jesus.

Finally, brothers and sisters, whatever is true, whatever is noble, whatever is right, whatever is pure, whatever is lovely, whatever is admirable—if anything is excellent or praiseworthy—think about such things. Whatever you have learned or received or heard from me, or seen in me—put it into practice. And the God of peace will be with you.

All this goes to show that PEACE is unlocked when we…

Pay
Exclusive
Attention to
Christ's
Excellence.

Christ's excellence can be seen in all the good things that have happened to us and that surround us (James 1:17). The stories we read in the Bible speak of how good He is. When we pay exclusive attention to these things then our 'child soul' falls into line behind the command of the Bible and we build a life of faith that can unlock kingdom results.

I learn to cultivate a winning disposition by thinking on the things that unlock love for God, love for people and love for who He has made me to be (Matthew 22:36, 37). A faith focus causes me to value my life, my future, others around me whereas a fear focus causes me to devalue my life, my future and the people who are around me.

Conversation with God:

Father God, I choose to draw faith conclusions about myself, my future and others rather than fear based conclusions. I choose to **Pay Exclusive Attention to Christ's Excellence.** *I take my eyes off my lack and fix my eyes on Jesus as my all sufficiency. My soul is satisfied by the Spirit of God in me and I choose to produce value that builds others up today.*

Day 12: The Winning Mindsets in the Meeting Room

Your Mindset creates your Reality

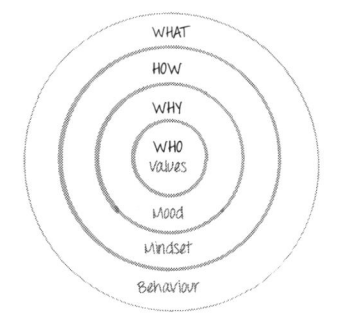

As followers of Jesus Christ we operate in an unseen reality. We have already established that everything around us comes from inside the human heart and that everything visible started in an invisible place. It originated in the heart of man but then a desire was translated into a planned action in the human mind. In the 'meeting room' of our mindset, the plan to make what is invisible visible is drawn up.

In Romans 7 and 8 the Apostle Paul helps us to see the internal battle that lies within everyone who follows Jesus. Our mindset is our choice; if we are unhappy with the mindset - our frame of mind - then this can be changed. In Romans 7 Paul helps us see the hopeless state we find ourselves in without Christ. To attain our full potential, we require the power of Christ in us.

Romans 7:23-25: *I see another law at work in me, waging war against the law of my mind and making me a prisoner of the law of sin at work within me. What a wretched man I am! Who will rescue me from this body that is subject to death? Thanks be to God, who delivers me through Jesus Christ our Lord!*

Paul says that there is a law, a set of beliefs, determined to pull us into the wrong mindset. This wants us to plan wrong actions that bring destructive results. We need God to help us stay fully aware of this internal struggle and to pray and agree with the Spirit of God inside of us that will put in place the right mindset for today.

We need to settle within ourselves before we go into today which mindset we are embracing. You are a champion and you have to agree with the Champion of Christ in you to adopt the winning mindset.

Romans 8:5-8: *Those who live according to the flesh have their minds set on what the flesh desires but those who live in accordance with the Spirit have their minds set on what the Spirit desires. The mind governed by the flesh is death but the mind governed by the Spirit is life and peace. The mind governed by the flesh is hostile to God; it does not submit to God's law, nor can it do so. Those who are in the realm of the flesh cannot please God.*

Paul asks in 1 Cor 2:16: *Who has known the mind of the Lord so as to instruct him? But we have the mind of Christ.*

The fact we have the Spirit of God at work in our hearts and therefore our soul child is under his watchful eye means that we can adopt the mindset of Christ which enables us to achieve kingdom results. As we look at the six kingdom conversations later in the book you will see the kind of mindset Jesus had and therefore the mindset you can adopt each day to win in life for God's glory.

Our Mindset is Created through the Thoughts we Agree on

When I agree with a thought I am choosing to make a plan for definite action which will set in motion a series of events. A filter is created through the thoughts we have agreed with. Over time these create strongholds or strong convictions that are difficult to change.

Let me give you an example. Is there a particular situation that triggers a deep feeling that affects how you behave? It doesn't matter how hard you seem to try, that trigger gets you every time. This is a stronghold that the enemy establishes in our belief system that controls us and prevents us from winning. We cannot alter these strongholds on our own.

Paul says in 2 Cor 10:3:4-5: *For though we live in the world, we do not wage war as the world does. The weapons we fight with are not the weapons of the world. On the contrary, they have divine power to demolish strongholds. We demolish arguments and every pretension that sets itself up against the knowledge of God, and we take captive every thought to make it obedient to Christ.*

The power to defeat any stronghold and to alter the landscape of our beliefs lies in the name of Jesus because he defeated it when he went to the cross and rose again. When we unleash the power of Christ's identity within us, our belief system can be changed to become like His belief system and therefore we can rule our life under His authority.

The message version says this: We use our powerful God-tools for smashing warped philosophies, tearing down barriers erected against the truth of God, fitting every loose thought and emotion and impulse into the structure of life shaped by Christ (2 Cor 10:5,6).

Whenever I have a thought or a feeling I need to ask, 'Does this fit into the shape of who Jesus is?' If it does not then if we hold onto it then it becomes an obstacle to us cultivating a winning conversation.

Very often we contemplate thoughts that we think fit with our lives forgetting that it is no longer I who live but Christ who lives in me. We must stop any thought or feeling from squatting in a life that belongs to Jesus.

My authority to evict these thoughts or emotions comes from Christ and not simply from 'positive thinking.'

Col 2:9-10: *For in Christ all the fullness of the Deity lives in bodily form, and in Christ you have been brought to fullness. He is the head over every power and authority.*

With Christ in me I have every power and authority backing the choices I make in agreement with him. This power is multiplied when I agree with others as Jesus reveals in Matthew 18:19-20: *"I tell you that if two of you on earth agree about anything they ask for, it will be done for them by my Father in heaven. For where two or three gather in my name, there am I with them."*

Get in the Right <u>Lane</u> and the Right <u>Frame</u> of Mind

The Bible says that you are in a race and the track is marked out for you. You have been awarded the medal already as a champion. Now you have to outwork what has been gifted to you. Like an athlete in a race you have to maintain a winning posture. The writer to the Hebrews tells us how.

Heb 12:1-3: *Therefore, since we are surrounded by such a great cloud of witnesses, let us throw off everything that hinders and the sin that so easily entangles. And let us run with perseverance the race marked out for us, fixing our eyes on Jesus, the pioneer and perfecter of faith. For the joy set before him he endured the cross, scorning its shame, and sat down at the right hand of the throne of God. Consider him who endured such opposition from sinners, so that you will not grow weary and lose heart.*

To get in the right lane and right frame of mind before you enter the day, decide what you are:...

Leaving

What mindset (set of thoughts) is going to slow you down in your race? Put off the old mindset and embrace the new attitude (Eph 4:23).

Longing for

Through prayer let the Spirit of God intensify what you want to see happen (2 Tim 1:6). Let the Spirit of God take you on a tour of what God is going to do through you in the future.

Leveraging

Christ has already been this way before and He lives in you. You have what it takes; there is no doubt. To doubt it is to doubt Christ's ability, so leverage that same Spirit that lives in your spirit core (Rom 8:11).

Conversation with God:

Father God, help me only to entertain the thoughts and feelings that fit with WHO I am in Christ Jesus. Reveal any stronghold of beliefs that is holding me back and through the power of your Word help me to hold onto the new belief until the old belief is demolished. I thank you that I live in the authority of Jesus who is all powerful and so I praise you because I am an overcomer.

Day 13: Winning Determination

Living Determined to make our decisions follow our goals

The Kingdom Mindset Mix

In order to unlock the kingdom results that are part of our Kingdom assignment it is vital that we try and distil from the Bible what a Kingdom mindset looks like. Each of the six internal conversations of the Kingdom we are looking at flows through the filter of the following six Kingdom mindsets.

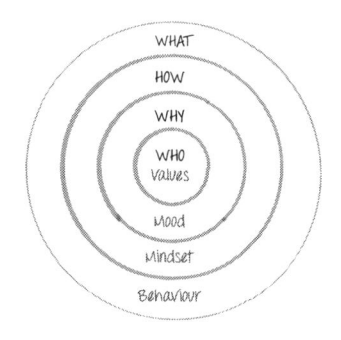

Remember when you agree on these words in faith you unlock the mindset and set your actions up to have a Kingdom impact.

Progress Mindset

Kingdom expansion starts with my development

When we pray the Lord's Prayer and utter the words, 'Let your Kingdom come, your will be done on earth as it is in heaven,' we are in fact praying that this happens first in our lives. Many have debated as to whether the Kingdom has come or is coming. The reality is **both**. (See these verses that show it is both present and future: Luke 17:20-21; 19:11ff). The Kingdom has come as an external reality through Christ but it also resides as kingdom potential inside those who put their faith in Jesus. Our job as Kingdom people is to embrace the journey of unlocking the Kingdom in us so that it can progress to its climax and fulfilment. For this to happen we have to become lovers of the Kingdom process.

While fully God and yet fully human, Jesus put himself under the same limitations as you and I. (Phil 2:7) It was not until he was aged 30 that he stepped onto the public scene of his ministry. So what was he doing in the 18 years from the time when he was lost at the Temple (Luke 2:41-51)? Those 18 years are summed up in one verse in Luke 2:52: *And Jesus grew in wisdom and stature, and in favour with God and man.* Jesus embraced personal development and growth to get him ready for his public moment.

Patiently pursue your goal knowing that if Jesus had to go through the process to prepare Himself, so do we.

Conversation with God:

Father God, help me not to try and bypass your process but prioritise that which will grow me toward the goal you have given to me. I approach this day ready to see your Kingdom expand my thinking.

Determined Mindset

Kingdom prominence starts with helping others to have the courage to climb higher

When I determine daily to devote myself to my purpose and the people with whom I come into contact, my prominence will take care of itself. In Romans 15:4 Paul encourages us to choose today to allow what has gone before to stir a new level of determination: *For everything that was written in the past was written to teach us, so that through the endurance taught in the Scriptures and the encouragement they provide we might have hope.*

As you encourage yourself in God you create an enduring mindset. This creates the platform that allows you to maintain a consistency of encouragement to those around you. As you encourage widely today you will increase not only the capacity for others to endure but your own capacity increases too.

May the God who gives endurance and encouragement give you the same attitude of mind toward each other that Christ Jesus had, so that with one mind and one voice you may glorify the God and Father of our Lord Jesus Christ (Romans 15:5-6).

Conversation with God:

I thank you Father that through my conversation with you I am lifted up, elevated in my soul. I have prominence in this world because of who I am in you. I am determined to lift others up today. Let others feel bigger as a result of my conversation with them.

Confident Mindset

Kingdom influence is about me getting out the way and allowing God to reach out through my God-confidence

My confidence does require me to be someone I am not in order to connect to others. I simply have to make myself available everyday to be a tool in God's hand through my conversations. Paul openly admitted that his natural disposition was timid when face-to-face with people: *By the humility and gentleness of Christ, I appeal to you—I, Paul, who am "timid" when face to face with you, but "bold" toward you when away* (2 Cor 10:1). He clearly wrestled with the tension of humility and boldness. However his influence came when he led out of God-confidence. He wrote to Timothy about this bold and confident spirit that we have in Christ: *For the*

Spirit God gave us does not make us timid, but gives us power, love and self-discipline (2 Tim 1:7).

Life's journey is about me getting out of the way and letting the power and strength of God to invade the world through my life. Paul said *for it is God who works in you to will and to act in order to fulfil his good purpose* (Phil 2:13). With God it's more about *letting* God work as opposed to *getting* God to work.

Conversation with God:

Father God, I choose to let you work through me today. I step into my world with God-confidence and choose to raise my level of confidence through my conversations today with those I know and through new conversations. I am your Kingdom influence to my world today.

Diligent Mindset

My Kingdom value will become value to the world around me as I maintain a diligent mindset

Everything I need to unlock my future is in my present. While what I have may not look anything like the future, it is the seed of what is to come. So what will unlock it? The answer is a diligent mindset. As I feed off Christ's appreciation of me, I produce appreciation of everything entrusted to me knowing that my mindset of diligence is the water that will grow the seed and over time produce a valuable harvest.

Let us not become weary in doing good, for at the proper time we will reap a harvest if we do not give up (Gal 6:9).

With a supernatural process we often require supernatural patience. Through adopting the diligent mindset of Christ I can step out of my weariness and go again with renewed enthusiasm.

Conversation with God:

Father, I thank you that I am seen as worthy of Christ's blood being spilt on the cross and I declare that I am not my own; I am yours. Everything I have is yours and I will express my appreciation toward you and others through my diligent mindset today. I know that as I continue to clarify my future goal, my faithfulness in the present will unlock an amazing future.

Persevering Mindset

The Kingdom assignment requires divine resilience which is unlocked through faith and perseverance

When I give my current challenges a future context, I unlock the perseverance to keep turning up to the problem. By adopting the Kingdom mindset of perseverance I can choose to celebrate what my challenges are and will produce in me.

Romans 3:3-4: *Not only so, but we also glory in our sufferings, because we know that suffering produces perseverance; perseverance, character; and character, hope.*

I would not want to shortcut the problem because I do not want to short circuit in the face of future challenges. I embrace this time because I will look back in the future and smile at how God's glory seeped out through my weakness.

Conversation with God:

Father, I thank you that there is MORE resilience in me than I think and that you entrust me with my current challenges in order to build my capacity for future opportunities. While I can often wonder WHY at times like this I know that you know WHY and that is good enough for me. Help Christ's perseverance to flow through my veins today!

Sincere Mindset

Leave a Kingdom impression on those you talk to through your sincere interest in the lives of those meet

In a suspicious world those who build relationships with *sincerity* will be remembered. People feel insincerity when we are simply 'behaving' our way toward our goals. However, when they sense and feel genuine value through our approach and attitude toward them we will build a platform that creates room for the Kingdom message we carry. This starts from a heart that is exposed to Christ's genuine love which creates in us a sincere mindset toward others.

Now that you have purified yourselves by obeying the truth so that you have sincere love for each other, love one another deeply, from the heart (1 Peter 1:22).

Peter's letter reveals that our sincere activity unlocks the purity of Christ in our lives. We are made pure through our salvation but we can experience that provision the more we outwork our faith through letting Christ sincerely value others through our lives.

Conversation with God:

Father, I choose to surrender any temptation I have to use my relationships to get what I want. I want to sincerely love the people you have entrusted and will entrust to me. You loved me because you are love. I choose to love others because I no longer live but you live in me.

What we Frame, we Form

Take a moment today when you go over your NOT YET goal to surrender your old mindsets and embrace the mindset of Christ so that His Kingdom can come today in and through your life.

Day 14 - The Winning Choices in the Assembly Room of Actions

Kingdom Behaviour

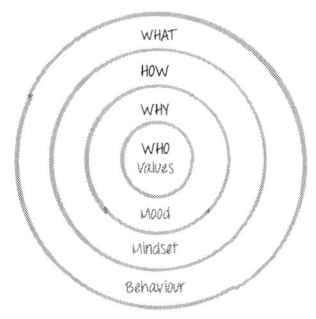

In order to unlock the Kingdom results that are part of our Kingdom assignment it is vital that we try and distil from the Bible what Kingdom behaviour looks like. Each of the six internal conversations of the Kingdom we are looking at have a corresponding Kingdom action.

COMMIT wholeheartedly

Kingdom prominence is unlocked when what I commit to do I can do as I would for Christ

If my conviction is wholehearted commitment then I have to make sure that I follow through. To not follow through means I am at risk of accepting a lesser standard and this decreases God's opportunity to work through me. The message of Christ is wholehearted commitment in following Him and I want my actions to be His message.

Col 3:16-17: *Let the message of Christ dwell among you richly as you teach and admonish one another with all wisdom through psalms, hymns, and songs from the Spirit, singing to God with gratitude in your hearts. And <u>whatever</u> you do, whether in <u>word or deed,</u> do it <u>all</u> in the name of the Lord Jesus, giving thanks to God the Father through him.*

If I cannot follow through with wholehearted commitment then I either have a belief problem or a capacity problem. If I am doing too much then I will produce results that will go unnoticed. Christ's challenge is to *let your light shine before others, that they may see your good deeds and glorify your Father in heaven* (Matt 5:17). If wholehearted commitment does not lie behind my actions then his glory will remain hidden in me.

Conversation with God:

Father, forgive me for any apathy that is in me. I choose to be devoted, full of expectancy and determined to commit wholeheartedly to what has been entrusted to me today.

COMPLETE well

Kingdom resilience is unlocked when I complete my commitments

Our actions reinforce our beliefs. Therefore if I want to develop a deeper passion for Christ and the Kingdom work I have been given, I must learn to complete on my *commitments*.

Paul challenged the church at Corinth, with regards to a financial commitment that they had made, to complete the commitment within the realms of what was possible.

2 Cor 8:11-12: *Now finish the work, so that your eager willingness to do it may be matched by your completion of it, according to your means. For if the willingness is there, the gift is acceptable according to what one has, not according to what one does not have.*

Paul recognises that sometimes what we thought we could do we cannot quite fulfil. However, the key is the heart behind the action. The Message version of the same passage contains the phrase *the heart regulates the hands*. What we do with our hands is what we really believe in our hearts. We are to complete on our commitments with the means we have available to us.

King Solomon recognised that our passion level increases when we learn to complete and not just come up with exciting ideas.

Ecclesiastes 7:8: *The end of a matter is better than its beginning, and patience is better than pride.*

Conversation with God:

Father, help me build resilience today through learning to commit to tasks within my capacity to complete them. I know that as I am faithful with little, you will entrust me with MORE. Help me with those commitments I have not completed; help me to do my best to bring them to a conclusion in a way that makes you look good.

CONTRIBUTE to solve problems

The Kingdom touches those to whom I give relief

If Jesus was walking this earth and you had 24 hours with him my guess is you would take him to see as many of the people you know as possible. You would be confident that they would believe in Him as He helped solve their current problems. Well Jesus has commissioned you do exactly what you would want Jesus to do for you. You have a Kingdom relevance that means you can help alleviate the burdens that people are carrying through your sincere willingness to contribute toward making them walk away from you lighter than when they first started talking to you.

Gal 6:2-4: *Carry each other's burdens, and in this way you will fulfil the law of Christ. If anyone thinks they are something when they are not, they deceive themselves. Each one should test their own actions.*

While you cannot solve every problem, your faith unlocks a helpful mood which causes you to promote others selflessly ahead of your own needs. In doing so people remember you and watch how you always have the help you need in your relationships as you pursue your winning purpose.

Conversation with God:

Father, help me not to withhold good from those to whom it is due, when it is in my power to act (Proverbs 3:27). Today I choose to contribute to bring solutions so that people experience progress and breakthrough in their lives. I know you see all that I need and as I seek your Kingdom advancement in the lives of others I know you will tend to all that I need (Matt 6:33).

CONNECT widely

The Kingdom influence grows as your connections grow

When Jesus was asked what the Kingdom of God looks like and what it can be compared to He pointed to the mustard seed (Luke 13:19). The mustard seed was not going to produce anything like the majestic and towering cedar trees that we read of in the Old Testament. It produced a common garden weed. The significance of the illustration was not so much in the size of the plant as in its invasive nature - in its ability to push past every obstacle. It relentlessly pursues places where it has not yet spread, not giving thought to its small beginnings.

We are often our biggest critics and are aware of our apparent insignificance. However, we carry the Kingdom when we carry Christ. Therefore when we let the Kingdom advance through new connections we become like the mustard plant reaching into new places. Kingdom influence increases and opportunities with it.

Our approach should reflect what Paul speaks of in Phil 2:3-5:

Do nothing out of selfish ambition or vain conceit. Rather, in humility value others above yourselves, not looking to your own interests but each of you to the interests of the others. In your relationships with one another, have the same mindset as Christ Jesus...

Very often we are more concerned with how we look when there are opportunities to connect with people we do not know. We would naturally rather follow our default which is an exclusive belief. However, now you are in His Kingdom, you have an inclusive belief that will lead to the behaviour of connecting beyond your 'usual' people.

Conversation with God:

I thank you Father that your Kingdom is relentlessly growing and you want to do this through my life. I thank you for the example of Jesus who connected widely and saw His influence spread. Help me to do the same today when I have opportunity to meet new people.

CONSTRUCT imaginatively

Kingdom expansion comes through the new 'thing' God wants to introduce through you

When it comes to solving problems we have to believe that with the Creator God living in us through his Spirit we can think differently. We know that our minds can be transformed which enables us to create new patterns of behaviour that reflect God. I believe this also leads to creating the new thing that will come from our winning purpose.

Maybe you are struggling to see anything that looks similar to the NOT YET goal that you have? I would suggest you should not be surprised because you are unique and so is your legacy; you are part of a new thing that God is doing. (Isaiah 43:19).

Proverbs 25:2 says: *It is the glory of God to conceal a matter; to search out a matter is the glory of kings.*

God is not hiding his provision <u>from</u> you; He is hiding it <u>for</u> you.

I love hiding gifts for my children to find. It is not that I purposely want them not to have them. I want to enjoy the process with them of uncovering what they have not possessed.

God's glory will be revealed in those who uncover what He has hidden for them. So decide today to think differently and pursue the Kingdom of God through the creative gift of your imagination.

The Message version of the verses we mentioned from Gal 6:2-4 say this: *Make a careful exploration of who you are and the work you have been given, and then sink yourself into that.*

Conversation with God:

Father, transform my thinking so that today I can put to work the imagination that you have blessed me with. I want to construct through my life solutions to problems that bring you glory. I want to see the expansiveness of your nature unlocked through my life.

COMPETE differently

The Kingdom makes a difference through my difference

My Kingdom value is unlocked when I pursue my difference that makes a difference.

I am called to stand out, to be different. I am nowhere called to blend in. How do I do this when I have an ordinary life, an ordinary job, in an ordinary place? Decide today to do things with uncommon care, to compete against how the majority would carry out tasks. As you do this, see how you become more valuable to your world.

I do not try and become valuable to feel valuable because my appreciation comes from Christ. However, I want those in my world to experience this value through what I produce.

Paul used sporting examples to help us catch this kingdom principle of competing differently.

1 Cor 9:24-27: *Do you not know that in a race all the runners run, but only one gets the prize? Run in such a way as to get the prize. Everyone who competes in the games goes into strict training. They do*

it to get a crown that will not last, but we do it to get a crown that will last forever. Therefore I do not run like someone running aimlessly; I do not fight like a boxer beating the air. No, I strike a blow to my body and make it my slave so that after I have preached to others, I myself will not be disqualified for the prize.

A mere competitor is happy to compete in the same way that others do. However you are a champion not just a competitor.

Conversation with God:

Father God, I thank you that I am valued by you. I want to express this value to the people around me through my behaviour. I want to show uncommon care towards them. I want to compete differently today from how I did yesterday knowing that this belief and behaviour unlocks the glory that you have put in my life (2 Cor 4:7).

Section 3: The Winning Team— I Value People

Day 15: The Winning People in my Life

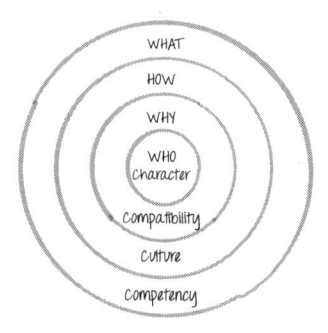

As Christians we need a community of believers to outwork our relationship with Jesus. This community should be diverse and yet united around the common mission of the church to make disciples.

The focus on the winning team is especially focussed around the people who will have a direct and deliberate impact on our lives as we seek to cultivate a winning conversation and aim to fulfil our winning purpose.

As Christians we seek to influence and be influenced. Whilst all relationships have a level to which influence will flow both ways, I am choosing to focus on the relationships that are developing me, helping to unlock my Kingdom potential.

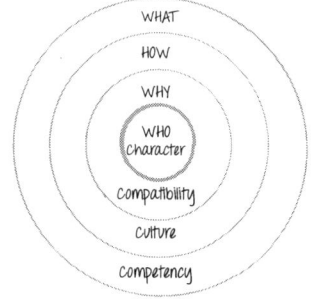

Who - The Character of a Person

People who inspire me to be more like Jesus

The central role of any relationship that I choose to influence me is to help bring out the nature of Christ in my life. Whether it is choosing someone to coach or to marry me, one question really does and should be the lynch pin.

'Does this person inspire me to be more like Christ?'

No one is perfect and when we draw close to any human being we will realise that they looked better from a distance, as indeed do I. Remember, broken people are more relatable than 'perfect' people. However, within a broken person there has to be a pursuit and desire for Christ-likeness that brings a challenge to us in this relationship.

Paul said: *Follow my example, as I follow the example of Christ* (1 Cor 11:1). We need people who exemplify the principles of the Word of God. After all it is the Living Word, and the most effective way of learning is through demonstration and example.

Shared beliefs are an essential core foundation for your winning team in life.

Why - The Compatibility of a Person

Humility is the unifying force of the Kingdom

I look for humility in the people I want to influence me. Humility creates a consistency with which a team of people can become one. It is the emulsifying force that enables a community of people to project Christ. The Kingdom goal according to King Jesus is unity or oneness. John's gospel chapter 17:21-22 captures this thought in a significant prayer of Jesus: *'May ....all of them may be one, Father, just as you are in me and I am in you. May they also be in us so that the world may believe that you have sent me. I have given them the glory that you gave me, that they may be one as we are one.'*

The glory of God is unlocked through unity and unity requires humility. Like me, you want great people to influence you. Jesus helps us understand what greatness in the Kingdom looks like in Matthew 20:26-28: *'Not so with you. Instead, whoever wants to become great among you must be your servant, and whoever wants to be first must be your slave - just as the Son of Man did not come to be served, but to serve, and to give his life as a ransom for many.'*

What does humility look like? Humility is when a person is more interested in serving your needs than you serving theirs (note: I said needs not wants).

SECTION 3: THE WINNING TEAM

How - The Culture of a Relationship

People with whom I can build on my God-given emphases

Our values (PRIORITIES) are the branches that grow from the roots of our beliefs (PRINCIPLES). Values are what we seek to emphasise and prioritise as important. We can learn from people who do not share the same values. In fact it is vital that we broaden the kinds of people with whom we speak. However when it comes to developing a winning team of people you do life with, shared values are essential. You need to prioritise with others in order for that environment to grow what is in you. Your values are your Kingdom 'flavour.' Disunity of values creates a culture clash and this tears relationships apart.

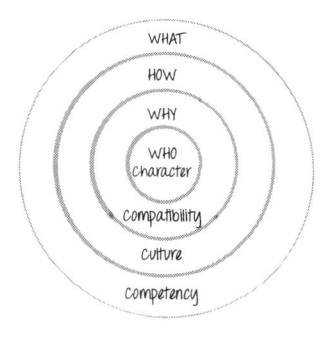

Remember however, this is not about WHAT we do; it is about HOW we do it.

It is important that we do not confuse cultural values with style. Style is a WHAT not HOW. Cultural values transcend style. The values shared in this book are not the sole property of any country or group of people. They are Kingdom values based on Kingdom beliefs.

When Jesus preached the Sermon on the Mount He helped us as Christians understand the difference between beliefs and values. Jesus said in Matthew 5:7: *'Do not think that I have come to abolish the Law or the Prophets; I have not come to abolish them but to fulfil them.'*

Jesus came to emphasise a new HOW. He was not changing the principle. An example would be verse 21ff: *'You have heard that it was said to the people long ago, "You shall not murder, and anyone who murders will be subject to judgment." But I tell you that anyone who is angry with a brother or sister will be subject to judgment.'*

There is no change of belief. God does not tolerate murder. However Jesus prioritised how this belief applies not only to our behaviour but to our thought life. He raised the bar, deepened the conviction and re-established the standard of this belief.

What - The Competency within a Relationship

People who inspire me to get better through their example

We need to be surrounded by people who have competencies that complement our weaknesses. 1 Corinthians 12 provides the image of the Church as the Body of Christ. This communicates the Kingdom principle of interdependence. For me to grow in life, I need people with certain strengths that help promote the things that I need to get better at. Whilst this passage is not speaking exclusively about interdependence of gifts, the principle applies.

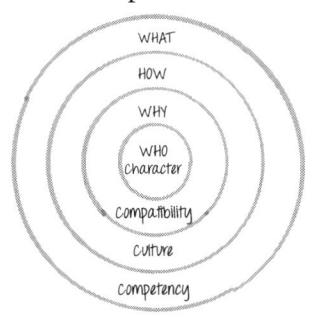

What are the areas of life that I need to get better at? Out of the six conversations I look at in this book, there are many things that I identify as important to live the winning life. However, other people do some of these things far better than me. I need these people to keep getting better and help me get better. Whether its ways to connect with people, ability to prioritise or being creative in being generous, I want, and need to get better. I need these people and these people need me.

In 2 Corinthians 8 Paul praised the competency of the Macedonian church for their level of generosity. He also lauded the personality traits of Titus, championing his ability to be enthusiastic and use his own initiative.

We need people who inspire us to win.

Conversation with God:

Father, I recognise that I need people. Help me overcome the barriers that stop me asking for help and seeking input from others. Humble my heart and Holy Spirit help me to start to identify people who can invest in me as I seek to invest in others.

SECTION 3: THE WINNING TEAM

Day 16: - The Winning People around my Purpose

We each have a unique assignment that God has for us, however we cannot fulfil this on our own. We need the help of many other people to achieve our winning purpose. This is not achieved through asking others to prioritise our wants. When we seek to serve the purpose and plans God has for others, others will feed into our purpose. As we have established in this book already, it is about doing things in the correct order. In serving others we unlock our Kingdom potential and purpose.

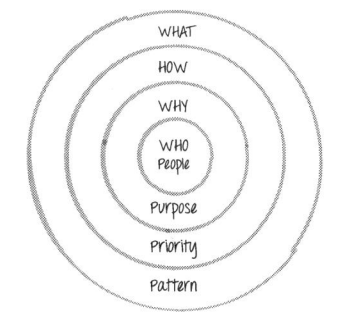

Step 1: WHO - The kind of people in my team

There are four kinds of roles that we see in the bible that are required for a winning team.

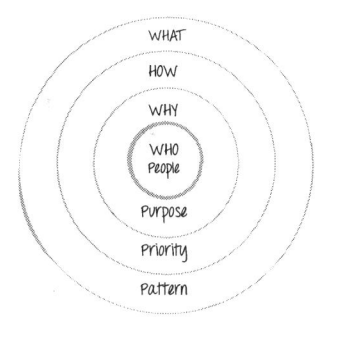

Counsel - We need people who provide counsel

There are specific times when we need counsel and we need to know who these people are or be willing to find suitable counsel if our situation is unique. We usually need these people when we face significant decisions and/or facing crisis.

Proverbs 11:14

For lack of guidance a nation falls, but victory is won through many advisers.

God has hidden resources in our relationships and one of those hidden treasures is experience and perspective. As human beings we can often be led by emotion in a decision, however we need people who are emotionless about our context (emotionless does not mean heartless) and can bring a level perspective helping us spot any blind spots we might be missing because we have convinced ourselves that everything is good to proceed in the way we feel we should go.

Counsel can be sort from numerous sources, but it is essential that the more important the decision we make the more aware this person is of biblical counsel. Paul says that *All Scripture is God-breathed and is useful for teaching, rebuking, correcting and training in righteousness...*(2 Tim 3:16) We need people who can use the standards of the bible and apply them to our context.

Coaching - We need people who will coach us

These people are a consistent voice into our lives and have oversight of our winning purpose. We need people who can see our plans in order to help us bring them to pass.

Prov 20:18 *Plans are established by seeking advice; so if you wage war, obtain guidance.*

Coaching is a form of discipleship. Jesus helped the disciples shape up for life without him so that they could fulfil their Kingdom mission as the early apostles of the church. We need someone to coach us and we need to be coaching at least someone else. A coach is given permission to be brutally honest.

Proverbs 27:17 *As iron sharpens iron, so one person sharpens another.* Coaching is a two way process. While one person may be designated the coach and leads through great questions, both people are sharpened in the process.

It is my belief that coaching is a 21st century interpretation of discipleship. Coaching can be used in a faith context or a non-faith context. Coaching is essentially people and life development and has a holisitic benefit. I believe every able person should aspire to coach to some degree, especially Christians.

Community - We need people with whom we share a common unity

There are biblical disciplines that require a community within which they can be practiced. Our participation in this community is essential to our growth. As we serve these people we will discover it to be an avenue through which some of our close team around our purpose will be found.

A healthy community that is devoted to one another around Jesus will experience and enjoy the favour of God. It was this favour that saw the early church expand with such momentum.

Acts 2:42-47 Devoted to one another

They devoted themselves to the apostles' teaching and to fellowship, to the breaking of bread and to prayer. Everyone was filled with awe at the many wonders and signs performed by the apostles. All the believers were together and had everything in common. They sold property and possessions to give to anyone who had need. Every day they continued to meet together in the temple courts. They broke bread in their homes and ate together with glad and sincere hearts, praising God and enjoying the favour of all the people. And the Lord added to their number daily those who were being saved.

It is amazing what happens when a group of people are committed to the success of the whole team as opposed to their individual success. The result is nothing short of extraordinary. With Gods involvement that extra-ordinary takes on a supernatural dimension.

Collaboration - We need people with whom we work closely alongside on specific tasks and projects

As we will see through the 'Expansive Conversation', the Kingdom of God is unlocked when we collaborate, unlocking the joint potential of a group of people who are in agreement. An inspiring biblical example of such collaboration is found in the book of Nehemiah. Nehemiah identified his winning goal of rebuilding the city walls of Jerusalem. He was only a cup bearer to the King, and had no such experience of this engineering feat. However, he pulled together a winning team and we read this in this Old Testament book:

Nehemiah 5:16-17

Instead, I devoted myself to the work on this wall. All my men were assembled there for the work; we did not acquire any land.

Furthermore, a hundred and fifty Jews and officials ate at my table, as well as those who came to us from the surrounding nations.

These men united together and accomplished this huge task within 52 days! That is the power of Kingdom expansion when people unite around a task that is on God's heart.

Step 2: WHY - The purpose for why they are in my team

The principle of synergy is found in Deuteronomy 32:30 where we understand that while one man can chase a 1000 men, two men can chase 10,000. The sum total of the individual parts combines to have an exponential effect. However, the key is HOW the two or more individuals come together.

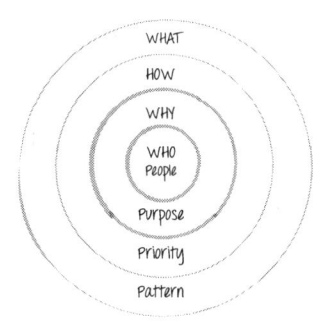

When we are meeting up with people pray beforehand and ask God to help you discern before and during how you can not only learn from the person you are meeting but also how you might be able to serve them. When we involve God we strengthen our relational connections as we understand from ECC 4:12 *Though one may be overpowered, two can defend themselves. A cord of three strands is not quickly broken.*

Step 3: HOW - The prioritising of key environments in my involvement with others

Close - Jesus moments with a disciple

Jesus had a number of close moments with the one disciple or the three disciples. One of his most significant close moments was with Peter in Matthew 16:13-20 when he was able to unlock specific revelation about Peter's kingdom assignment. In the western church we are not so focussed on creating these intimate and vulnerable moments. They require high intentionality and happen organically where as the other environments are often part of church programmes.

I would argue that close coaching/ discipleship moments are the missing piece that will unleash the power of the church in our generation, hence the desire to see coaching rise to the fore in the Church as a framework for effective discipleship in the 21st century. Close moments create high accountability which is essential when our default sinful natures are naturally lazy and self-serving.

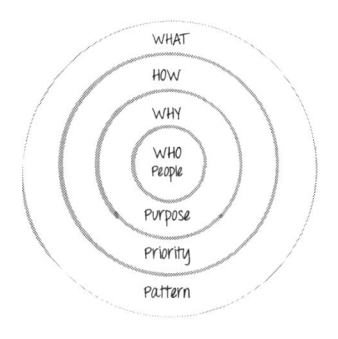

Unlocking your Kingdom potential requires you to be involved, even initiate close moments. These do not have to be intense affairs, some of my most significant moments have taken place in coffee shops whilst talking. These rarely feel like an urgent priority to us, but I would suggest that these conversations can do more than many days of work in terms of shaping how we progress our purpose.

Core - Jesus moments with the disciple group

Jesus exemplifies the rhythm we need to emulate if we are to unlock our kingdom potential. Jesus knew that with only three years on earth to perform his ministry He needed to invest in those who would live beyond Him. His legacy was more important than the demands of consumer crowds.

Matt 11:1 After Jesus had finished instructing his twelve disciples, he went on from there to teach and preach in the towns of Galilee.

When it comes to developing a winning team around my purpose, I need to follow Jesus' example and identify a core group of people that I can either pull together or be part of through which I can serve others and in turn unlock my kingdom potential.

Crowd - Jesus moments in the crowd

Jesus called the disciples to be *fishers of men* (Matt 4:19) and I believe this analogy had a wider significance than simply being a relevant analogy to communicate to a group of fishermen their new calling. Jesus' crowd ministry was a means of casting the net of the Kingdom message out in order for many *fish* to jump into the net.

There are crowds of people that you need to visit in order to go fishing for people who are beyond your normal circles. Key shifts in the progress of your purpose rely on you pushing the boundaries of the circles you operate in.

Step 4: WHAT - The pattern of involving these roles and environments with others.

No one other than yourself (or your coach) will instruct you to pull together a healthy pattern for developing yourself through these environments. If like me you want to see the harvest (the results) of your purpose then note what Solomon points out about the ant in Proverbs 6:6-8

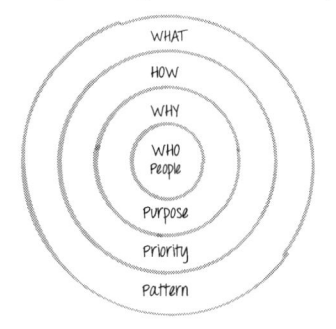

Go to the ant, you sluggard; consider its ways and be wise! It has no commander, no overseer or ruler, yet it stores its provisions in summer and gathers its food at harvest.

Your provision is stored away in the people you serve. As you find how you can help them win, so you in turn will experience incredible wins that you could never have imagined.

Conversation with God:

Father God, I thank you that you have provided all that I need through people in the body of Christ, the church. Reveal to me the people I am to lean into to help me move forward in your plans and purposes. I thank you for Christ's example operating across the different groups of people. While I am aware of the environments I find most challenging; my commitment to see others built up and there potential unlocked means I will do whatever it takes.

Day 17: The Winning Evaluation

One day we will all stand before God and give an account for our lives. That day will be the ultimate evaluation. As I have already mentioned, our acceptance of Jesus as our Lord during our lifetime is our requirement for access to heaven, and then our reward will be based upon the quality of our living for Jesus whilst on earth.

We can either make that day a moment to look forward to, because every day we are building toward a result that will please God, or we can be like the lazy servant in the Parable of the Talents who buried his head in the sand thinking he could excuse his way out of his lack of results.

The way to prepare for that day of evaluation is to create a rhythm of evaluation so we can see how we are actually doing rather than how we feel we are doing. We have already established that feelings are unreliable and a dangerous leader for our lives. We need more objective criteria.

Once again we see from the Bible that our results are our own responsibility.

So how do we unlock greater results?

Evaluation requires a benchmark

In Romans 7, Paul helps us understand the role of the Jewish law. Jesus came and fulfilled the law; He did not come to get rid of it (Matt 5:17). So what is its function now that Jesus had superseded it?

This is the question Paul answers:

What shall we say, then? Is the law sinful? Certainly not! Nevertheless, I would not have known what sin was had it not been for the law.

The law is a <u>benchmark</u> to show the distance that exists between God's standard and our best efforts. It makes for frustrating comparison. However, it is important that frustration exists otherwise we would not ask the question, 'How is the gap between where God wants me to be and where I am going to be bridged?'

This is what benchmarks do; they produce frustration through providing clarity on how well we are doing so that we can make decisions in order to close the gap.

Paul is vulnerable in the book of *Romans* and reveals his inner struggles. As he paints a picture of his internal conflict, I'm sure you will be able to identity with his frustration.

His description is really one of a civil war - a struggle between two sides who live in the same place but want total possession and rule. The two sides Paul speaks of are his sinful self (defaults) and his spirit self (design). Paul shares his frustration that despite his best of intentions to do what is right and good, in other words back his spirit self, the sinful self seems to take over every time.

I need something more! For if I know the law but still can't keep it, and if the power of sin within me keeps sabotaging my best intentions, I obviously need help! I realise that I don't have what it takes. I can will it, but I can't do it. I decide to do good, but I don't really do it; I decide not to do bad, but then I do it anyway. My decisions, such as they are, don't result in actions. Something has gone wrong deep within me and gets the better of me every time (The Message).

Paul struggles to act on his best intentions. Every time he is overthrown by his sinful defaults, doing what makes him feel good and look good. With every decision to do good, he is aware of the likelihood that he will not be able to follow through.

It happens so regularly that it's predictable. The moment I decide to do good, sin is there to trip me up. I truly delight in God's commands, but it's pretty obvious that not all of me joins in that delight. Parts of me covertly rebel, and just when I least expect it, they take charge.

Evaluation leads us to revelation - Find the Missing Piece

Paul's self-evaluation and benchmarking against the law brought him first into a feeling of hopelessness. This is why many of us do not evaluate because it is better to believe everything is going well in ignorance rather than face up to the pain of the mess that lies within.

I know that when I am in control of my finances I have no problem visiting my online banking, I have no problem stepping on the weighing scales when I am in the flow of regular exercise. However when I have neglected these areas I am reluctant to face them for fear of how it will make me feel. I do not want the feeling of hopelessness. People avoid dentists and doctors for the same reason.

Paul faced up to the pain of his personal reality and when he realised the distance between where he was and where he needed to be he was able to ask the revelation question:

What is it that I do not know that is stopping me progressing?

When we get a true picture of our results we are able to get clarity through asking this question. Paul's revelation took him to the limit and it was at this point that he was ready to discover a way past the problem.

I've tried everything and nothing helps. I'm at the end of my rope. Is there no one who can do anything for me? Isn't that the real question? The answer, thank God, is that Jesus Christ can and does. He acted to set things right in this life of contradictions where I want to serve God with all my heart and mind, but am pulled by the influence of sin to do something totally different.

Kingdom clarity lies on the other side of honest benchmarking.

Evaluation leads us to rebellion - Stop the Subtracting Element

Finding the answer is one thing, but then taking the steps to back the new creation, the winning you, is essential. It means everything within you needs to rebel against the default settings of your old identity and back your design, the new identity in Christ Jesus. As Romans 8:1-2 says:

With the arrival of Jesus, the Messiah, that fateful dilemma is resolved. Those who enter into Christ's being-here-for-us no longer have to live under a continuous, low-lying black cloud. A new power is in operation. The Spirit of life in Christ, like a strong wind, has magnificently cleared the air, freeing you from a fated lifetime of brutal tyranny at the hands of sin and death (The Message).

Paul is not being over-dramatic in his imagery; this quite literally is the fight of YOUR LIFE. Everything you can hope and dream is counting on you backing the Spirit of Christ over self. It's the tag team match of eternity as you and the Spirit of Christ seek to dethrone the opposing team of sin and self.

They aren't going to take it lying down.

As Paul continues in verses 3-4 of Romans (The Message):

God went for the jugular when he sent his own Son. He didn't deal with the problem as something remote and unimportant. In his Son, Jesus, he personally took on the human condition, entered the disordered mess of struggling humanity in order to set it right once and for all. The law code, weakened as it always was by fractured human nature, could never have done that.

While the spiritual significance of this may appear obvious, you might be wondering what this has to do with me achieving practical goals like losing weight, setting up in business, starting a family. The reality is that we are integrated beings. Everything we fail to action in life is ultimately rooted in a failure of our belief system. It is a spiritual problem. The apple lying under the tree is a result of the roots under the ground. People get worn out trying to achieve goals through trying to influence behaviour patterns. What we need to change is our beliefs. This is why Paul was able to ask the rebellion question: *What is it that I need to stop doing and why?*

He knew that he needed to stop striving in his own strength because he did not have what it takes to make up the failure gap between himself and the benchmark of the law. In fact he would kill himself trying. He needed to let go of striving and let God work through him.

Evaluation leads us to revolution - Establish the New Law

With a new governing power on the inside, Paul moved to a new focus that would unlock new opportunity. All he had to do was welcome the new government every day. So in Romans 8:9-11 he writes:

> *But if God himself has taken up residence in your life, you can hardly be thinking more of yourself than of him. Anyone, of course, who has not welcomed this invisible but clearly present God, the Spirit of Christ, won't know what we're talking about. But for you who welcome him, in whom he dwells—even though you still experience all the limitations of sin—you yourself experience life on God's terms. It stands to reason, doesn't it, that if the alive-and-present God who raised Jesus from the dead moves into your life, he'll do the same thing in you that he did in Jesus, bringing you alive to himself? When God lives and breathes in you (and he does, as surely as he did in Jesus), you are delivered from that dead life. With his Spirit living in you, your body will be as alive as Christ's!*

When we think of Christ as the new governing power in our lives, we should remember how Jesus fulfilled the prophecy of Isaiah 9:6:

For to us a child is born, to us a son is given, and the government will be on his shoulders. And he will be called Wonderful Counsellor, Mighty God, Everlasting Father, Prince of Peace.

The mantle for governing is on Jesus' shoulders!

The Jewish people mistook this to mean a physical change of government that would dominate other world powers. However, the Kingdom of God is an invisible government that shapes all that is seen, including our own spirits. This is why the governing power of Christ needs to be established in our lives. When it is, we opt to back his revolution against the old power of sin.

When answering the revolutionary question *'What new discipline do I need to start doing?'* Paul knew that it was all about his internal conversation being led by Jesus as the new head of state and ruling power. As long as he kept backing it, he would keep living in the victory of the Champion who is Christ. That is why he says in Romans 8:15-17:

This resurrection life you received from God is not a timid, grave-tending life. It's adventurously expectant, greeting God with a childlike "What's next, Papa?" God's Spirit touches our spirits and confirms who we really are. We know who he is, and we know who we are: Father and children. And we know we are going to get what's coming to us—an unbelievable inheritance! We go through exactly what Christ goes through. If we go through the hard times with him, then we're certainly going to go through the good times with him! Message

The revolution does not make us exempt from failure and frustration. This is the battle of life and it is the battle that causes us to draw more from Christ as our source and in doing so to become more like him. The revolution means that we have the ability to live a winning life regardless of what is happening to us.

Winning in life is ultimately about preparing us for an eternity with God where the win will be complete and the winning crowns for champions distributed! (James 1:12, ESV).

RESOLUTION - A New Normal is Created

What can I put in place to make sure I keep doing this?

Paul encourages the church at Galatia to stay informed not ignorant. He encourages them not to be deceived by how they feel things are going.

If anyone thinks they are something when they are not, they deceive themselves. Each one should test their own actions. Then they can take pride in themselves alone, without comparing themselves to someone else, for each one should carry their own load (Galatians 6:3-5).

When we live a Kingdom life, we are in a war which means the most dangerous position to be in is complacent. You will build momentum in unlocking Christ's potential in you but always stay alert (1 Peter 5:8) because the enemy is looking for any lapse in focus. You will be tempted at times to feel like everything is going well. While you must maintain a grateful mood, you must also stay aware of the facts. Jeremiah 17:9 reminds us that *the heart is deceitful above all things.* Tomorrow we look at the importance of accountability which helps us stay alert and focussed.

Paul answers the resolution question *'What can I put in place to make sure I keep doing this?'*

The key is maintaining awareness of what God is doing in us and for us. There will be times when we feel weary and weak, susceptible to the enemy but the Holy Spirit is our counsellor, the ultimate coach who is our prayer partner around the clock. You could not ask for a better prayer partner! As Romans 8:26-28 says:

Meanwhile, the moment we get tired in the waiting, God's Spirit is right alongside helping us along. If we don't know how or what to pray, it doesn't matter. He does our praying in and for us, making prayer out of our wordless sighs, our aching groans. He knows us far better than we know ourselves, knows our pregnant condition, and keeps us present before God. That's why we can be so sure that every detail in our lives of love for God is worked into something good.

When we live in awareness of our new status in Christ, the challenges that come with dreaming and thinking big make the adventure all the more appealing!

In any challenge we face, we do not have to be afraid of benchmarking and the clarity it brings because we have the certainty of our hope in Jesus, that through him we can do <u>*all*</u> *things* (Phil 4:13).

Conversation with God:

Father God, I thank you that I can come into your presence and examine my heart. Your Word helps me to evaluate how I am doing. Even when I fail you, you do not condemn me (John 3:17) but you help me learn to live again (John 10:10). I thank you that I can live from a point of victory (1 Corinthians 15:57) and my failures help me identify the Christ potential that has yet to be unlocked.

Day 18: The Winning Accountability

The demands of a champion

Any serious athlete with their hearts and minds set on winning understands the need to put self-imposed demands on themselves in order to unlock the potential that is inside them. They will involve other voices to help bring parameters and boundaries to their behaviour in order to keep them on a winning course. This is the heart of developing a winning team. You need a community of champions.

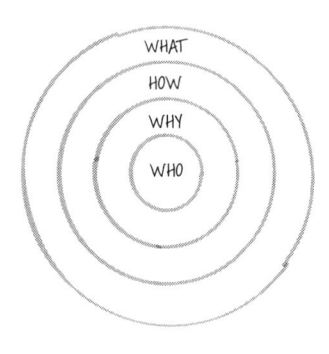

Paul had no one to place demands on him to do what he did. He placed them on himself. As he writes in 1 Corinthians 9:19-23:

Even though I am free of the demands and expectations of everyone, I have voluntarily become a servant to any and all in order to reach a wide range of people: religious, nonreligious, meticulous moralists, loose-living immoralists, the defeated, the demoralized—whoever. I didn't take on their way of life. I kept my bearings in Christ—but I entered their world and tried to experience things from their point of view. I've become just about every sort of servant there is in my attempts to lead those I meet into a God-saved life. I did all this because of the Message. I didn't just want to talk about it; I wanted to be in on it! Message

Paul wanted to be in on what God had for him and this required self-imposed constraints.

We need to set parameters for our lives through right relationships. This helps to unlock the MORE than is in us.

In Proverbs 29:18 it says, *Where there is no revelation, people cast off restraint; but blessed is the one who heeds wisdom's instruction.*

Let me rephrase that as a positive statement: *Where there is revelation (vision or a winning goal) people embrace restraint and are blessed because they invite the instruction of wisdom.*

Paul set us an example of 'no holds barred' Christianity - the brutal belief that Christ's best comes out of setting ourselves tough tests. By doing this we crave for the grace of Christ in us to be released.

This is why Paul continues in verses 24-27 of 1 Cor 9 to say this:

You've all been to the stadium and seen the athletes race. Everyone runs; one wins. Run to win. All good athletes train hard. They do it for a gold medal that tarnishes and fades. You're after one that's gold eternally.

I don't know about you, but I'm running hard for the finish line. I'm giving it everything I've got. No sloppy living for me! I'm staying alert and in top condition. I'm not going to get caught napping, telling everyone else all about it and then missing out myself. Message

Determine that you are not going to miss out on the future God has for you and get brutal with embracing *the winning accountability.*

The three demands we place on ourselves are:

i) Accountability - Put the demand in the hands of another

What makes you turn up to work? What makes you file your tax return? What makes you pay your bills? Someone has placed a demand on you and they expect a result. You are being held to account. It is only when we involve others and empower them to hold us to account that we can move from intention to action.

Accountability is God's idea to help us win. This is why He said right at the beginning, It is not good for man to be alone. This principle applies in any context, not just marriage. We are not designed to win alone. As the Message version of Ecclesiastes 4:9-10 reads: *It's better to have a partner than go it alone. Share the work, share the wealth. And if one falls down, the other helps.*

Accountability is an act of humility. To those we make ourselves accountable we are saying. 'I need you to make this happen and cannot achieve it without you.' This works against the grain of our prideful self but this is part of the revolution; we have to die to self and embrace the strength of others. When we do this, we are in fact tapping into the strength of the Body of Christ. There is limitless potential within the Body of Christ if we put the demands on it.

ii) Authenticity

Failure is a key part of the journey of a champion.

The team that surrounds a champion has to be aware that

failure is part of the journey and be mature enough to handle it properly. Any team that has helped produce a champion will have used failure as a means of bringing progress.

Every airplane is fitted with a black box which is designed to collate information when the airplane fails. The idea is that in every past disaster there is a gift for the future -new knowledge that brings improvement and progress. I like to think of it this way, 'in every black box of my failure is a gift box for my future success.'

We need authentic relationships where we can have frank discussions designed to open the black box and uncover the truth for our future. The reason we cannot do this effectively on our own is because we are emotionally tied in to the choices and decisions we have made. We need someone who is not led emotionally in those situations to help shed light.

Even when we have a positive belief about failure it does not go all the way and anaesthetise us from the pain. We all need encouraging voices to help us through and to prevent us taking shortcuts to minimise short term pain (Heb 3:13).

Jesus created a team environment where failure was not a cultural taboo. Peter and Judas failed around the same time. The difference was that Peter's relationship with Jesus was authentic; Jesus could have the conversation with Peter that could take the pain of Peter's failure (Luke 22:34ff) and turn it into his platform (Acts 2:14). Judas was not open to authentic conversation and therefore failure caused him to crash and burn. When Jesus reinstated Peter (John 21:15-19), Peter learnt what it was like to unpack failure in a relationship where there was no judgment but an empowering expectation of what Peter could go on to do.

Authenticity is not an excuse to fail but simply realising that it happens and that the process of sanctification (being made like Jesus) that we read of in John 17:17 needs a truthful conversation if it is to be outworked. Jesus welcomes us as we are to approach Him because we are never made good enough as a result of our performance. We are only made right through His grace. When we truly experience His grace we never want to stay the way we are. We are inspired and motivated by his love to achieve a higher level. We do this not by living <u>for</u> His approval but by living <u>from</u> His approval.

iii) Agreement

A champion not only accepts that failure is part of the journey but in fact works hard at creating the possibility of failure in order to improve. When we agree on a goal we set ourselves up for the possibility of failure. This is why many avoid goal setting because it's too painful and exposes true intentions. However, the process of failing and succeeding through goal setting with others means that they get to know the real me. This level of relationship, while vulnerable, actually creates permission to encourage and permission to challenge.

How many times have you had a conversation with someone who you know intended to do something but never did it? You said to yourself, 'I knew when they said they would do it that they wouldn't!' Sound familiar? People have said it when you and I have made public our intentions. This kind of conversation, kept to ourselves, helps no one. We need to give permission for people to hold us to account and ask 'Why didn't you follow through with your intention?'

Proverbs 27:5-6 says: *Better is open rebuke than hidden love. Wounds from a friend can be trusted, but an enemy multiplies kisses.*

In one sense we are inviting people to cause us pain, because the truth hurts. However, this form of brutality is simply killing off my old identity and giving way to my new Christ identity.

Find a Coach and become a Coach

The goal behind the winning dice (see www.thewinningconversation.com for more details) is to help create a tool for coaching. Whether it's relational or professional, coaching is part of unlocking the potential in you.

In Matthew 5:19 Jesus says: *Whoever practices and teaches these commands will be called great in the kingdom of heaven.* The rhythm of practicing and teaching is the tension that creates forward motion in the Kingdom and gets the potential that is in us out of us.

The more we encourage and build others up, the more we are built up (1 Thessalonians 5:11).

Conversation with God:

Father God, help me to be vulnerable enough to ask for help in becoming the person you want me to be. I realise that I cannot do this on my own. You have designed me to be accountable and authentic with others and not afraid to make agreements about what I am seeking to achieve for you. So help me to be transparent and open in my relationships.

SECTION 4: BE MORE PROMINENT

Section 4: Be MORE prominent

Day 19: The Winning Conversation makes you MORE Prominent

Devotion unlocks the door of **Prominence**

Kingdom Key: *You are a city on a hill. You are the light of the world. A city that is set on a hill cannot be hidden* (Matthew 5:14).

When I host the prominent conversation I become:

1) MORE Others-Driven

Confidence comes from focussing on others more than myself

When we centre our lives on serving the needs of other people we unlock the Christ potential inside us. The key to effective serving is to identify with the suffering of those we are trying to help. This work is deeply spiritual. The more spiritual our work, the more fulfilling it is and the greater potential there is for God to make us prominent in the eyes of others for His glory.

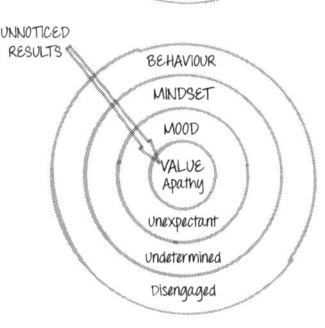

Making disciples is ultimately about connecting spiritually with people and exampling Christ so that they experience heaven on earth. As Jesus said in Matthew 28:-18-20 (ESV):

All authority in heaven and on earth has been given to me. Go therefore and make disciples of all nations, baptizing them in the name of the Father and of the Son and of the Holy Spirit, teaching them to observe all that I have commanded you. And behold, I am with you always, to the end of the age.

Being exposed to the reality of other people's suffering is a necessary part of our personal development. It softens our hearts and causes us to realise that our lives must count for more than just material objects. Suffering is accordingly of great significance when it comes to unlocking a person's potential. The more others-driven we become the more we have to be prepared to suffer. But this suffering has a purpose. As Paul says in Romans 5:3-5 (NIV):

Not only so, but we also glory in our sufferings, because we know that suffering produces perseverance; perseverance, character; and character, hope. And hope does not put us to shame, because God's love has been poured out into our hearts through the Holy Spirit, who has been given to us.

Conversation with God:

Father God, you loved me so much that you gave everything in your son Jesus. I thank you that Jesus can identify and emphasise with my weaknesses (Heb 4:15). Help me to identify with the weaknesses and suffering of others. I want to unlock my kingdom prominence by being 'others-driven.'

2) MORE Aware of Your Journey

The big picture should drive the small decisions

Jesus knew that the big picture for Him was to start the Kingdom of God on earth so He proceeded to line up His choices in order to achieve that bigger goal. The first step for Him was to usher in the Kingdom among His own people, the Jews. His devotion kept His eye on the bigger picture while making the daily choices of reaching the Jewish people throughout His three years of ministry.

Jesus coached His team to stay aware of the big picture of the Kingdom while maintaining the narrow focus of their current assignment. We see evidence of this in Matthew 10:6 when Jesus tells them, Go rather to the lost sheep of Israel. Jesus knew there was an order to His work. He carried the same desire as the Father, that no one would miss out on the Kingdom (2 Peter 3). But He also knew He had to be ruthless with His priorities. This focus helped Him put parameters around what He did. That is why in: Matthew 15:24 He insisted, *I was sent only to the lost sheep of Israel.*

The big picture of the Kingdom of God and its advancement has been established for believers. God is willing to work with us on the business of devoting ourselves in a focused way so that we will be effective in our unique assignment.

Are all the small choices we make made against this backdrop?

If we get the order right, then we receive heaven's assistance.

As Jesus says in Matthew 6:33:

Seek first His Kingdom and His righteousness, and all these things will be given to you as well.

3) MORE Compassionate

Compassion creates clarity

Jesus demonstrated how devotion to our cause unlocks compassion. The deeper our devotion, the greater clarity we receive in our prioritising. In the process, our motivation moves up the gears. So we read in Matthew 9:36-38:

When He saw the crowds, He had <u>compassion</u> on them, because they were harassed and helpless, like sheep without a shepherd. Then He said to his disciples, "The <u>harvest is plentiful</u> but the workers are few. Ask the Lord of the harvest, therefore, to <u>send out workers</u> into His harvest field."

In the verses above, Jesus saw through the eyes of His devoted heart and this unlocked compassion. It caused Him to re-clarify the vision of readiness of 'the harvest' and this motivated Him to tell the disciples to pray and seek out more workers because people were ready to be reached.

4) MORE Loyal

Loyalty to others builds a bigger world for you to live in

Our prominence as Kingdom people is unlocked through our loyalty and love toward one another. When people come into an experience of a loving community where the interests of others are a priority over self-interest, they will take notice. As Jesus said in John 13:34-35:

A new command I give you: Love one another. As I have loved you, so you must love one another. By this everyone will know that you are my disciples, if you love one another.

Prominence is the result of consistent devotion. Consistent devotion is the disciplined belief that drives us. If we rely upon an externally inspired driver, our devotion will be inconsistent and will fail to be distinctive to the majority of people because they also work according to an outside-in pattern.

Paul reveals the Kingdom key of deep love and loyalty amongst believers. This produces prominence in a world vying for attention. As he says in Romans 12:9-13:

Love must be sincere. Hate what is evil; cling to what is good. Be devoted to one another in love. Honour one another above yourselves. Never be lacking in zeal, but keep your spiritual fervour, serving the Lord. Be joyful in hope, patient in affliction, faithful in prayer. Share with the Lord's people who are in need. Practice hospitality.

5) MORE Affectionate

Prominence in the eyes of others is powered by our emotional capacity

We need Christ to unlock our emotional potential. In the Kingdom of God my love toward someone is like a bill that I owe. As Paul puts it in Romans 13:8:

Let no debt remain outstanding, except the continuing debt to love one another, for whoever loves others has fulfilled the law.

We do not ask, 'Shall I love?' It's a command I embrace. I tell myself 'I want to' value and love others. This level of devotion in our spiritual core will unlock emotion and affection that we did not know existed in us. This should be no surprise because actually the emotion and affection comes from Christ in you. Heaven invades the lives you interact with, if you let it!

6) MORE Noticeable

Our prominence should be determined by the size of the cause and not by the size of the personality

The drive of your Kingdom cause is to let Christ love people through you. Whatever the context of your winning goal, the heart of each cause remains essentially the same. Ask yourself, 'How can I bring heaven to earth through my Kingdom mission?' Whether it's a classroom, a factory, a business, an office or interacting with other parents, you are on a Kingdom assignment.

When working on your cause, avoid getting caught up with the prize of getting noticed. Remember the Winning Conversation is about the right order. When we shift from the process to the prize we veer into the losing conversation that will result in apathy. There will be times when you are not noticed and if you are prize focused then you will start to make decisions based on a wrong WHY to feed the insatiable appetite of *affection* from the outside in.

Get your eyes off yourself and focus on the goal of the cause, those to whom Christ has called you to bring hope. Picture them now. When they become your focus you will fire on all your emotional cylinders and be amazed how your supply does not run dry because heaven is working its limitless supply through you. As you give out, so the supply of heaven will flow. As Jesus said in Luke 6:38:

Give, and it will be given to you. A good measure, pressed down, shaken together and running over, will be poured into your lap. For with the measure you use, it will be measured to you."

7) MORE Discerning

When a person's true cause is themselves they will drain and not motivate you

Jesus had discernment about those who wanted to approach

Him as consumers. He knew when someone had a valid need and when someone was treating him like a product. So, for example, He discerned that the woman with the issue of blood had a genuine call upon His resources. As we read in Luke 8:45-48:

"Who touched me?" Jesus asked.

When they all denied it, Peter said, "Master, the people are crowding and pressing against you." But Jesus said, "Someone touched me; I know that power has gone out from me." Then the woman, seeing that she could not go unnoticed, came trembling and fell at His feet. In the presence of all the people, she told why she had touched Him and how she had been instantly healed. Then He said to her, "Daughter, your faith has healed you. Go in peace."

We need to discern at what point we are simply feeding someone's 'soul addiction' rather than helping them find their source in Jesus.

Allowing someone to over-consume from us can cause 'mission drift' and distraction. Our goal is to hook them up to the Kingdom supply of Christ Jesus who is our all sufficient one (Col 1:13-20).

Kingdom prominence comes when we operate with discernment.

Ask the Holy Spirit today to give you the gift of discernment (1 Corinthians 12:7-11; James 1:5).

Day 20: The Winning Voice of Devotion

DEVOTION unlocks the door of PROMINENCE

Kingdom Key: *"You are the light of the world. A city that is set on a hill cannot be hidden"* (Matthew 5:14).

To be a person of devotion I have to immerse myself in the demands of God's design that are going to lead me into right feelings. The more I immerse myself in the *belief* that *I am devoted* to God and to people, the more prominent I will become.

Paul says in Galatians 2:20: *I have been crucified with Christ and I no longer live, but Christ lives in me. The life I now live in the body,*

I live by faith in the Son of God, who loved me and gave Himself for me.

This means WHO I am is WHO He is.

My Kingdom purpose requires me to have adopted my new identity and to choose each day to live from the Christ core.

Because of Christ's nature in me I can declare each day that:

i) I AM Chosen

God has chosen me

The fact that we are chosen needs to be a belief we continually affirm. If we truly adopt this belief it actually deals a death blow to our self-doubt. God has hand-picked me at this time for a specific purpose. A true revelation of this raises my level of devotion toward him to the exclusion of everything else.

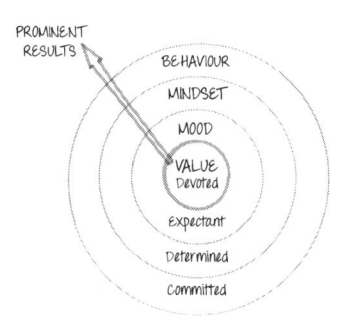

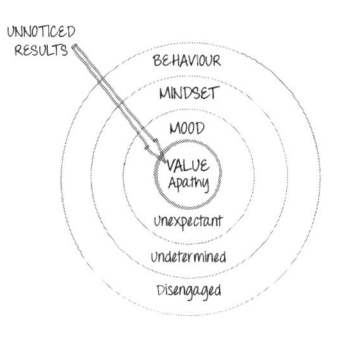

Kingdom Key: You did not choose me, but I chose you and appointed you that you should go and bear fruit and that your fruit should abide, so that whatever you ask the Father in my name, He may give it to you (John 15:16).

Conversation with God:

Father God, help me to get clarity on the reason you have chosen me to be alive at this time. Show me why I am alive at this time in history?

ii) I AM a Change Agent

I am the change God wants to see in the world

Jesus said, *"You are the light of the world,"* which means that you are to be the change that He wants to see in this world. You can see powerful transformation if you are willing to devote yourself to God's cause for your life. However, it will not happen without a fight; it will not happen without the winning voice of devotion. As Jean Nidetch says, "It's choice - not chance - that determines your destiny."

Every day I have to devote myself 100% to choosing the cause and I have to be willing to sacrifice whatever it takes to unleash my Kingdom potential.

Kingdom Key: "You are the light of the world. A town built on a hill cannot be hidden. Neither do people light a lamp and put it under a bowl. Instead they put it on its stand, and it gives light to everyone in the house. In the same way, let your light shine before others, that they may see your good deeds and glorify your Father in heaven" (Matthew 5:14-16).

Conversation with God:

What desire for change have you put in me, God? What must I do to see that take place in me first? What does that look like?

iii) I AM the Size of my Foundation

The height of your promotion is determined by the depth of your devotion

Jesus Christ could not have dug deeper foundations than to step into His own creation and become sin for us in order that we might be made right with God and have an opportunity to unlock heaven's potential in our lives (2 Corinthians 5:21). The depth of His devotion established the heights of our salvation. In Christ we are now seated in heavenly places in Christ Jesus (Eph 2:6-7) but in order to unlock the heights of heaven's potential on earth we must increase our levels of devotion.

Remember if Christ is in you, the levels of devotion you can reach are far beyond that which you can imagine (Matt 26:39).

Kingdom Key:

And being found in appearance as a man, He humbled himself by becoming obedient to death— even death on a cross! Therefore God exalted Him to the highest place and gave Him the name that is above every name, that at the name of Jesus every knee should bow, in heaven and on earth and under the earth, and every tongue acknowledge that Jesus Christ is Lord, to the glory of God the Father (Phil 2:8-11).

Conversation with God:

Father God, what are the 'grand design' changes that I sense I may be required to make to follow my cause?

iv) I AM my Uniqueness

It's not about making life easier for us but making it better for others

My pursuit should not be where the 'herds' go but an exploration of where I am different. I believe that Christ's assignment for your life lies in your difference - the very thing that sometimes you get embarrassed by but are passionate about. If I am going to build my life around a single focus, then it has to be my difference - my cause, my reason for being, my 'because.'

Kingdom Key: For we are his workmanship, created in Christ Jesus for good works, which God prepared beforehand, that we should walk in them (Ephesians 2:10).

Conversation with God:

What is the uniqueness God crafted into my life before I was born? How could it be linked to the things I am sometimes embarrassed about?

v) I AM being Trained by my Pain

The pain of the process makes you fit for your purpose

Devotion sets me up for a challenging and painful process but as long as I keep the purpose of the pain in front of me then I can press through to completion knowing that God's eternal purposes are being carried out on my character.

Kingdom Key: Dear friends, do not be surprised at the fiery ordeal that has come on you to test you, as though something strange were happening to you. But rejoice inasmuch as you participate in the sufferings of Christ, so that you may be overjoyed when His glory is revealed (1 Peter 4:12-13).

Conversation with God:

Father God, what pain do I carry that you are using to prepare me for my purpose?

Vi) I AM focused on one Person

A picture stirs desire in me which motivates me to keep going

In Luke 19:41 it was the picture of Jerusalem that caused Christ to weep. The sight of the city stirred up His Shepherd-heart to reach out to lost sheep.

There is a picture that resonates with the cause God is calling you to devote yourself to. A vision, a dream or a goal is simply a picture of the future you want to see. Without this image, apathy sets into our spirit.

Kingdom Key: "'In the last days, God says, I will pour out my Spirit on all people. Your sons and daughters will prophesy, your young men will see visions, your old men will dream dreams' (Acts 2:17).

Conversation with God:

Father God, what picture could I focus on that will create a burning desire in me when I feel myself slipping into apathy?

vii) I AM shaping my Convictions

A conviction is like the rudder of a ship; it carries incomparable power to turn around the toughest situations over time.

It is Christ's voice of devotion that keeps the other voices in the boardroom of our belief on track and moving in a uniform direction.

Create more time and space for His voice to speak. The more you hear His voice through His word, the deeper your belief goes and the more you will become increasingly convinced. Your conviction is what you have become convinced of. The more convinced you become the more conviction-led you will become in your decision-making.

Immerse yourself in your established convictions and you heighten your awareness of what God is doing around you. You see the jigsaw pieces God is giving you - the pieces of information, the contacts, the opportunities that you can collect along the journey to take the vision from the unseen to the seen.

Kingdom Key: That is why I am suffering as I am. Yet this is no cause for shame, because I know whom I have believed, and am <u>convinced</u> that He is able to guard what I have entrusted to Him until that day (2 Tim 1:12).

Conversation with God:

Father God, what are the things you are currently convincing me of? How will this belief potentially shape my future if I keep strengthening it?

viii) I AM Steadfast

Not everyone will champion my convictions and when this brings natural disappointment I will use it to further solidify what I believe

While convictions are developed internally, God can use everything externally to strengthen them. The more I have to persevere with the seed of my conviction, the greater the potential harvest can be reaped.

Kingdom Key: And let us not grow weary of doing good, for in due season we will reap, if we do not give up (Galatians 6:9).

Conversation with God:

Father God, what disappointments and discouragements have tempted me to become unstable in my convictions? How can I use this positively to reinforce what I believe regardless of the reaction I get from others?

ix) I AM Dying to Win

The feeling of dying precedes the greatest feeling of WHY you are alive

Paul honestly admits that our devotion to Christ and the process of outworking His assignment causes death in us. When our old defaults are put to death, this gives way to experiencing Christ's resurrection power. This creates an even greater clarity about the way Christ's life in me is meant to impact the world around me.

Kingdom Key: What is more, I consider everything a loss because of the surpassing worth of knowing Christ Jesus my Lord, for whose sake I have lost all things. I consider them garbage that I may gain Christ (Phil 3:8).

Conversation with God:

Father God, what do I avoid doing because of the feeling of death it creates in me? How is this actually setting me up for success rather than setting me back from success?

x) I AM Discovered through my Weakness

My weakness is the gateway to my greatest strength

My old identity is not the real me. It is simply the 'me' I have learned to accommodate in my body. When the weakness of this identity is exposed it creates a crack through which the new life of Christ can breakthrough. This is why weakness becomes strength and a point of celebration for the believer, because it gives way to the new creation, the new me in Jesus.

Kingdom Key: But He said to me, "My grace is sufficient for you, for my power is made perfect in weakness." Therefore I will boast all the more gladly about my weaknesses, so that Christ's power may rest on me (2 Corinthians 12:9).

Conversation with God:

Father God, what battles and weaknesses are you using to form strength in me?

SECTION 4: BE MORE PROMINENT

Day 21: The Winning Mood of EXPECTANCY

DEVOTION unlocks an EXPECTANT mood in me.

KINGDOM KEY: *"You are the light of the world. A city that is set on a hill cannot be hidden"* (Matthew 5:14).

My WHY purpose is to do the 'good work' which I was created to do (Eph 2:10). The vision of my life was prepared by God before I was even born (Jeremiah 1:50).

Expectancy Eradicates Uncertainty

A feeling of uncertainty can cause us to recoil and pull back from looking for and taking new opportunities. During moments of uncertainty we tend to increase our grip on what we already possess for fear that we will lose what we have. However, when we choose to relegate our feelings below our devoted belief, we bring our mood back into alignment and ignite expectancy and hope. Faith is the expression of certain devotion which stirs a mood of expectation.

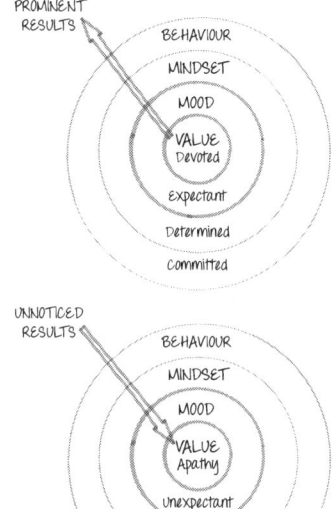

Hebrews 11:1 says: *Now faith is confidence in what we hope for and assurance about what we do not see.*

Expectancy enables me to ride the waves

Our feelings are in constant motion like the waves of the sea. At times they appear steady and at other points a storm can cause them to erupt with uncontrollable force with the potential to be devastating. Whilst we cannot escape from the turmoil of feelings, the Kingdom Key of devotion provides a means to re-balance ourselves when we are tossed around by life's storms.

David was a man who was aware of his soul script. He understood that our soul can be re-balanced through meditating on the Word of God and reflection in the presence of God. In Psalm 42:5 we see him speaking to his soul 'child' commanding it to follow the 'parent' of his Spirit...

Why, my soul, are you downcast? Why so disturbed within me? Put your hope in God, for I will yet praise Him, my Saviour and my God.

David highlights the power of our conversation with God and how it changes how we feel about ourselves, others and our future in many of the Psalms he wrote.

Expectancy is a state not an event

When we consistently affirm our convictions we create a consistent mood. The more convinced we become of what we believe the tighter the rein we have on our feelings. It is important that we understand this should be a proactive discipline and not simply used to react when our feelings run away with themselves.

In his letter to the church at Rome, Paul was setting out key Christian truths that would become a key reference point for the believers. Paul helped them to see that maintaining a consistent focus on a future hope was essential and part of the Christian discipline.

But if we hope for what we do not yet have, we wait for it patiently. Rom 8:25

Unlock a devoted soul script through immersing yourself in God's word (the bible)

We can stir our mood of expectancy for greater things by immersing ourselves in these verses:

When I immerse myself in this verse I value myself with a devoted belief:

I value myself as someone who is devoted to make a difference

I have a future inheritance that is out of this world and I can expect to see great things while I am alive

Romans 8:17 says: *Now if we are children, then we are heirs – heirs of God and co-heirs with Christ, if indeed we share in His sufferings in order that we may also share in his glory.*

I can expect fruit to come from my life because I am connected to the source, Jesus

John 15:16 we read: *You did not choose me, but I chose you and appointed you so that you might go and bear fruit—fruit that will last—and so that whatever you ask in my name the Father will give you.*

<u>**When I immerse myself in this verse I value others from a devoted belief:**</u>

I value others because I am devoted to make a difference

I make myself ready to add value to others

Colossians 3:12 we read: *Therefore, as God's chosen people, holy and dearly loved, clothe yourselves with compassion, kindness, humility, gentleness and patience.*

I serve Jesus as I serve others

Colossians 3:23, 24 we read: *Whatever you do, work at it with all your heart, as working for the Lord, not for human masters, since you know that you will receive an inheritance from the Lord as a reward. It is the Lord Christ you are serving.*

<u>**When I immerse myself in this verse I value my future from a devoted belief:**</u>

I value my future because I will make an even bigger difference

Because my future is greater than I can imagine, God chooses to reveal only as much as I can handle

1 Corinthians 2:9,10 we read *"What no eye has seen, what no ear has heard, and what no human mind has conceived"— the things God has prepared for those who love Him— these are the things God has revealed to us by His Spirit.*

When I involve God in my planning I can do so with assurance and expectancy

Phil 1:6 we read *...being confident of this, that he who began a* *good work in you will carry it on to completion until the day of Christ Jesus.*

Proverbs 16:3 we read *Commit to the Lord whatever you do, and he will establish your plans.*

Conversation with God:

Father God, I choose to put aside the thoughts, feelings and impulses that do not fit with who you are because it is no longer I who live but Christ who lives in me. I put off the old me and put on the new me. May my thoughts be your thoughts, my feelings your feelings and my impulses your impulses. I step into this day knowing that you are working through me to grow your Kingdom.

Day 22: The Winning Mindset of being Determined

DEVOTION unlocks a DETERMINED mindset in me and this is HOW I approach my day

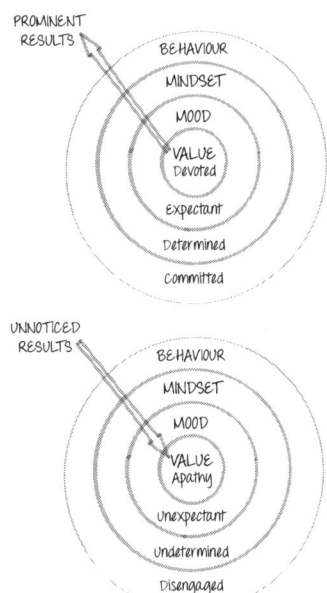

KINGDOM KEY: *"You are the light of the world. A city that is set on a hill cannot be hidden"* (Matthew 5:14).

Paul tells us in 1 Corinthians 2:16 that *We have the mind of Christ.* This is not about knowing all the thoughts of Jesus necessarily but our access to Christ's pattern of thinking. We have this when we build our lives around the commands of Christ in the Bible.

The winning conversation was demonstrated through the way Jesus lived his life. Jesus was devoted, lived with expectancy and had a determined mindset. Because our identity is found in Christ we can adopt the mindset of Christ. As Paul says in Colossians 3:2-4:

Since, then, you have been raised with Christ, set your hearts on things above, where Christ is, seated at the right hand of God. Set

your minds on things above, not on earthly things. For you died, and your life is now hidden with Christ in God. When Christ, who is your life, appears, then you also will appear with Him in glory.

1) Determined in my Focus through Quiet Reflection

Quality choices require quality times of reflection

Kingdom Key: *Jesus often withdrew to lonely places and prayed* (Luke 5:16).

Why did Jesus withdraw to pray in solitude? When you have a burning desire to fulfil a plan, focus is key. Focus is not about a constant intensity and pressure to be 'productive'; it is about cultivating and maintaining a rhythm of effective choices that get me to where I am going while growing through the journey.

Many people tried to place demands on Jesus that if He had allowed would have pulled Him off course. However Jesus was disciplined about taking time alone with the Father in order to simply be Himself with no demands placed upon Him. This is why He could say that when we come to Him and spend time with Him, His *yoke is easy and…burden is light* (Matthew 11:30).

Unless you guard regular times of quiet reflection your focus becomes blurred and the quality of your choices deteriorates. While times of reflection feel far from urgent they are of upmost importance if we are to avoid futile busyness. During these times I can focus on Christ who is my soul source and gain clarity on the people at the heart of my cause. The clearer the picture of the person I am to help, and the more time I soak myself in that, the stronger the desire I have to make a difference.

Solitude therefore solidifies our convictions. In a world of competing voices, devotion is given prominence and its voice echoes through the day whenever I allow it to speak. While many think the one who shouts the loudest gets noticed, the reality is that they are ignored as quickly as they shout. It is the voice of devotion that counts. We need to set ourselves apart to hear it.

Further reading: Psalm 62:5; Psalm 46:10.

2) Determined to Embrace Moments of Development

I can become better rather than bitter

Christ's nature can trump any feeling of bitterness that I start to cultivate through focusing on what others do to me or how they treat me. Therefore I choose to embrace Christ in this moment and focus exclusively on Him. This creates the right response in my soul and unlocks the mind of Christ in me.

Kingdom Key: Eph 4:31-32 says: *Get rid of all bitterness, rage and anger, brawling and slander, along with every form of malice. Be kind and compassionate to one another, forgiving each other, just as in Christ God forgave you.*

When I act quickly on a bitter thought and exchange it for a positive thought it protects me from developing a warped mind filter. When I allow bitterness to grow it shapes the lens through which I make my life choices. This will not only cause trouble for me in the future but potentially many others I have influence over.

Kingdom Key: Hebrews 12:15 says: *See to it that no one falls short of the grace of God and that no bitter root grows up to cause trouble and defile many.*

Read the story of Saul and David. Saul becomes bitter but David exemplifies how to become better through the voice of devotion (1 Samuel 18-24).

3) Determined to impact the Lives of Others

I grow self-importance when I make others feel important

Dishonour is the result of pride. Dishonour is to take from someone else in order to bolster one's self-importance. When you are connected to Christ as your source, you have no fear of a lack of supply to feed your need of affection. You will become prominent as you make others feel prominent. As Proverbs 11:25 says: *The generous soul will be made rich, and he who waters will also be watered himself* (NKJV).

You can live a life that seeks to outdo others with honour and watch as promotion takes care of itself!

Kingdom Key: Romans 12:10: *Be devoted to one another in love. Honour one another above yourselves.*

Further reading:

2 Tim 2:20-21 (KJV): Honour prepares you for the assignment God has for you

James 4:6 (NIV): God graces us with favour when we elevate others above ourselves

4) Determined to Adopt the Change I want to See in my World

I can initiate the change I want to see

Jesus created a serving epidemic through exhibiting what He wanted to propagate. He wanted His disciples to understand that prominence in His kingdom came through modelling humility. He wanted them to become like Him and so He treated them as He wanted them to treat others. *For I have given you an example, that you should do as I have done to you* (John 13:15).

Change is subject to you; you are not subject to change. You were created to have dominion over creation not for creation to dominate you (Gen 1:26)!

Further reading:

1 Tim 3:2: Act your way into the position you seek to obtain one day.

1 Tim 4:12: Prominence is not subject to experience but it is established through maturity.

1 Cor 11:1: Become someone worth copying.

5) Determined in my Willingness to Embrace the "Unreasonable" Demands of the Cause

When my cause feels "unreasonable," I know it is growing me

Jesus set "unreasonable" demands for me because they are required to pull the potential that is inside us out of us. In order for us to find true life we have to go through a process of losing and finding - losing old beliefs and finding new beliefs. *Whoever finds their life will lose it, and whoever loses their life for my sake will find it* (Matt 10:39). We lose on the way to winning in the Kingdom of God.

Further reading:

Luke 14:26-27: Jesus offends the mind to test the heart.

Mark 10:21: The one thing I do not think I can do is the one thing that will unlock everything I've wanted to do.

6) Determined even in the Midst of Crisis

Crisis creates the opportunity to refine my priorities

Times of devotion with God deepen your sense of security in the midst of apparent uncertainty. Psalm 1:2-3 says that blessed is the one *whose delight is in the law of the Lord, and who meditates on His law day and night. That person is like a tree planted by streams of water, which yields its fruit in season and whose leaf does not wither— whatever they do prospers.*

Listening to your own toxic conversation makes you feel smaller but speaking the word of Jesus to yourself makes you feel bigger. Call out greatness from your life today!

Further reading:

John 16:33: What you are going through has been overcome by Jesus who lives in you. You are an overcomer!

Psalm 34:17-20: You can make it, because you have been delivered out of all your trouble. The deliverer lives in you.

7) Determined in my Approach

If I cannot do it with everything I have, I cannot commit to it

The measure that I put into an activity or an opportunity will determine the measure that I get out of it. I therefore have significant control over my results through my approach.

Luke 6:38: *Give, and it will be given to you. A good measure, pressed down, shaken together and running over, will be poured into your lap. For with the measure you use, it will be measured to you.*

Further reading:

Luke 14:28: Establish the required cost of an activity and do it if you are able to give it what it deserves.

8) Determined to Equip my Successors

My success depends on me preparing others for success

When you look back, what do you wish someone would have done for you, now that you are aware of it? While you cannot go back in time, you can unlock your potential by doing for others what you wish others had done for you in your past.

Matthew 7:12: *So in everything, do to others what you would have them do to you, for this sums up the Law and the Prophets.*

Your obligation to those coming behind you is also your opportunity!

Romans 15:1: *We who are strong ought to bear with the failings of the weak and not to please ourselves.*

9) Determined in my 'Followship'

I apprentice myself to those further on than me because my progress demands it

It makes sense that those who follow learn actively to honour the leader. This creates an empowering environment for that leader to flourish. In doing so, the followers benefit from a stronger leader (Heb 13:17). The quality of fruit I feed off from my leaders is in some way down to my ability to refresh them.

Honouring creates a lift that will bring about a benefit for everyone, producing greater results for the cause to which truly devoted people are in submission.

Heb 13:17: *Have confidence in your leaders and submit to their authority, because they keep watch over you as those who must give an account. Do this so that their work will be a joy, not a burden, for that would be of no benefit to you.*

10) Determined to Create moments of Movement

I am addicted to making others feel bigger

When I take a moment to sharpen another person I sharpen myself. By helping to sharpen others I create bigger people who in turn will help me to grow bigger!

Proverbs 27:17: *As iron sharpens iron, so one person sharpens another.*

Encouragement protects others from making bad choices. Our encouragement given out also refreshes us emotionally.

Hebrews 3:13: *Encourage one another daily, as long as it is called "Today," so that none of you may be hardened by sin's deceitfulness.*

When I lift others up, God gives me a lift up. As we give affection, we draw affection from Christ.

1 Peter 5:5-6: *In the same way, you who are younger, submit yourselves to your elders. All of you, clothe yourselves with humility toward one another, because, "God opposes the proud but shows favour to the humble."*

Conversation with God:

Father God, I thank you for the truth of your word. As I mediate on it may it unlock the winning mindset I need to see your Kingdom come and your will be done in my life today!

Day 23: The Winning Behaviour of committing wholeheartedly

"WHAT I do today will be driven by WHO I am. My choices will reflect my character."

Today we look at some practical ways to look at how you can develop the winning conversation that will make you MORE prominent in life. The more you inform the right choices, the more you activate the results.

Devotion is the lead voice of the six sat around the meeting table of our beliefs. Devotion leads the discussion because everything forms around our cause. Our cause is the reason for our lives; it is our 'be-<u>cause</u>.'

Devotion needs to lead the boardroom of my beliefs and be the reminder that it is my picture of my preferred future that will lead the conversation. Therefore I must practice HIGH commitment in the choices that I make today.

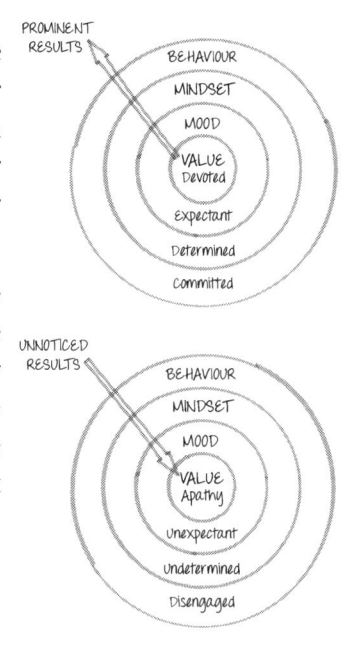

Experience the Reality of your BE-CAUSE

We have already talked about the power of our imagination and the ability we all carry to use images to stir us emotionally to action. Today I want to achieve two things. The first is this: I want to help you experience your goal in your imagination.

Results are produced by certain intention multiplied by intense action. Therefore the clearer the picture we have, the more we can see, feel and experience the result before we reach it. Our imagination produces the image that eventually becomes what we incarnate in our choices.

Certain Intention = WHO + WHY

Certainty is about combining clarity and desire

WHO

If we are agreed that a cause starts and ends with a person, then WHO is the person or group that you want to serve through your purpose?

Can you see the face of the person and the context of the person/people your cause is trying to effect? If it is a group of people then imagine what they might be doing now. The clearer the profile of the recipient/beneficiary, the more clarity you acquire about what you have to do to serve them.

It is important that you keep clear about WHO your cause is about. Life is full of opportunities and choices and the challenge is to stay on a determined and defined path once you know your cause. People and organisations move off course when they lose sight of the objective.

Moment to pause: Look at an image(s) of the WHO behind your cause

WHY

Why do you want to bring a lift to that person or group? What is it that motivates you about them? What is it you seek to change in their life that will raise their life experience? What would you say to that person now about your plan and what would be their reaction? It is a great idea to talk through your cause with those people or those who represent that group. Their reaction to your goals will help inform you when you build and clarify your LIFE Map.

Use your imagination to see the end goal. What does is look like, smell, taste, feel or sound like? The greater the detail the more certainty you create. This intensifies your belief and expectancy in the end goal.

Moment to pause: Imagine the outcome of the change you are going to bring

Determined Action = HOW + WHAT

Determined action is about a clear plan backed by high levels of desire that produce consistent choices which get you to the end goal.

HOW

Imagine yourself living in the reality of your end goal. What would life look like? How would you behave? How would you approach your time? How would you apportion your time? What finance would you have? What relationships would you anticipate carrying forward? What demands would there be on your body and so what health regime would be required? What approach would be needed to sustain and increase the results you would be seeing?

When our minds spend time thinking about this the reality produces clarity on the difference between now and then. This may appear like two worlds. If your goal is big enough then going to a place in your mind when you are thinking about this will feel like you are visiting another planet. This may feel like fantasy to others but if it is built on a foundation of certainty that this is how things will be then it becomes fuel to make the necessary changes in HOW you currently live your life.

Moment to pause: Write down a short journal entry of a future day as if you were already living in the fulfillment of what you are trying to achieve. Now you have created a benchmark in your mind that will help steer you in your choices today.

WHAT

The way to pursue the cause is to act like the person you are becoming. The changes to how you live your life will not happen by chance; you need to adopt the winning mindset which informs the winning behaviour and activates the winning results. One way to help you challenge your current behaviour in the light of your goal is to find people who are already successfully serving the people you also want to serve, or people who have successfully served another group but have demonstrated they have navigated the path to achieving their goals. By default we like to swim in a pond that makes us look big. However, while this will stroke our ego it does nothing for us unlocking our potential. We need to be a small fish in a big pond so we can see how bigger fish swim!

Moment to pause: What can I do today that will create an action to drive deeper my conviction of the future I will obtain?

Plan a Rhythm of Resistance that Creates Positive Experience

The second thing I want to help you establish today is a pattern of daily challenges.

One thing I have found extremely useful is to have a challenge each day that keeps me a producer and not a consumer—that keeps me focussed on others and not myself. These challenges create moments of movement not only in others but also in you as you give. Those who are generous with their words and actions build a bigger life but those who withhold encouragement and acts of kindness shrink wrap their lives!

Daily Challenges that Keep Giving

I find that having a small daily routine that challenges me to act in line with the winning conversation is really powerful.

I have found that daily challenges:

Keep me Stirred

It is amazing how small acts of kindness can keep us stirred and in touch with people. It ignites a childlike excitement about life whilst all the time building a platform with people. It keeps my eyes off myself and on the cause, which is people.

Keep me Stretched

Our selfish and self-serving defaults are so strong that a selfless action everyday keeps me producing and not consuming. It creates a moment where I have to decide to point my value outwards rather than pulling value from the outside-in. It reminds me of my commitment to the winning conversation.

Keep me Sensitive

It is amazing how we can quickly become desensitised to the needs of others. Our daily pursuits will centre round our needs without us being aware of it, to the extent that we can become numb to the needs of those around us. Daily challenges keep us sensitised to the needs of people because they break our focus from 'our own small worlds' and encourage us to step into someone else's world.

Over the years I have refined and changed my daily challenges.

Here are my daily challenges. You can create your own that help you stay stirred, stretched and sensitive. Invite the Holy Spirit to guide the planning and outworking of your acts of kindness that they may open up unexpected opportunities to bring influence.

Monday—Motivate on Monday

Share a motivational thought with someone at the start of a new week

There are quick and easy ways of sharing these thoughts with many people with the media outlets we have available. In order to increase the difficulty level, decide on a person who you feel needs encouragement because of the season of life they are in and share it face-to-face. Alternatively, share it over the phone. The more personal the thought becomes, the more powerful the impact is.

Tuesday—Talk up Tuesday

Share with someone how they are getting it right in something they do

The winning conversation is about seeing other people win. When we make clear to someone that what we have seen them do is praiseworthy, it produces a very clear encouragement to raise the bar in that area. When someone encourages me in my public communication it encourages me in that area to do more in the future. Talking others up with them present is powerful.

Wednesday—Wow on Wednesday

Give a gift to someone that takes them by surprise

Generosity is a powerful tool and you can really have fun with it. Whether it is buying someone a coffee in the cue at the coffee shop or having a gift delivered to a person's home or workplace, this raises the value placed on that person. Gifts given for no obvious reason—e.g. a birthday—reinforces the value you seek to bring to that person.

Thursday—Thank you Thursday

Communicate your thanks to someone for WHO they are

The words, 'thank you,' are greatly underestimated. Demonstrating appreciation unlocks powerful emotion that creates motion in others, whether you do it through a handwritten note or a phone call. To take the time to communicate your gratitude adds a value to the person that far outweighs the cost of the giver.

Friday—Fresh connection Friday

Kick-Start a conversation and show interest in someone you do not know

When a challenge involves an unknown person it can feel more difficult. Fear of how a person may react often prevents people pushing beyond the familiar. However, the more difficult a challenge may feel the greater potential there is for a positive result. New connections can lead to new relationships and new opportunities to serve the needs of other people. I have been surprised by the ways I have been able to help and support fresh connections that I have made over the years.

Saturday—Step up Saturday

Read, watch or listen to content that will challenge you to raise your game.

The weekend provides the perfect opportunity to invest in yourself. Saturdays are great for getting hold of content that will inspire or instruct you to think and act in new ways. The earlier in the day you get to access the content the longer you have to chew it over. When meeting up with friends or spending time with family you have opportunities to talk it over, creating deeper levels of understanding.

Sunday—Stand back Sunday

Reflect on the week that has gone and the week ahead

Reflection is powerful and Sunday still provides a great opportunity for me not to feel the pressure and demands of a world 'at work' and to take time to think. Thinking time is never an activity that feels 'urgent' but it is vitally important. Viewing the week ahead and building our approach and strategy can release a level of effectiveness that produces significant results. Worshipping and serving alongside other Christians in a bible based and Christ centred church is a key part of this reflection.

Take time to revisit your 'Life MAP' and prepare to 'move through the gears,' (See day 61) increasing the momentum of the winning conversation in your life.

Increased Difficulty leads to Increased Results

In order to bring new depths to the winning conversation I encourage you to increase the difficulty level on your daily challenges. Imagine the daily challenges as weights on a dumbbell. The more you increase the weight and repetitions the greater the resistance you will feel, but the greater the potential results you will also experience.

The more the daily challenges become a habit the more enjoyment we get out of life.

Day 24: The Winning Evaluation

Benchmark which mindset you have when it comes to the PROMINENT conversation.

The fruit of my actions will reveal the root of the conversations I host. Today we are looking at 10 questions or statements we make based on situations we find ourselves in. I encourage you to be brutally honest as to which response most fits you. Tally up how many you answered according to which voice and make a decision to go back under the bonnet of your inner conversations to strengthen your foundation as a champion. If you feel frustrated then that is not a bad thing as long as you focus that frustration on making certain that you commit to hosting the winning conversation.

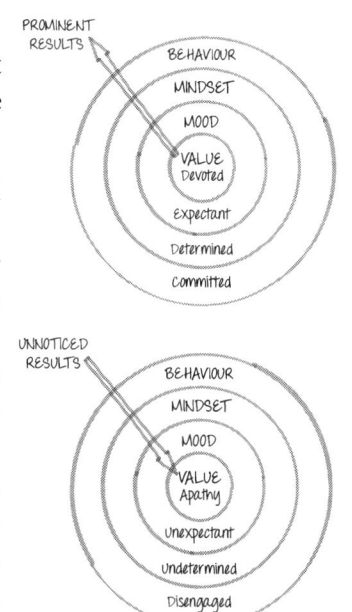

1) **Success of others—What do you do when others are successful?**

Consumed - I avoid the success of others because it makes me feel small. I will find fault in those who are succeeding to feed my sense of self-worth

Complacent - It is easier to deal with the success of others when you do not push too hard to pursue goals. There is nothing to compare against.

Competitor - I will learn from those who are successful.

Champion - I will help others learn from those who are successful and significant and celebrate what they have achieved.

2) **Generosity—How do you view generosity?**

Consumed - I give when there is an obvious benefit for doing so, even if that is just to give the appearance of generosity.

Complacent - I give sporadically, depending on how finances are at the time and the need that presents itself to me.

Competitor - I give regularly to worthy causes because I believe in contributing to society.

Champion - I create a rhythm of giving in order to intensify my level of devotion. Therefore my basis for giving is out of a need to give rather than the just nature of a cause.

3) **Friends—How do you view friendship?**

Consumed - Friends are about what they can do for me.

Complacent - Friends are about fun and enjoyment, sharing and caring.

Competitor - Friends fill my emotional tank. They are important relationships that provide a resource for the cause.

Champion - Friends are a community from which anything healthy in my life will grow. Therefore I must invest in community.

4) **Partner—How do you view your partner?**

Consumed - They are there to add to my life.

Complacent - They are someone I have got used to having around whom I must appreciate from time to time.

Competitor - I give my best when they give their best.

Champion - What I give is a choice I make and not based on what I receive in return.

5) Difference—How do you view those who are different from you?

Consumed - I view the differences of others as a disadvantage and seek to gather around me those who are similar. I have no time for people who don't think like me.

Complacent - I appreciate everyone is different but prefer those in my own tribe.

Competitor - I need different kinds of people to achieve the goal. I encourage discussion and openness between people in order to enrich life and achieve better decisions.

Champion - I seek to unlock the difference in others in order to help them succeed, regardless of whether it helps me towards my goal or not. I work hard at bringing people together—even those who repel each other—to get a blend of the differences. The bigger the repel, the greater potential for synergy. This requires skill and clarity of vision.

6) Up line leaders—How do you respond to those you report to?

Consumed - I give them what they require when I am treated well. I have no problem being involved in conversations that discuss how those leading should be performing better.

Complacent - I stay clear of dissenting conversations but do not actively discourage them. I just keep my head down and my aim is to go unnoticed.

Competitor - I exceed expectations in my performance. I avoid conversations that seek to demote those who lead me.

Champion - I seek to understand the challenges they face and actively do my best to create solutions regardless of reward. I try to focus everyone on solutions not problems.

7) Opposition—How do you respond to opposition?

Consumed - I will give as good as I get when others oppose me. I cannot be seen to be a doormat.

Complacent - I keep my head down and because of this I do not receive much opposition.

Competitor - I will not respond and give my energy to opposition. I will keep on track with the goals I know to be right.

Champion - I will use any opposition as an opportunity to demonstrate my pursuit for their best regardless of my internal feelings toward them.

8) Competition—How do you see competition?

Consumed - I seek to demote any competition in order to gain a competitive advantage.

Complacent - I accept my place in the pecking order and get on with life.

Competitor - I stay focused on what I have set out to achieve and don't allow competition to detract me.

Champion - I seek to learn and understand from competition and even seek opportunity for collaboration without deviating from the course.

9) Resentment—How do you view resentment?

Consumed - I put distance between me and them because otherwise I will react badly.

Complacent - I bury it and am good at compartmentalising.

Competitor - I can rise above any action that creates a feeling of resentment by focusing more on the goals ahead than the present negative circumstances.

Champion - I keep the conversation going and overcome feelings of resentment by promoting what I see others can become through acts of kindness and words of encouragement.

10) Coaching—What are you doing about getting a coach?

Consumed - I am waiting for someone to offer.

Complacent - I have met up with a coach and I try to make it happen regularly but struggle for time.

Competitor - I meet up with a coach and download from them.

Champion - I seek to add value to the coach and to coach others with what is being learnt, becoming a channel not just a reservoir.

PRACTICE V POTENTIAL of the PROMINENT conversation

Based on the answers to the above questions, how many times could you honestly say that your answer was that of a 'champion'?

Consumer:	1-2 times
Complacent:	3-5 times
Competitor:	6-8 times
Champion:	9-10 times

My Overall POTENTIAL: I AM A CHAMPION

MY Overall PRACTICE: I HAVE BEEN A _____

In order for my practice to match my potential I have identified the following three things I can do to unlock the champion in me:

1_____

2_____

3_____

Day 25: The Winning Accountability

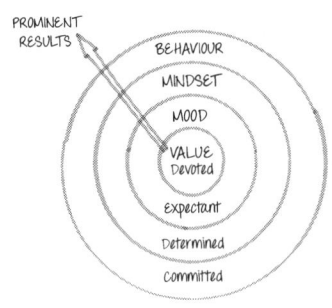

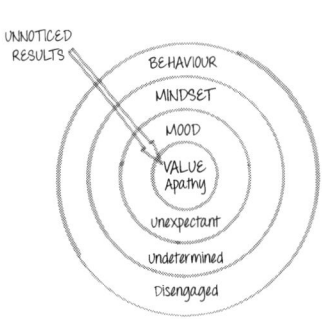

Pulling this whole week under the title of 'play the ace and not the joker' enables us to be able to review this conversation quickly. Using the dice in spare moments throughout the day, or in a small group, helps me to focus on the inner conversation of devotion.

The Winning Dice—*Play the Ace and not the Joker*

My prominence is directly linked to the value I place on the lives of other people.

A devoted person seeks to extract the highest value from life and does so by placing the greatest value they can on people. To play the ace in a game of cards is, in most games, to play the most powerful card. It carries the highest value and helps you win. Contributing in a positive way to people is involves an action that adds the highest value to another life. A person who hosts the devoted conversation becomes convinced that in every situation it is right to add value even when there are often reasons not to do so.

When a group of people agrees that this is the expected norm they collaborate to create an enriching environment that is healthy and therefore produces growth and results. This makes the group stand out because it is not the social norm to act this way. This unlocks more prominence for them and the cause they represent.

To play the joker is to use the card that carries the lowest value, the losing card. When we demote rather than promote people we usually do so in the belief that making the other person look bad and feel bad will in some way raise our prominence. While it may gain attention it will not produce lasting prominence.

There is MORE prominence in you when you play the ace and not the joker!

Step 1: RECALL Together

Here is a quick review of what it means to play the ace and not the joker so we can stay on course for allowing DEVOTION to have the loudest voice, thereby drowning out APATHY. Here is a description based on what we have looked at this week:

What does it look like to play the ace?

- We celebrate others even when we feel uncelebrated
- We're quick to respond positively to those in authority
- We go out of our way to make someone else look good
- We are sensitive to those in need
- We own the job of protecting the group/organisation/leaders/managers for the sake of the cause because reputation and credibility affects everyone
- We actively put others first
- We willingly make sacrifices to help others
- We go further than expected, beyond the call of duty
- We place a higher value on our finances, time and health because of the demands that will be required from the cause
- We find a coach/mentor from whom to receive but also to promote and encourage for their contribution

What does it look like to play the joker?

- We allow familiarity of life, relationships and resource to breed contempt
- We make ourselves look good at someone else's expense
- We demand to be honoured and promoted
- We put our wants before the needs of others
- We assume privilege

- We often talk without thinking
- We create relational alignment in order to 'climb the ladder.'

Step 2: REVIEW with others

Get together weekly with people who are committed to developing the winning conversations on the journey of this book. This week discuss the following:

i) What cause have you clarified so far?

ii) Who could you be coached by in order to support their cause but also receive advice and instruction on your journey?

iii) How could we support one another through the demands of pursuing the cause?

iv) Has there been a time when we have allowed ourselves to play the joker and not the ace?

v) How would our relationships be enriched by 'playing the ace'?'

Step 3: REFLECTION to be shared

Now create a reflection that you can share with someone in your group or someone else that you are coaching to be a champion in life. Why not take the time with your children, loved one, or friend and share what you have learnt? Simply sharing this reflection will accomplish much in your life and deepen relationships, enriching them with vulnerability and moments of movement.

Follow our basic structure:

i) What I realised for the first time/again this week is ….. (Share a thought that is authentically you)

ii) The change I need to make is ….. (Share the action point you are in agreement over)

iii) Can you help me make it …… ? (Invite help and create accountability)

Once you have developed the habit of doing this why not decide to turn your thoughts into a blog or even take your coaching to another level. There is so much in you connected to your commitment to stretch yourself.

THE WINNING KEYS

Section 5: Be MORE Resilient

Day 26: The Winning Conversation makes you MORE Resilient

PASSION unlocks the door of RESILIENCE

Kingdom Key: You are the house on the rock.

"Therefore everyone who hears these words of mine and puts them into practice is like a wise man who built his house on the rock" (Matthew 7:24).

When you get the revelation that Jesus Christ fully lives in you, you understand that you carry an incredible inner strength. There is a tenacity and zeal inside you that has not yet been fully seen. You carry a power and authority source that is beyond your natural strength.

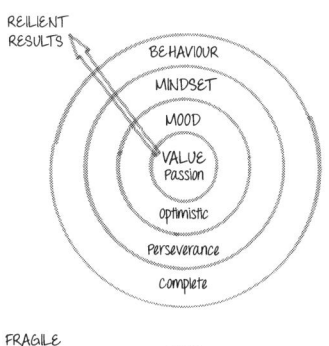

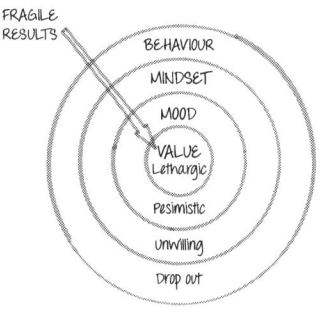

When I host the RESILIENT conversation I become…

1) MORE aware of the calm in the storm

Determine to respond rather than react to the storm

When you realise that you host the voice of passion in the boardroom of belief you realise that regardless of what is happening around you, Christ who is in you is stronger.

In Mark 4 the storm got into the soul of the disciples and they reacted in panic. Jesus however allowed the calm in him to speak to the storm. *'He got up, rebuked the wind and said to the waves, "Quiet! Be still!" Then the wind died down and it was completely calm.'* Christ is now in the boat of your life. You have a Kingdom resilience that you can use when the storms of life arise.

1 John 4:4: *The one who is in you is greater than the one who is in the world.*

2) MORE aware of a problem's potential

My problems can create more capacity in me

With Christ's potential in you the problems and challenges you face are opportunities to unlock a more spacious place for you to operate in your Kingdom assignment. Like me you will pray for the space but will not necessarily be asking for the problem that will give way to it. The children of Israel faced many battles before they took possession of the Promised Land but each challenge was proving their potential to handle the future they so desired.

Exodus 23:30: *Little by little I will drive them out before you, until you have increased enough to take possession of the land.*

The problems you face are building capacity to sustain the new space God will move you into.

Further reading:

Psalm 18:19: *He brought me out into a spacious place; He rescued me because He delighted in me.*

Psalm 31:8: *You have not given me into the hands of the enemy but have set my feet in a spacious place.*

3) MORE self-confident

Confidence is built from suffering upward

I carry the confidence of Christ in me who is the hope of ALL glory (Col 1:27). Christ-confidence is unlocked when the suffering

I face causes me to depend on Him more. Like a person jumping on a trampoline, the harder they hit it, the higher they bounce. The more my challenge forces me to have faith and 'bounce' off Christ in total dependence, the more the springs of His confidence launch me higher into His glorious purposes. I can bounce off my confidence in Christ knowing that it will unlock His glory!

The Apostle Paul in Eph 3:10-13 helps us to see the depths of God's potential available to us that will launch us to incredible heights for Him!

His intent was that now, through the church, the manifold wisdom of God should be made known to the rulers and authorities in the heavenly realms, according to His eternal purpose that He accomplished in Christ Jesus our Lord. In Him and through faith in Him we may approach God with freedom and confidence. I ask you, therefore, not to be discouraged because of my sufferings for you, which are your glory.

4) MORE accepting of challenge

Let the storm produce the wind for your sails

I accept the challenge in the storm because its force will create motion toward the purposes and plans of God in my life.

I will not lose confidence I will dig deep and be strengthened in my God-confidence. This storm will help me and not hinder me <u>if</u> I stay <u>in faith</u>! I will **NOT** be disappointed.

Romans 5:3-5 (NLT): *We can rejoice, too, when we run into problems and trials, for we know that they help us develop endurance. And endurance develops strength of character, and character strengthens our **<u>confident</u>** hope of salvation. And this hope will not lead to disappointment.*

5) MORE persistent with passion

Passion balanced with patience produces deep resilience

Peter urges his readers to build passionate patience into the rhythm of their lives in order to experience MORE of Christ in their lives.

2 Peter 1:5-9 (The Message): *So don't lose a minute in building on what you've been given, complementing your basic faith with good character, spiritual understanding, alert discipline,* **_passionate patience_**, *reverent wonder, warm friendliness, and generous love, each dimension fitting into and developing the others. With these qualities active and growing in your lives, no grass will grow under your feet, no day will pass without its reward as you mature in your experience of our Master Jesus. Without these qualities you can't see what's right before you, oblivious that your old sinful life has been wiped off the books.*

Our persistent passion is dealing with the most important process of all, causing us to push our way out of the chrysalis of our old life into our new life in Christ. While we cannot always make sense of God's eternal processes that are taking place inside us, we realise the process is fuelled by our deep trust and confidence in Him. He hasn't made a mistake yet and He is not going to break the habit of eternity. You are in the master craftsman's hands!

Whilst enduring process can be frustrating, God creates an environment designed to enlarge us not to diminish us. Romans 8:22-25 (The Message): *The Spirit of God is arousing us within. We're also feeling the birth pangs. These sterile and barren bodies of ours are yearning for full deliverance. That is why waiting does not diminish us, any more than waiting diminishes a pregnant mother.* <u>*We are enlarged in the waiting.*</u> *We, of course, don't see what is enlarging us. But the longer we wait, the larger we become, and the more joyful our expectancy.*

6) MORE resourceful toward others

People feed from passion

Jesus both repelled people and compelled them to Him. His passion was contagious with people like Zachaeus who was transformed after a conversation with Jesus in Luke 19:8 to the point where we read:

Zacchaeus stood up and said to the Lord, "Look, Lord! Here and now I give half of my possessions to the poor, and if I have cheated anybody out of anything, I will pay back four times the amount."

At the same time Christ's passion caused others to react angrily toward Him and be repelled from Him, like the Pharisees in Luke 15:1-2:

Now the tax collectors and sinners were all drawing near to hear Him. And the Pharisees and the scribes grumbled, saying, "This man receives sinners and eats with them."

Choose today to be fuelled with Christ's passion and believe you can inspire people to be bigger regardless of their reaction. One thing is for sure: even those who react angrily are inwardly challenged.

7) MORE listened to

The passionate pursuit of my cause gives permission to others to pursue their cause

The potency of Jesus' passion and the audacity of His goal meant that people left what they were doing in a moment!

Mark 4:19-20 (ESV): *"Follow me, and I will make you fishers of men." Immediately they left their nets and followed Him.*

Believe today that there are people who want to catch what you have and who will be drawn into the cause that you are pursuing. Share your passion today and inspire others. Who knows who might follow you!

Conversation with God:

Father God, I thank you that you have called me to be like a rock that is resilient. I thank you for your Word because it ignites passion in me and unlocks confidence and faith which is an impenetrable substance. I draw more passion from Christ in me today.

Day 27: The Winning Voice of Passion

Passion is not WHAT I do, it is WHO I am

PASSION that unlocks the door of RESILIENCE

Kingdom Key: You are the house on the rock

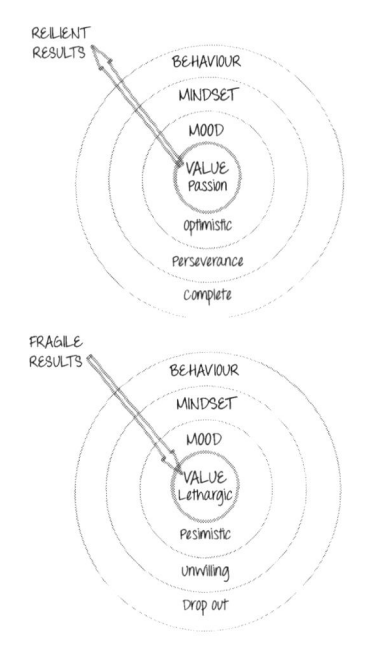

Therefore everyone who hears these words of mine and puts them into practice is like a wise man who built his house on the rock (Matthew 7:24).

To be a person of PASSION I have to immerse myself in my new identity in Jesus Christ. This belief will lead me into the right feelings. The more I immerse myself in the *belief* that I am passionate, the MORE *resilient* I will become.

Now I have Christ in me I have to die daily to the old me and live from the new me.

Paul says in Galatians 2:20: *I have been crucified with Christ and I no longer live, but Christ lives in me. The life I now live in the body, I live by faith in the Son of God, who loved me and gave Himself for me.*

This means WHO I am is WHO He is. I have adopted my new identity and I choose each day to live from the Christ core. I am passionate because Jesus is passion!

To unlock PASSION I have to believe that…

i) I AM stimulated from the inside-out

Initiate what you want to experience

Paul reminded his spiritual son Timothy that he could stir up the gift that was in him. Our internal passion does not require external stimulus but can be stirred up by a choice. The firmer I make the choice the greater the stir I create inside me.

Kingdom Key: 2 Timothy 1:6-7 (NKJV): *Therefore I remind you to stir up the gift of God which is in you through the laying on of my hands. For God has not given us a spirit of fear, but of power and of love and of a sound mind.*

The glorious and eternal hope of God resides in you, which tells me there is no end to the passion and enthusiasm you can stir up if you believe. Heaven is ready to be funnelled through you if you are willing and ready to receive!

Kingdom Key: *To them God has chosen to make known among the Gentiles the glorious riches of this mystery, which is Christ in you, the hope of glory* (Col 1:27).

Conversation with God:

Father, inspired by the hope in me today, help me to identity what I need to jump-start and initiate, driven by the passion of Christ in me.

ii) I AM grown through tension

When I am in tension I can create movement

When a tree grows it moves in two directions. It stretches up and pushes down.

Sometimes we can face circumstances that create a contradiction inside us. When God is stirring something inside us the things on the outside can feel uncomfortable. This is quite normal because pushing in two apparently different directions forms your growing pains toward maturity. The tension of growth in a tree leads to fruit on a tree and the same is true in your life.

Kingdom Key: *Consider it pure joy, my brothers and sisters, whenever you face trials of many kinds, because you know that the testing of your faith produces perseverance. Let perseverance finish its work so that you may be mature and complete, not lacking anything* (James 1:1-4).

Conversation with God:

Father God, what are you trying to produce in me through my current tension? What needs more tension in my life in order to produce the fruit that you are looking for?

iii) I AM born to stretch

Stretch brought me into this life and it keeps me alive!

Spiritual stretch is created through my faith goals. The greater revelation of WHO I am in Him, the greater the goal I can believe for. When I move towards this goal, the stretch begins. It is a stretch because a faith goal is often unusual and lacks logical sense to others. Faith is my expectation and confidence in what is NOT YET. This only makes sense to people of faith.

The prophet Isaiah was God's mouthpiece to the nation of Israel during a desperate era. The circumstances looked 'barren' and yet he prophesied stretch. Isaiah 54:1-4:

"Sing, barren woman, you who never bore a child; burst into song, shout for joy, you who were never in labour; because more are the children of the desolate woman than of her who has a husband," says the Lord. "Enlarge the place of your tent, stretch your tent curtains wide, do not hold back; lengthen your cords, strengthen your stakes. For you will spread out to the right and to the left; your descendants will dispossess nations and settle in their desolate cities.

This prophecy had echoes of Israel's founding father Abraham and his wife Sarah. When the promise of a son - and through him subsequent countless descendants - came to them they were barren. However they were told that through them a nation would be born. Sarah even laughed (Gen 18:12) when she heard the promise given, such was the 'stretch' between the goal and their current reality.

However when passion himself (Christ Jesus) sits at the boardroom of our belief, what is apparently ridiculous in the natural makes perfect sense in the supernatural because God multiplied by anything equals the possible.

Kingdom Key: *And without faith it is impossible to please God, because anyone who comes to Him must believe that He exists and that He rewards those who earnestly seek Him (Hebrews 11:6).*

Conversation with God:

Father God, show me how stretch has positively impacted my life so far? Which areas of my life need to be stretched? Help me to see where I can stretch my faith and reliance on you.

iv) I AM optimistic in the squeeze

My squeeze allows the world to see what He is made of

When I choose Christ to be the voice of passion in me, then an external squeeze can let His voice out through my optimism.

My job is to cultivate a passionate internal conversation that can infiltrate my external response to any challenges that I face.

Kingdom key: *For the mouth speaks what the heart is full of. A good man brings good things out of the good stored up in him, and an evil man brings evil things out of the evil stored up in him* (Matthew 12:34-35).

We can be optimistic when we are the authors of our own squeeze.

Jonathan and his armour-bearer found themselves in a squeeze created from their own decision to take on the Philistines because the fighting army did not have any weapons. They were flanked by two cliff edges - not wise if you want to get away should things go bad. However, they created a squeeze situation. The squeeze produced passionate optimism and this ignited faith which brought God to the table.

A miracle is instigated when I choose to take on a challenge bigger than I have the power to complete. This is true if the challenge calls forth a certainty and belief that God can finish what I cannot, if it is for His glory.

In that first attack Jonathan and his armour-bearer killed some twenty men in an area of about half an acre. Then panic struck the whole army—those in the camp and field, and those in the outposts and raiding parties—and the ground shook. It was a panic sent by God (1 Samuel 14:14-15).

Conversation with God:

Father God, show me how can I respond differently in the squeeze so that others get to see Jesus through me?

v) I AM disciplined in my response

I can increase in responsibility when I improve in my ability to respond

I can call on Christ to give me the strength and power to endure and be patient. He can and will help me choose my response in the moment and every response can build Kingdom resilience in me.

I taught my kids, and in turn myself, that when I feel that I can't do something, I can simply say to myself 'not me, but you Jesus.' That simple set of words ignites a winning conversation and unlocks the grace of Christ in me. Grace is the unmerited, undeserved and unlimited favour and assistance of God in a person's life.

You have no shortage of strength; you carry the 'glorious might' of heaven in you. Give God permission to act and you will be amazed even shocked at how you can let Him respond through you under the greatest of opposition.

Kingdom Key: *...being strengthened with all power according to his glorious might so that you may have great endurance and patience* (Colossians 1:11).

Conversation with God:

First replay the last time you reacted negatively...

Father God. I am sorry for the wrong way in which I reacted. I am sorry and want to learn from this so that next time people can see how I am different because you live inside of me.

Now think about how you are going to choose your response when something similar happens next time.

Father God, I commit now to choose a new way to respond with your strength and power working through me.

vi) I AM able to pause a trigger

Giving in to a reaction is to give up on an opportunity to build strength

In Romans 12:10-11 Paul reveals the link between our devotion for other people and our spiritual passion. When I do not <u>react</u> but <u>respond</u> in love, I unlock a new level of passion and Kingdom resilience.

Romans 12:10-11: *Be devoted to one another in love. Honour one another above yourselves. Never be lacking in zeal, but keep your spiritual fervour, serving the Lord.*

Conversation with God:

Holy Spirit, help me to see what triggers a reaction in me. In what way can I choose a more disciplined response so that your strength can be unlocked in me and I can be an example to those around me? Father God, help me in the moment I am tempted to react to draw on Christ in me.

vii) I AM future

My future goal will produce my present experience

A champion takes control and leads their feelings through training them to reattach themselves to a picture of a different, brighter future. The Apostle Paul held the tension of the NOW moment with the promise of an amazing future that had NOT YET happened in his letter to the church at Phillipi. In Phil 1:2 he said *For to me, to live is Christ and to die is gain.* This is why death to him was merely an entrance into a better future and therefore nothing to fear. Paul persevered through prison, court appearances, beatings, shipwrecks and attacks on his credibility by immersing himself in his future goal of being with Christ in eternity.

Conversation with God:

Father God, help me to see how my current challenge is training me for the future.

viii) I AM able

Relegate the feeling of being UNABLE below the belief that 'I am ABLE'

Living by faith is about activating the choice to call upon God and allow Him to work through us. When we feel unable to keep going we can dig deep into heaven's reserve and from the inside-out release a wave of belief. This wave builds from our Spirit, raising our soul's anticipation, reforming our mindset, causing us to choose new behaviour. I am the only limiting factor when it comes to drawing on heaven's reserve.

Kingdom Key: *Very truly I tell you, my Father will give you whatever you ask in my name. Until now you have not asked for anything in my name. Ask and you will receive, and your joy will be complete* (John 16:23b-24).

Conversation with God:

Father, what do I currently believe I am unable to do that needs to be challenged with my new belief? I lower my spirit like a bucket into the well of heaven's resource and draw it up into my soul. Realign my thinking and help me to act as one empowered by heaven.

ix) I AM able to pull my future into my now

My obstacle is simply the scenery along the route to winning

My perspective is determined by the belief 'glasses' I wear. These are the 'eyes of my heart' that Paul mentions. When I wear my faith 'glasses' and state my *winning purpose*, I instruct everything today to get behind that goal. Christ's voice of passion in me can instruct my spirit to lead my thought process. Whilst I do not leave my brains behind, when it comes to decision-making my feelings and thoughts follow the instinct of my renewed belief in who I am in Christ and what I believe He is going to do in and through me.

Kingdom Key: …having the <u>eyes of your hearts enlightened</u>, that you may know what is the hope to which He has called you, what are the riches of His glorious inheritance in the saints, and what is the immeasurable greatness of His power toward us who believe, according to the working of His great might that He worked in Christ when He raised Him from the dead and seated Him at his right hand in the heavenly places (Ephesians 1:18-20).

Conversation with God:

What do I believe about the obstacles I face? Father God, open the eyes of my heart so I can see how to progress.

x) I AM comfortable with change

I grow more through the discomfort of change

Following Jesus is about being transformed; change is therefore part and parcel of the journey. This involves forging into an unknown future and forgetting a past that seeks to hinder us. Change forces us to not put our hope in what can be seen because that can be shaken.

We are not just talking about external circumstances. Change can also create an internal feeling of grieving when the idea of change appears good but the process reveals the emotional attachments we have made with people, places and possessions and positions that are external to us. The process of dying to these things however can re-establish our security in God.

Passion for the change happening in us causes us to stir our faith and trust in God knowing that as we push into the unseen He will reveal the glorious future that God has for us.

Kingdom key: *But one thing I do: Forgetting what is behind and straining toward what is ahead, I press on toward the goal to win the prize for which God has called me heavenward in Christ Jesus* (Philippians 3:13-14).

Conversation with God:

Father, reveal the discomfort I am resisting that I really need to embrace.

Day 28: The Winning Mood of Optimism

Unlocking the power of WHY creates optimism

PASSION unlocks an OPTIMISITC mood in me.

Base verse: You are the house on the rock Matthew 7:24

"Therefore everyone who hears these words of mine and puts them into practice is like a wise man who built his house on the rock.

The Kingdom key of Passion unlocks my WHY which is my PURPOSE.

My purpose is the 'good work' which I was created to do. (Eph 2:10)

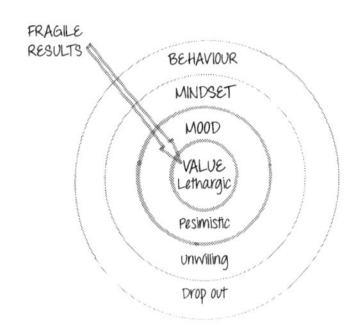

The vision of my life was prepared by God before I was even born. (Jeremiah 1:50)

I am having the RESILIENT conversation led by the voice of passion which means I choose to put myself in an OPTIMISTIC mood.

Good will always prevail

Let me revisit the story of Abraham and Sarah for a moment. In one of his letters, Paul refers to this inspiring story of Abraham and how he tenaciously held onto his promise from God that he and his wife Sarah would have a child. They trusted God despite being beyond child bearing years at the point of receding the promise and still having to wait a quarter of a century to have their firstborn.

Romans 4:19-20 Without weakening in his faith, he faced the fact that his body was as good as dead—since he was about a hundred years old—and that Sarah's womb was also dead. Yet he did not waver through unbelief regarding the promise of God, but was strengthened in his faith and gave glory to God…

A future promise and belief can lift us out of circumstantial pessimism and into the joy of an optimistic state. The mood of optimism views the peaks and troughs of life as the makings of a great life story. The Christ follower has the assurance that the story has ultimately been penned by God before the foundation of time.

When I choose to put myself in an optimistic mood I am deciding to enjoy and not simply endure the process. Sarah laughed (Gen 18:12) when she heard the promise given by God based on the odds stacked against them. Enjoy the process of cultivating a huge and hilarious goal. While many things in life do not 'feel' enjoyable, I can choose to enjoy what God is producing in me throughout the process. (1 Thess 5:18) Optimism is remaining cheerful and full of hope and allowing that powerful mood to navigate the choices of the day.

Optimism is confident presence

Optimism creates a hopeful confidence. Optimism is created when I have an internal supply of assurance. My supply in Christ is endless.

Col 1:11-12 *...being strengthened with all power according to his glorious might so that you may have great endurance and patience, 12 and giving joyful thanks to the Father...*

When I cultivate assurance through Jesus I then produce feelings of security in the lives of others. This is profoundly attractive.

Optimism is living to the optimum

The word optimistic comes from the Latin word optimum which means 'the best thing.' Optimism is a state of being hopefull, believing the best thing will prevail. The medical and scientific world now accepts the link between a person's daily disposition of hope and their ability to fend off sickness. There appears to be an intrinsic link between hope and our immune system and this is revealed in the bible.

Proverbs 13:12 *Hope deferred makes the heart sick, but a longing fulfilled is a tree of life.*

Unlock a passionate soul script through immersing yourself in the word of God (the bible)

The belief that our voice will make a difference will increase when we immerse ourselves in these verses:

When I immerse myself in this verse I value myself with a passionate belief:

I value myself as someone who has it in them to grow in any situation

I value myself because I carry Christ's goodness is in me. I carry the seed of a future harvest

Colossians 1:10-12 *...so that you may live a life worthy of the Lord and please him in every way: bearing fruit in every good work, growing in the knowledge of God, being strengthened with all power* *according to his glorious might so that you may have great endurance and patience, and giving joyful thanks to the Father, who has qualified you to share in the inheritance of his holy people in the kingdom of light.*

Christ passionately pursued me and so I passionately pursue who I am in Him

Philippians 3:12-14 *Not that I have already obtained all this, or have already arrived at my goal, but I press on to take hold of that for which Christ Jesus took hold of me. Brothers and sisters, I do not consider myself yet to have taken hold of it. But one thing I do: Forgetting what is behind and straining toward what is ahead, I press on toward the goal to win the prize for which God has called me heavenward in Christ Jesus.*

<u>**When I immerse myself in this verse I value others from a passionate belief:**</u>

I value others by encouraging and allowing them to draw on the strength that Christ has given me

God has strengthened and rescued me because he wants me to help strengthen and rescue others

2 Tim 4:17 *But the Lord stood at my side and gave me strength, so that through me the message might be fully proclaimed and all the Gentiles might hear it. And I was delivered from the lion's mouth.*

As Christ demonstrated passionate humility for me so I will do the same for others

Philippians 2:5 *In your relationships with one another, have the same mindset as Christ Jesus Who, being in very nature God, did not consider equality with God something to be used to his own advantage; rather, he made himself nothing by taking the very nature of a servant, being made in human likeness.*

<u>**When I immerse myself in this verse I value my future from a passionate belief:**</u>

I value my future by embracing the challenge of now knowing it is preparing me

My potential to keep going exceeds my future challenges therefore I have the potential to overcome this obstacle through Christ in me

Romans 8:37 *No, in all these things we are more than conquerors through him who loved us.*

God cares for me enough to allow my current challenge to prepare me for my future purpose

Romans 8:28 *And we know that in all things God works for the good of those who love him, who have been called according to his purpose.*

Conversation with God:

Father God, I choose to put aside the thoughts, feelings and impulses that do not fit with who you are because it is no longer I who you live but Christ who lives in me. I put off the old me and put on the new me. May my thoughts be your thoughts, my feelings your feelings and my impulses your impulses. I step into this day knowing that you are working through me to grow your Kingdom.

Day 29: The Winning Mindset of Perseverance

High level focus through persevering regardless

PASSION unlocks a PERSEVERING mindset in me and this is HOW I approach my day

Kingdom key: You are the house on the rock

Therefore everyone who hears these words of mine and puts them into practice is like a wise man who built his house on the rock (Matthew 7:24).

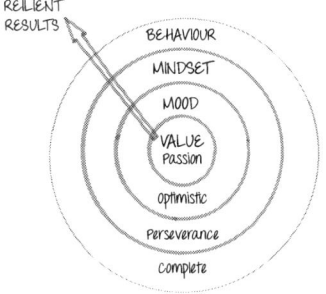

Paul tells us in 1 Corinthians 2:16 that We have the mind of Christ. This is not about knowing all the thoughts of Jesus necessarily but our access to Christ's pattern of thinking. We have

this when we build our lives around the commands of Christ in the Bible.

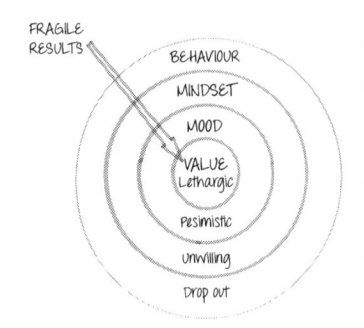

The winning conversation was demonstrated through the way Jesus lived His life. Jesus was passionate, lived with optimism and had a persevering mindset. Because our identity is found in Christ we can adopt the mindset of Christ.

Col 3:2-4:

Since, then, you have been raised with Christ, set your hearts on things above, where Christ is, seated at the right hand of God. Set your minds on things above, not on earthly things. For you died, and your life is now hidden with Christ in God. When Christ, who is your life, appears, then you also will appear with Him in glory.

1) Persevere regardless of the fights that choose you

I can pick the size of my fights

There are good fights and bad fights.

Paul's letter to Timothy reminds us that our 'fight' needs to be focused on a cause and not a personality.

Kingdom Key: *Fight the good fight of the faith. Take hold of the eternal life to which you were called when you made your good confession in the presence of many witnesses* (1 Tim 6:12).

The fight of faith is allowing Christ to overcome our negative, self-centred and sinful beliefs through surrendering our current beliefs for those belonging to our new identity in Jesus Christ.

To get caught up with the battles that we can see is to waste our energy. Our external fights are best dealt with when we unlock the resilience of our new nature. It is time to lay down the negative fights and pick the only fight worth fighting. All victories lie inside the fight of faith.

You were born to fight the good fight of faith and born to win!

Further reading:

Eph 6:10-18 Paul reminds us that our fights lie in the unseen and not the seen.

2) Persevere regardless by correctly labelling your feelings

I can reassign meaning to my feelings

As Christ followers we must remember *the heart is deceitful above all things, and desperately sick; who can understand it?* (Jeremiah 17:9 ESV) This means that we need another benchmark against which to measure our feelings, challenges and future. When we spend time processing these in the presence of Jesus and through reading the Bible we are able to access a true perspective. When our feelings start to shake us we need to stir up the commands and Word of God in us that will lead us into the future God has for us.

Further reading:

Heb 4:12: The Bible becomes the referee for our lives that helps to bring order when our soul is shaken and we feel unstable and unsafe.

Eph 1:18: Paul prayed for the church that they may be led by looking at life through transformed hearts rather than natural eyes that had become transfixed on what could be seen.

3) Persevere regardless by relegating practice below principle

I can make my practices follow my principles

When you do not feel like doing what you know you need to be doing, imagine the hand of the person you are trying to reach taking your hand and pulling you up from your lethargic state into your passionate purpose.

The author of our principles is Jesus Christ and He is holding out His hand right now and saying, *You of little faith…why do you doubt!* He is pulling you out of lethargy into passion. Take His hand today (Matt 14:31).

Further reading:

1 Corinthians 10:31: Paul helps us to see in this passage that when we do not feel like doing it for ourselves or for others, we allow the principle of doing everything for God to pull us out of our lethargic state.

4) Persevere regardless by drawing new conclusions

I do not have to settle for the conclusions I have; I can draw new ones

What are the statements we make about ourselves that we would want to change? What we verbalise we reinforce. As followers of Christ we develop a rhythm of surrendering our statements to Him allowing Him to have the final word. This helps to unlock the mind of Christ in us.

It is when the Christ follower learns to hold firmly to statements and promises of hope that we have in Christ that we uncover a deeper passion and therefore resilience that helps us to persevere regardless of what we are going through. When I worship God for who He is and thank Him for what He has done I create the right environment for new conclusions to be established in my heart and soul. I maintain a persevering mindset by making these new conclusions my confession.

Kingdom key: *Let us hold unswervingly to the hope we profess, for he who promised is faithful* (Hebrews 10:23).

Further reading:

2 Cor 12:9: There is a grace reserve with your name on that will always out supply the demand of your circumstance. Perseverance unlocks Christ's power and therefore we celebrate moments that lead us to acute dependency.

5) Persevere regardless through hiding inside your belief

I can take cover in the shelter of my impenetrable belief

Dig deep and discover Jesus in your situation. What would Jesus say to you in the moment of you being shaken? What He says becomes a tower of belief that you hide inside. His word is impenetrable. *The name of the Lord is a fortified tower; the righteous run to it and are safe* (Proverbs 18:10).

Further reading:

James 1:25: *But whoever looks intently into the perfect law that gives freedom, and continues in it—not forgetting what they have heard, but doing it—they will be blessed in what they do.*

6) Persevere regardless through turning annoyance into an assignment

I can turn my negative annoyance into a positive assignment

Your annoyance will be linked to questions you ask such as, 'Why does someone not fix this problem?' 'Why do people tolerate this?' 'Why are people remaining silent on this issue?' 'Why has someone not thought of a solution for this? Surely it's obvious.'

Persevering regardless is about proactively using what otherwise would cause you to quit to empower you to grow. The prophet Habakkuk was annoyed at the wickedness and evil he witnessed and the apparent lack of justice being administered by God. His complaint became his commission. The steps outlined in the winning conversation under this heading are inspired by his story found in the Book of Habakkuk.

Further reading:

Luke 10:2: Jesus often helped His disciples to see a problem because when we are looking through the eyes of faith, then opportunities lie behind problems.

7) Persevere regardless and you will produce what you are looking for

When you produce for others you unlock your own supply.

Proverbs 11:25: *A generous man will prosper; he who refreshes others will himself be refreshed.*

A person who is passionate does not wait for a feeling of security to come in order to give assurance to others. They produce assurance for others and in doing so create an increased personal sense of assurance. This means that I can kill off the sinful default of being a 'selfish cow' and choose the design which is to be a 'super cow', unlocking heaven's supply by supplying the needs of others.

Further reading:

Luke 6:38: Your intake is determined by your outlet. Let the supply demand from others increase the demand you place on Christ as your source and supply.

Phil 4:19: The supply of God's riches requires you to be a distributor of His supply.

8) Persevere regardless by creating constant incremental change

I can incrementally control my rate of change through daily changes that build resilience

We know that suffering produces perseverance; perseverance, character; and character, hope (Romans 5:4).

The personal 'suffering' we create by persevering beyond the point of comfort has a direct impact on our character formation. Due to us being immersed in the NOW moment, we are often the last to witness quite how these changes are impacting HOW we live and WHAT we do. Like the turning of a ship's wheel, the immediate action of turning the wheel feels like it has little or no impact on the overall direction of the vessel but over time it does change the course and ultimately the destination.

Further reading:

Exodus 23:30: The capacity to take on the new comes through a process of incremental changes designed to preserve what God entrusts to you in order to protect you.

9) Persevere regardless by learning to feel a choice before you make it

If it feels good tomorrow, I will do it today

Kingdom key: *Like a city whose walls are broken through is a person who lacks self-control* (Proverbs 25:28).

Every time I take control of my choices and do not give in to my feelings, thereby making them follow the principles that I am building my life around, I strengthen the 'city walls' of my life. Jesus said in Matthew 5:14 (NLT): *You are the light of the world—like a city on a hilltop that cannot be hidden.*

Every choice I make either weakens or strengthens the walls of my city and therefore the impact I have on the world around me.

As well as calling on the strength and power of Jesus to help me make strong choices, I can overcome temptation in the moment by visualising a picture of the future for which I am believing and ask myself, 'Am I willing to sacrifice the future for this moment of weakness?'

Further reading:

Eph 5:15-16: Evil sits alongside God-given opportunity. However opportunity is not always obvious. To resist evil/temptation is to unlock kingdom resilience that prepares you for promotion.

10) Persevere regardless by recycling the past into fuel for the future

I can make use of any experience to create momentum toward my goal

God is the master recycler. He does not waste an experience or event; He weaves the unlikeliest and even ugliest circumstances to add extreme value and beauty to the story of my life.

Kingdom Key: *And we know that in all things God works for the good of those who love Him, who have been called according to His purpose* (Romans 8:28).

The mindset of perseverance identifies a problem as potential. Paul prayed for the church at Thessalonica: *the Lord will direct your hearts into God's love and Christ's **perseverance*** (2 Thessalonians 3:5).

When Christ saw an obstacle He observed an opportunity.

In Him, you too have this mindset.

Rather than being filled with despair this mindset produces greater levels of hope. There is something desirable for us inside the undesirable challenges we face. Inside the undesirable lump of carbon is a diamond ready to be unearthed. It simply has to persevere through the combination of pressure and time.

There is a promise in the problem.

'The more problems the more passion' that can be unlocked and the greater the promise must be!

Choose your response today to fan the fire of passion with the oxygen of hope.

Further reading:

Gen 50:20: Inside every failure is a victory - behind every problem an opportunity and every disappointment can unlock more hope.

Conversation with God:

Father God, I thank you for the truth of your Word. As I mediate on it may it unlock the winning mindset I need to see you Kingdom come and your will be done in my life today!

Day 30: The Winning Choices of Completing aggressively

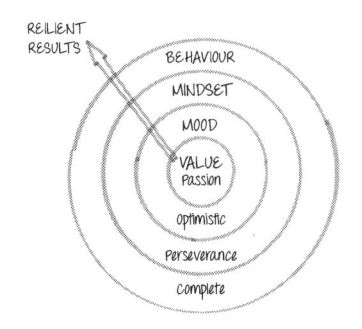

PASSION unlocks my ability to COMPLETE in life

Kingdom Key: You are the house on the rock

Therefore everyone who hears these words of mine and puts them into practice is like a wise man who built his house on the rock (Matthew 7:24).

The Kingdom key of Passion unlocks my WHAT which is the action to COMPLETE aggressively.

To be a winner you have to learn to fight. It is in the fight that the voice of passion will be required to produce the perseverance necessary to complete what God has started. My new identity in Christ is formed through the fight. It is Christ's resilience in me that will become part of my reputation as a finisher and not a quitter.

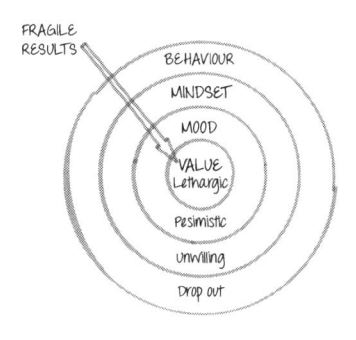

To unlock the Christ potential in me, my beliefs have to move from intention to action.

James 2:17: ... *faith by itself, if it is not accompanied by action, is dead.*

So what can you do practically to help unlock the potential of passion in the conversation of your life? How do you cultivate the resilience that allows you to cross the finish line of your goals aggressively?

FIGHT TO THE FINISH

You will need some time to prepare yourself for the day. While this could be at any time I believe first thing in the morning is the optimum time because it means that you are then in a state of readiness throughout the day.

The following steps are inspired by the story of Jacob who wrestled with God and through this process unlocked his new identity as Israel. We find this in Genesis 32:22-32.

FIGHT

Find a place
Immerse
Grab the new
Hold down belief
Test through practice

Find a place

When living the winning conversation, which requires an inside-out paradigm, it is vital that you find a place of stillness because how you set yourself on the inside will determine what makes itself to the outside world.

Jacob sent everything and everyone on ahead so that he could unlock the potential of his new identity.

Gen 32:23-24: *After he had sent them across the stream, he sent over all his possessions. So Jacob was left alone.*

Immerse yourself

Create an opportunity at the beginning of the day to read this book and/or other books that produce life-giving principles. Allowing these to soak into your thinking is vital as it feeds your belief system.

As well as this you can listen to material in the car or on the commute, read a book during break, and discuss with others. Create the immersive experience you need.

Jacob engaged his whole self in this place of solitude.

Gen 32:24: *So Jacob was left alone, and a man wrestled with him till daybreak.*

GRAB the new

Embodying the new conversation does not happen by chance; it happens by choice. It will be more of a wrestle than a soft encouragement to oneself. Such is the strength of our defaults.

Breakthrough in our lives does not happen without discomfort or pain. Perseverance is required when our old, sinful identity needs killing off and the new is brought into place. Jacob was not leaving that place until he experienced personal breakthrough.

Gen 32:25-26: *When the man saw that he could not overpower him, he touched the socket of Jacob's hip so that his hip was wrenched as he wrestled with the man. Then the man said, "Let me go, for it is daybreak."*

Two moves are critical in a wrestling fight: the grab and the hold:

THE GRAB:

Jacob held on!

Gen 32: 26b: *But Jacob replied, "I will not let you go unless you bless me."*

Here is what has to happen during our fight in order for the new identity to break through:

Galvanise Gratitude
Review and realign
Affirm I AM
Believe I CAN

Galvanise *Gratitude*

Decide on at least three things to be grateful for every day. Think about these and allow the emotion of gratitude to oil your passion motor. Never underestimate the power of gratitude.

Review *and realign*

When reviewing the previous day or the day so far, are there any actions I need to take? Do I need to ask forgiveness from someone? What did I do right? What needs more investment? Where have I left the course and need to steer back onto the right path? Doing this daily means smaller changes. The longer the gap between reviews the more severe and difficult the changes. Doing this daily increases assurance and confidence and builds resilience.

Affirm *I AM*

Every investment and correction starts at WHO I AM. So what do I need to affirm today? This book is designed to be a continuous conversation. Read some of it every day and stay on course.

Believe *I CAN*

Make a definite decision that you can and remind yourself what you CAN now do. Remember it will require FIGHTING talk with yourself and brutal honesty.

Jacob discovered WHO he was and this meant he could operate at a new level of resilience in WHAT he did from this moment on. This resilience prepared him for the years ahead when he would need to persevere to experience the fullness of God's blessing for his life.

Gen 32:28: *Then the man said, "You will no longer be Jacob, but Israel, because you have struggled with God and with humans and have overcome."*

THE HOLD:

Hold down belief

When we hold down a belief long enough it will create the change of mood, mindset and behaviour we long to see. In wrestling, the hold is the final move that leads to victory. The one performing the move holds the opponent until submission is communicated by either the opponent or referee. Hold a belief long enough and the internal components of your soul, mind and body have to submit to it.

Test through practice

Only an experience will solidify the belief so FIGHT to decide what challenge you will embrace today to set another brick in the building that represents the grand design of WHO you are. Imagine yourself operating the winning conversation in a situation you choose to encounter today.

If we repeat this process daily then the beliefs we hold down and the practices we implement become our habits. If our habits are the shaping force behind the person we become then we need to give them daily health checks. What are the habits with which have I made a personal agreement to develop? Which habits am I keeping and which am I breaking? What habits do I need to start?

Sometimes we need to stir up a positive aggression that will create forward progression. We do this through creating a controlled crisis. As believers we create a controlled crisis internally through inviting the Holy Spirit to test us.

David says in Psalm 139:23: *Search me, God, and know my heart; test me and know my anxious thoughts.*

David knew that if he could test the heart and pass, then everything he did would carry the hallmark of God's success.

Paul said in Romans 12: *Do not conform to the pattern of this world but be transformed by the renewing of your mind. Then you will be able to test and approve what God's will is—His good, pleasing and perfect will.*

Internal transformation and innovation come through our plans and mindsets coming under the spotlight of the Holy Spirit. By doing this we unlock the good, *pleasing and perfect will* of God.

When completing and/or reviewing your life MAP, make sure you take time to do this in prayer and in the quiet place where the Holy Spirit can test its resilience.

Day 31: The Winning Evaluation

Benchmark which mindset you have when it comes to the RESILIENT conversation.

The fruit of my actions will reveal the root of the conversations I host. Today we are looking at 10 questions or statements we make based on situations in which we find ourselves. I encourage you to be brutally honest as to which response most fits your nature. Tally up how many you answered according to which voice and make a decision to go back to your inner conversations to strengthen your foundation as a champion. If you feel frustrated then that is not a bad thing as long as you focus that frustration on making certain your commitment to hosting the winning conversation.

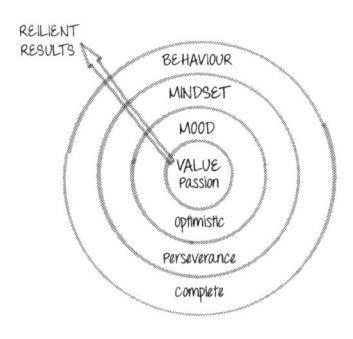

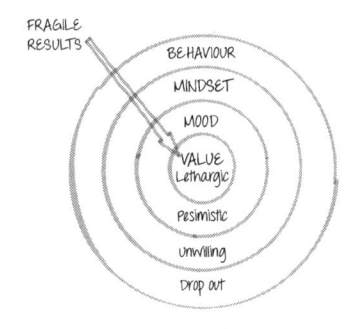

FRAGILE
RESULTS
BEHAVIOUR
MINDSET
MOOD
VALUE
Lethargic
Pesimistic
Unwilling
Drop out

1) Capacity—Can your capacity be increased and how?

Consumed - My capacity is something I don't give much thought to, I fill my time and when it's full it's full.

Complacent - My capacity can possibly be increased when the opportunity comes to offload responsibilities. I'll just wait and see.

Competitor - I actively seek to get more into my life in order to grow my capacity and yet this can produce an adverse effect I struggle to complete things. I guess that's just the price of busyness.

Champion - I actively seek to grow my capacity through tackling and completing the right tasks. I understand that my capacity is not grown through busyness but effective use of my time.

2) Wholeness—Do you treat your emotional, mental, spiritual and physical components equally?

Consumed - I do not think that they are equally important.

Complacent - I try to think about all four as I see their benefit but I am not actively looking to grow each area.

Competitor - I know they are all vital to my wellbeing but I tend to favour one over the rest.

Champion - It is vital that I learn to invest in each area as this gives lift to my whole being. Balancing my accounts helps me unlock my potential.

3) Confidence - Is confidence something you actively seek to develop?

Consumed - Confidence is connected to the type of personality you are. A person can become more confident but this is limited by their personality type.

Complacent - I feel more confident when others encourage me based on what I have done. Therefore the more I get around people who encourage me the more confident I will become.

Competitor - I will not shy away from opportunities to grow my confidence. When they present themselves to me I will evaluate them.

Champion - Confidence is grown through my willingness to embrace challenge. I will daily challenge myself to step beyond what is comfortable which will deepen my convictions and build confidence in me. My level of confidence is in my hands.

4) Completion—How important is it to complete what has been started?

Consumed - Completing tasks is admirable but not essential.

Complacent - Completing tasks that have the highest importance is important and trying best to do the same with other tasks is advisable.

Competitor - I attempt to complete everything but with my desire to grow I always have more to do than I can possibly complete.

Champion - Completion is vital. Therefore I will take time to assess my ability to complete a challenge. Self doubt decreases the more I take on bigger challenges and commit to complete them.

5) Enthusiasm - How do you view enthusiasm?

Consumed - It is good to be enthusiastic but this can only be expected in those areas people like.

Complacent - Enthusiasm is important to achieving a good result. Enthusiasm, however, is unpredictable and not always within a person's control.

Competitor - Enthusiasm is very important because how I feel while doing something is important not only for the quality of result but also those I may lead. I do not always display my enthusiasm outwardly.

Champion - Enthusiasm is a choice that is imperative if I am going to attribute any resource to a task. The more demonstrative my enthusiasm the more I feel enthusiastic inside and the more energy the task receives.

6) Reaction—Is my reaction my responsibility?

Consumed - People can make you react a certain way and therefore they must accept the responsibility. I never want people to think I am a 'doormat.'

Complacent - Sometimes reacting to another person is inevitable and so it depends on the circumstances.

Competitor - Reaction is never a good thing. It is better not to say anything and just keep going.

Champion - Taking the time to think through a response that builds strength is essential. Avoiding any kind of response is not helpful, especially with those in a team environment, as trust erodes when situations are not confronted.

7) Rest—Is rest important?

Complacent - Rest becomes boring and counterproductive and so I fill my spare time with mindless pursuits.

Consumed - Rest is a luxury that I can afford when things quieten down from my busyness.

Competitor - Cramming my week and then finding space to relax at the weekend or when on holiday feels productive and the right way to go about life.

Champion - Rest is vital to build resilience. It needs to be weaved into the rhythm of the week. Resilience is not built on constant activity. Rest is a place I should be working from not working for.

8) Disappointment—What do you do when you feel disappointment?

Consumed - I avoid disappointment by not setting goals. If something good happens then I will celebrate. However I do not want disappointment in my life. Previous disappointments have taken the wind out of my sails.

Complacent - Disappointment can set me back for a period and even a season of my life, but eventually I get back to the place I was before.

Competitor - I get down when I am disappointed and I am prone to focusing on other areas of my life until the disappointment wears off.

Champion - Disappointment is a perspective and not the deciding factor in my life. I must learn to evaluate moments when I feel disappointed. The moment disappointment happens is the best time to sharpen conviction.

9) Thoughts—Is it important to manage your thoughts?

Consumed - I do not spend much time thinking about the way I think. I do not see the significance.

Complacent - Managing my thought life is very important but I do not have anything in place to do this.

Competitor - Every now and again I have to spend time sorting my thinking out. When my mindset is clearly affecting what I want to do I make sure I do something about it.

Champion - Managing my thoughts needs to be part of my daily rhythm. I actively try to understand what I am unaware of as I know I am not consciously aware of many of the thoughts that are shaping my actions.

10) Exercise—How important do you rate physical exercise?

Consumer - It is great if you are that kind of person but most of the time it is a necessary evil.

Complacent - Being physically in shape is important and I attempt to use the latest methods to achieve fitness. However, this often starts with enthusiasm but dissipates after a short period of time.

Competitor - I have a plan to stay physically fit and try my best to keep to it.

Champion - I have fitness goals because I know growing this area will influence the other capacities in my life. Physical endurance creates endurance mentally, emotionally and spiritually.

PRACTICE V POTENTIAL of the RESILIENT conversation

Based on the answers to the above questions, how many times could you honestly say that your answer was 'champion'?

Consumer: 1-2 times
Complacent: 3-5 times
Competitor: 6-8 times
Champion: 9-10 times

My Overall POTENTIAL: I AM A CHAMPION

MY Overall PRACTICE: I HAVE BEEN A _____

In order for my practice to match my potential I have identified the following three things I can do to unlock the champion in me:

1_____

2_____

3_____

Day 32: The Winning Accountability

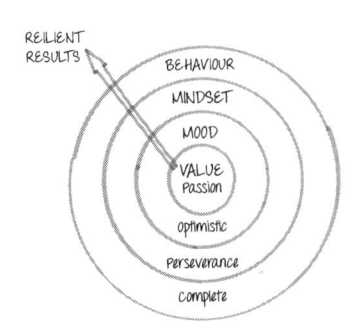

Pulling this whole week under the title of 'be stirred and not shaken' enables us to be able to review this conversation quickly. Using the dice in spare moments throughout the day, or in a small group, helps me to focus on the inner conversation of passion.

The Winning Dice—**Be stirred and not shaken**

Resilience is a person's inner strength.

The only way to develop resilience is by persevering regardless through challenging situations.

When you are stirred, you begin to shake the potential that has become settled. When it comes to carbonated drinks the last thing you want to do is shake the bottle. The shaking produces a build up of pressure and when the pressure increases beyond the ability of the container to hold it, it will explode. When we do not learn to handle the pressures and challenges of life correctly, this is what happens to us. The challenges do us harm rather than bring us value.

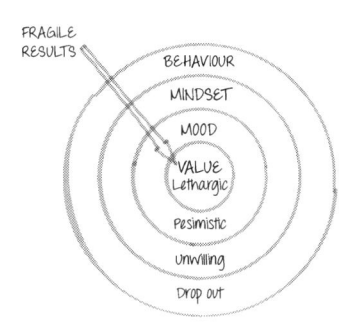

I hope I have achieved my aim through this conversation, to create a paradigm shift in each one of us so that we realise that every challenge is indeed a gift. It is an opportunity that can produce something of real value. The key is in our response. If we recognise that every shaking can help us to realign our focus to an unshakeable principle then our lives can be more like bottles of freshly squeezed juice. These containers encourage the consumer to shake the bottle well before drinking in order to get the best possible taste. The act of shaking shifts the goodness from the base of the bottle to the rest of the container. This is what challenges can do in your life. They cause the principles in our belief system to produce fruit in our emotional, mental and physical lives.

An unsettling feeling can in fact be the start of a fruitful period. You can run from this and look again for what produces the settled feeling but you will close the door on a new season of results if you do. You have to ask what you want more—a feeling or a new result? Your next steps will prove your genuine desire.

In sharing this principle with others and the community where you work and play we are aiming to create a cultural expectation. There are many times when we do not feel up to doing something. Sometimes people require a word or challenge that shakes them into action. However, with the 'winning conversation' we choose to stir what is in us and choose to be up for it before feeling up to it. We make a decision that helps our thoughts and feelings to follow the right pattern.

When we stir up enthusiasm, this is a discipline that relies on internal and not external stimulation. We can stir ourselves into action. We can choose to be passionate rather than wait for something or someone to make us feel passionate.

We stir our imaginations to solve problems and find alternative ways of doing things when what we do is shaken. However, every day we can choose to stir up our thinking so that we discipline ourselves to embrace change by choice rather than circumstance.

Similarly, we get old on the inside when we stop seeking new ways of doing things and we become content with what we have already learnt rather than seeking to learn new things. We want adventure, change and new things and so we choose to make that happen rather than wait for it to happen by chance.

Here is a quick review of what is required if PASSION is to have the loudest voice, drowning out LETHARGY.

Step 1: RECALL together

You can choose to stir yourself from the inside-out or be shaken from the outside-in. The two choices reflect WHO you have determined to be.

What does 'being stirred' look like?

You learn to confide in faith, counsel your feelings and consult the facts

You do not allow your circumstances to set your attitude

You are consistent in setting the bar high in all things

You do not need telling to 'step up'

You have an internal desire to do and be better

You are always up for new challenges in order to see greater results

You like to mix things up because freshness is more important than predictability

You exude the freshness of new life

You sense the strength of your core identity in conversation and practice

You are disciplined in all areas of life—mental, physical, emotional as well as spiritual.

What does it mean to be 'shaken'?

You will easily take things the wrong way

You are highly sensitive and defensive

You are insecure regarding change because what you do is your security

You will go underground during difficult times

Your attitude is set for you

You think other things/people are to blame for the way they are

You let feelings lead you

You allow misery to get on the inside

People feel like they are treading on egg shells around you

People cannot guess what mood you are in from day to day

Productivity and effectiveness will be directly linked to how well things are going in your life, not in spite of what is going on

Step 2: REVIEW with others

With people who are committed to developing the winning conversations get together weekly throughout the journey of this book and this week do the following:

i) Share a time when you were shaken? Knowing what you know now, what would you have done differently?

ii) Give an example of someone who has inspired you because

they stirred up what was in them and persevered?

iii) Who do you want to model this to in your circle of influence?

iv) How can you help others create assurance in their lives?

v) What were the key limitations that you know are going to be the hardest to overcome? How could the person or group you are talking to help you overcome them?

vi) Do you have any wins to celebrate now? Inspire one another with your stories.

vii) What wins do you want to celebrate one week from now, six months from now and one year from now?

Step 3: REFLECTION to be shared

Now share a reflection with someone in your group or someone else that you are coaching to be a champion in life. Why not take the time with your children, loved one, or friend over coffee to share what you have learnt. Simply sharing this reflection will accomplish much in your life and deepen relationships, enriching them with vulnerability and moments of movement.

Follow our basic structure:

i. What I realised for the first time/again this week is ….. (share the thought)

ii. The change I need to make is …… (share the action point)

iii. Can you help me make it (Invite help and create accountability)

Once you have developed the habit of doing this, why not decide to turn your thoughts into a blog or even take your coaching to another level? There is so much in you and it is directly connected to your commitment to stretch yourself.

Section 6: Be MORE memorable

Day 33: The Winning Conversation makes you MORE memorable

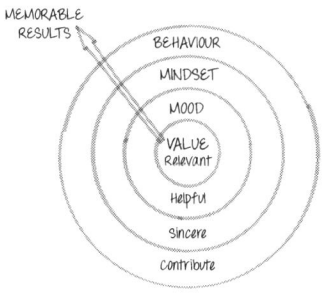

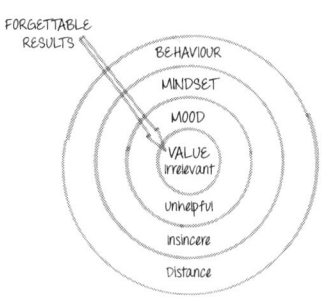

RELEVANCE that unlocks the door to being MEMORABLE

Kingdom Key: We are distinctive fruit

No good tree bears bad fruit, nor does a bad tree bear good fruit. Each tree is recognised by its own fruit. People do not pick figs from thorn bushes, or grapes from briers (Luke 6:43-45).

When I host the voice of Christ's relevance in the boardroom of my belief I can become MORE memorable through my conversations with others. Unlocking this Kingdom key enables us to *build a platform* with people so that the message of our lives and ultimately the Gospel can be heard and experienced. Our challenge is that we are in the information age which means that the amount of voices we compete with is immense. The content of our conversation has to add 'standout' value to the person we converse with to have any lasting impact.

The Psalmist says: *Open your mouth and taste, open your eyes and see, how good God is. Blessed are you who run to Him* (Psalm 34:8).

Now that God lives in you through His Spirit, you are to produce the fruit that tastes good. Psalm 34 says *blessed are you who run to Him*. As you use the Kingdom key of Christ's relevance in you, people will start to come to you because your character and therefore your conversation taste good. The fruit of your conversation will become like vintage wine, distinct from common everyday conversations. People will also be *blessed when they run into you* because you will learn to become memorable in your first impressions. Your awareness of the Kingdom in you and of practicing this key will make you memorable.

Jesus said I am the vine and in His analogy those who believe in Him are the branches. He said: *This is to my Father's glory, that you bear much fruit, showing yourselves to be my disciples* (John 15:8).

Our very reason for being alive is to produce this memorable and distinctive fruit. John in his Gospel goes on to reveal that this fruit would flow from our love for Jesus and our ability to learn how to love others more effectively. When we produce this fruit we unlock greater kingdom opportunity.

You did not choose me, but I chose you and appointed you so that you might go and bear fruit—fruit that will last—and so that whatever you ask in my name the Father will give you. This is my command: Love each other (John 15:16-17).

When I host the MEMORABLE conversation I become:

1) MORE intriguing

The riches of life are unearthed through the value of my conversations

Jesus conferred value to people in his conversation. Even when dealing with the woman caught in adultery, He challenged the crowd by saying *He who is without sin cast the first stone!* Upon hearing this, the crowd put down their rocks and dispersed. He then said lovingly to the woman, *now go and sin no more* (John 8:1-11).

When you seek to add value - even when everyone else devalues

SECTION 6: BE MORE MEMORABLE

- your conversation become even MORE intriguing and therefore memorable.

2) MORE attuned to how people feel

The right words at the right time make you a 'go to' person

Col 4:5-6: *Be wise in the way you act toward outsiders; make the most of every opportunity. Let your conversation be always full of grace, seasoned with salt, so that you may know how to answer everyone.*

Every conversation is an opportunity to leave a Kingdom impression. From the questions you ask through to what you affirm about a person to their face, you have an opportunity to bring heaven to someone's life today. While the enemy seeks to destroy the value in people's lives (John 10:10), you have the ability to preserve the God-value in someone through a seasoned conversation that leaves a person built up and encouraged.

Col 4:5-6 (The Message): *Use your heads as you live and work among outsiders. Don't miss a trick. Make the most of every opportunity. Be gracious in your speech.* **The goal is to bring out the best in others in a conversation**, *not put them down, not cut them out.*

When we seek to bring the best out of the people we meet today through questioning and affirming, we leave the fingerprints of Christ on their lives.

God has wired people to connect to such a conversation, so test His design and ask the Holy Spirit to guide you in your conversations. He will guide you.

4) MORE focussed on building a platform

When you think your conversations are not taking effect, keep talking!

A harvest is the result of a God-ordained process and not an event. When we focus on the process of building relationships through adding value and taking the opportunities to do good, then we can leave the harvest to God. You carry Christ and He is relevant. Do not veer from this belief and enjoy watching God at work through you!

Gal 6:9: *Let us not become weary in doing good, for at the proper time we will reap a harvest if we do not give up.*

5) MORE attentive to others' priorities

Prioritise others and others will prioritise you

Many of the gifts of the Spirit are given to the Church in order to make us more effective in our conversations so that the Kingdom of God can grow. The gifts of discernment, faith and prophecy give us the ability to have divine understanding about a person's problem and to give words that unlock a person's situation. (1 Cor 12:7-11)

I believe the gifts of the Spirit are most powerful in the day-to-day conversations we have. They do not have to be spoken with supernatural eloquence in a church building. They can simply be uttered from a genuine heart in an everyday conversation through which you desire to see the Kingdom of God come in a person's life.

Proverbs 15:23: *A man has joy in giving an appropriate answer, and how good and delightful is a word spoken at the right moment—how good it is!*

You can bring joy and hope to people by listening to the voice of the Holy Spirit. To do this our focus cannot be on ourselves; we have to focus our whole being on God and the person with whom we are talking. When we are thinking about ourselves we block the process. We fear saying the wrong thing, looking foolish, and becoming self-conscious. These are classic manoeuvres of the enemy.

6) MORE committed to moments of movement

Our memory favours those who move us

The relevant voice of Christ in you will enable you to feed the soul of those who are starving for affirmation and to be valued. A person never forgets a great restaurant that served them a great meal and if we leave people feeling valued they will never forget how we made them feel.

Proverbs 15:4: *The soothing tongue is a tree of life, but a perverse tongue crushes the spirit.*

Our conversation can be soothing, counteracting the sharp tongues of cynical and destructive voices that exist in a person's life. Whether those voices are spoken at them or those destructive voices are inside them, we can bring healing.

Proverbs 16:24: *Gracious words are a honeycomb, sweet to the soul and healing to the bones.*

The river that flows from the Temple brings healing. The river today flows from the throne of God and through the Temple of your life (Ezekiel 47:1-12; Revelation 22:1-3).

7) MORE authentic

People connect to my authenticity not my 'perfection'

Jesus was perfect and yet at no point do we see Him wave this in the faces of the people He was trying to influence with the Kingdom. His ability to show acceptance to the worst of sinners made Him a target for the proud religious and a magnet to the broken.

In Luke 7 Jesus gives us a key to cultivating love within our internal conversation - a love that will spill over into our external conversation. The more we realise how far we have fallen and experience daily the true grace and forgiveness of Christ, the more love we cultivate which in turn spills over into our conversations with others.

Luke 7:41-43: *"Two people owed money to a certain moneylender. One owed him five hundred denarii, and the other fifty. Neither of them had the money to pay him back, so he forgave the debts of both. Now which of them will love him more?"*

Simon replied, *"I suppose the one who had the bigger debt forgiven."*

"You have judged correctly," Jesus said.

The more we appreciate the desperate position from which we have been rescued, the more people will be able to connect with our authenticity. People want to connect to REAL people. The more real we get with ourselves, the more people can connect with us.

Day 34: The Winning Voice of Relevance

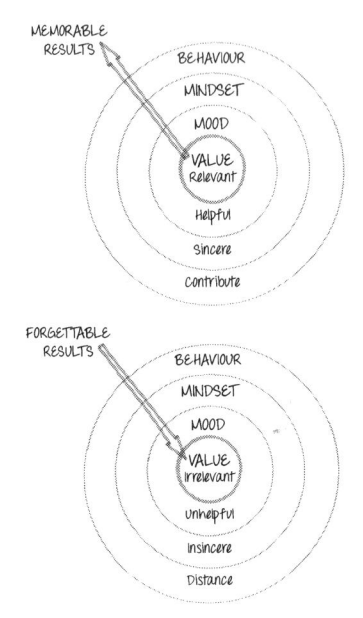

Relevance that unlocks the door of being MORE **Memorable**

Kingdom Key: We are distinctive fruit

No good tree bears bad fruit, nor does a bad tree bear good fruit. Each tree is recognised by its own fruit. People do not pick figs from thorn bushes, or grapes from briers (Luke 6:43-45).

To be a person of RELEVANCE I have to immerse myself in my new identity in Jesus Christ. This belief will lead me into the right feelings. The more I immerse myself in the belief that I am relevant, the more memorable I will become.

Since I have Christ in me then daily I have to die to the old me and live in the new me.

Paul says in Galatians 2:20: *I have been crucified with Christ and I no longer live, but Christ lives in me. The life I now live in the body, I live by faith in the Son of God, who loved me and gave himself for me.*

This means WHO I am is WHO he is. I have adopted my new identity and I choose each day to live from the Christ core.

I am relevant because Jesus is relevant!

To unlock RELEVANCE I have to believe that…

i) I AM committed to inconvenience

My inconvenience is someone else's convenience

When we look at the path of discipleship that Christ has called us to, there is nothing convenient about it. Jesus quite literally made His home in 'inconvenience'. He chose not to settle for any of life's comforts because He was so mission focussed.

Kingdom Key:

As they were walking along the road, a man said to him, "I will follow you wherever you go." Jesus replied, "Foxes have dens and birds have nests, but the Son of Man has no place to lay His head" (Luke 9:57-58).

While He was not commanding us all to be nomadic, He demonstrates the power of deliberate inconvenience. When we practice being inconvenienced we avoid the temptation of mission drift. Inconvenience keeps us leaning into the voice of the Holy Spirit, sharpens our faith and keeps us on the critical path of the mission, enabling us to maximize Kingdom results.

Conversation with God:

Father God, help me today to manage the tension of being focussed on my winning purpose while at the same time being ready to be inconvenienced for the sake of your Kingdom through my conversations with others. I believe 'unplanned' Kingdom opportunities lie in wait for me. I ask that you heighten my awareness of your Spirit's leading in the day that lies ahead.

ii) I AM a source for others

Help others expand to become more expansive

People will not always recognise or verbalise that they need what you have. However, you carry Christ and therefore you are relevant. Have confidence focusing on what you <u>do have</u> rather than what you lack. A lack of something does not remove the opportunity to focus our current resource on our desired outcome. John and Peter did this in Acts 3:4-7 and look at the miracle that took place!

Kingdom Key:

Peter looked straight at him, as did John. Then Peter said, "Look at us!" So the man gave them his attention, expecting to get something from them.

Then Peter said, "Silver or gold I do not have, but <u>what I do have I give you.</u> In the name of Jesus Christ of Nazareth, walk." Taking him by the right hand, he helped him up, and instantly the man's feet and ankles became strong (Acts 3:4-7).

John and Peter were equipped with the spiritual gift of healing and they used what they did possess rather than focus on their inability to give finance. This act of service to the crippled man expanded his life opportunities because he could now walk.

We are called to expand the lives of the people we interact with. At the very least we can do this through simple words of affirmation and encouragement. Words are powerful and bring transformation. Some people have lacked words of affirmation to the point that they have forgotten how it feels. Our affirmation not only adds value but opens up the opportunity for us to add future value through establishing a relationship.

While we can increase our resources and communication skills in order to relate to people, we also need the power of the Holy Spirit to be effective when we are looking for Kingdom results. The baptism in the Holy Spirit was given to the Church as a means of empowering us for fulfilling our Kingdom assignment.

Pray that God will fill you with the Holy Spirit and activate spiritual gifts in you. You can receive them by faith for the Kingdom assignment. They become tools through which God can use you to add 'heaven's' value to people. They help people experience a loving God who wants to interact with them.

The more you cultivate the relevant conversation, the more you will *eagerly desire spiritual gifts* (1 Cor 12/14).

Conversation with God:

Father, help me to be aware that I carry Christ Jesus who is the source with which people need connecting. Help me not to focus on what I lack but on what I have. I ask you to fill me with the Holy

Spirit. I desire the gifts of the Spirit in order to supernaturally impact the lives of those with whom I have conversations. As I speak, give me a God-confidence like that of John and Peter.

iii) I AM compatible

I become compatible when I become compassionate

People will not always communicate that you have connected on a deep level with them. Sometimes people are so unused to people adding sincere value to them that they do not know how to react. Sometimes this absence in their lives causes people to be suspicious of motives. However, keep building a platform with them, adding value that builds credibility, and over time see how it changes the dynamic of your conversation with them.

Keep acting out of conviction. Do not simply add value to the people you find it easy to talk to; add value to your enemies.

People who dislike us are simply exhibiting an internal dislike that they have for themselves. The more challenging we find it to add value to someone the more compassion is unlocked inside us. Remember, the greater the demand in what we set out to achieve, the more potential there is to unlock.

Kingdom Key:

Romans 12:14-17 *Bless those who persecute you; bless and do not curse. Rejoice with those who rejoice; mourn with those who mourn. Live in harmony with one another. Do not be proud, but be willing to associate with people of low position. Do not be conceited. Do not repay anyone evil for evil. Be careful to do what is right in the eyes of everyone.*

Adding value to people can create an unexpected reaction. Do not let that knock you off course. Remember, live inside-out. Stay helpful and sincere in your compassion towards others and allow God to take care of the rest. You may not see the harvest of your compassion, but the key is to stay obedient.

Conversation with God:

Father, strengthen the conviction of relevance within me. I want Jesus to show Himself to those with whom I struggle to connect. Help me demonstrate compassion through my conversations today. I commit the results to you.

iv) I AM an open book

My authenticity is my appeal

The openness and vulnerability of Jesus' human nature enabled His close disciples to connect deeply with Him. In Matthew 26 Jesus exposed the sorrow of His soul and the feeling of being overwhelmed with Peter, James and John.

We become more relevant when we allow others to see into our soul.

Jesus demonstrated that strong leadership is not about covering weakness but allowing others to draw alongside during moments of weakness. Interdependence in a team requires permission from every person involved, especially the leader.

Kingdom key:

Then Jesus went with his disciples to a place called Gethsemane, and He said to them, "Sit here while I go over there and pray." He took Peter and the two sons of Zebedee along with Him, and He began to be sorrowful and troubled. Then He said to them, "My soul is overwhelmed with sorrow to the point of death. Stay here and keep watch with me" (Matthew 26:36-38).

When we learn to allow others in on our challenges we will be amazed at the relevant connection that is created. This deepens unity and unity unlocks the glory of God on earth.

Conversation with God:

Father, help me to be open with people and confident that exposing my weaknesses will not bring disconnection but will deepen my connection with people. Remove any fear of vulnerability that I may have or distrust I carry because of how I have been hurt in the past by those to whom I've been honest and open.

vii) I AM a solution

Listen hard enough and you will hear a problem you can solve

You are to be a solution bringer. While we can commit ourselves to increasing our competency in deciphering problems and bringing solutions, our key assets are heaven-inspired.

One of the primary roles of the Holy Spirit is to guide and instruct us. The Holy Spirit is ready to equip you with irresistible wisdom which people will remember you for (John 16:13). In Luke 21 Jesus said that even under pressure and in the most extreme situations the Holy Spirit will inspire us to have relevant words that form influential and memorable conversations.

Luke 21:15: *I will give you words and wisdom that none of your adversaries will be able to resist or contradict.*

Conversation with God:

Father, I ask your Holy Spirit to give me the gift of wisdom. Grant me wisdom today so that I can use Kingdom keys to bring a relevance to the lives of the people around me. Help me recall lost information that I once obtained to bring back to remembrance anything that will add Kingdom value to people's lives today (John 14:26).

viii) I AM built to resonate

Only the real me will resonate with others

When Jesus spoke, the hearts of His listeners resonated as they sat and listened. He sought to understand their position in order to lead them gently onto the Kingdom path. Whether it was the woman caught in adultery or Zacchaeus the Tax collector, He positioned himself in their world at their level and then brought gentle but uncompromising truth.

Paul carried this same passion to be relevant.

1 Corinthians 9:22-23:

To the weak I became weak, to win the weak. I have become all things to all people so that by all possible means I might save some. I do all this for the sake of the gospel, that I may share in its blessings.

Conversation with God:

Father, I choose today to step into other people's worlds by asking appropriate but searching questions that allow me to communicate the simple fact they can belong in relationship with me before they believe. Help me demonstrate acceptance that causes their hearts to resonate with the love you want to show through me.

ix) I AM a 'lifter' of people

I am lifted when I lift others

When I 'lift up' other people through positively affirming them and encouraging them I too am uplifted.

As I create 'fruit' that helps to satisfy the needs of others, my soul is satisfied.

Kingdom Key:

Proverbs 18:20-21: *From the fruit of their mouth a person's stomach is filled; with the harvest of their lips they are satisfied. The tongue has the power of life and death, and those who love it will eat its fruit.*

Conversation with God:

Father, help my tongue to be ready to lift people up and elevate them today, not with words of flattery but sincere value and love. May I bear fruit through my conversations and not waste the energy you have entrusted to me today.

x) I AM always leaning in

I am learning when I am leaning

The Apostle Paul operated from a 'relevant' conviction when he visited the Areopagus in Athens. As well as holding conversations in religious venues, Paul often ventured into marketplace meetings in order to connect people from wider society to the Kingdom message.

Acts 17:22-23: *Paul then stood up in the meeting of the Areopagus and said: "People of Athens! I see that in every way you are very religious. For as I walked around and looked carefully at your objects of worship, I even found an altar with this inscription: to an unknown god. So you are ignorant of the very thing you worship—and this is what I am going to proclaim to you.'*

While many Christians would have focused on the sinful practice of the Greeks in worshipping idols, Paul presented himself as someone who was interested in their culture in order to build a platform for his own message.

If you want to be memorable, become someone who develops a hunger to learn. We can learn from anyone and everyone. Our willingness to learn actually builds a memorable connection because people love to feel valued. When we show interest in what others value they will show interest in what we value. While learning from others we can find common ground useful for communicating our message in a way that others can relate to and understand.

Kingdom Key:

The heart of the discerning acquires knowledge, for the ears of the wise seek it out (Proverbs 18:15).

Conversation with God:

Father, help me to position myself with the humility of Christ as a learner today. Help me to ask good questions that value people and what you have put in them. Help me connect what people already understand to what they do not yet understand about you and your Kingdom.

Day 35: The Winning Mood of helpfulness

RELEVANCE unlocks a HELPFUL mood in me

Kingdom Key: We are distinctive fruit

No good tree bears bad fruit, nor does a bad tree bear good fruit. Each tree is recognised by its own fruit. People do not pick figs from thorn bushes, or grapes from briers (Luke 6:43-45).

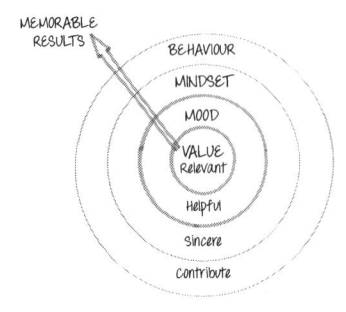

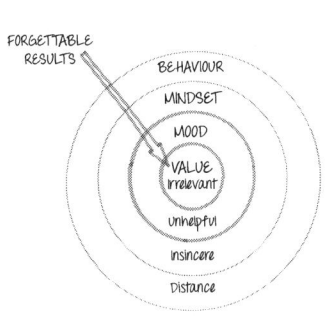

The Kingdom key of Relevance unlocks my WHY which is my PURPOSE.

My purpose is the 'good work' which I was created to do (Eph 2:10).

The vision of my life was prepared by God before I was even born (Jeremiah 1:50).

I am having the MEMORABLE conversation led by the voice of relevance which means I choose to put myself in a HELPFUL mood.

A helpful mood brings clarity to my voice

Many believers can be left waiting for clarity of purpose before progressing forward with their winning goal. Clarity however follows when we act upon what we do know. As we seek to help others through acts of service, we build up an understanding and knowledge of where our strengths and passions lie.

Don't push your way to the front; don't sweet-talk your way to the top. Put yourself aside, and help others get ahead. Don't be obsessed with getting your own advantage. Forget yourselves long enough to lend a helping hand (Phil 2:3-4: The Message).

Many believe that to get ahead we need to clamber over one another to scale the heights of 'success.' However, success in the Kingdom means serving others. When we serve the common good, with an uncommon attitude, then uncommon results will follow.

Helpfulness makes me value conversations more

Kingdom opportunity lies inside the conversations ahead of you today. Keep asking yourself the question, 'what help can I bring to this person?' See how your helpful mood creates a sincere desire to find a solution that serves that person. Cultivating this mood deeply enriches your life and opens up opportunities for the message of the Gospel to be shared.

Helpfulness sown is helpfulness reaped

Knowing that I am to become heaven's distribution for God's resource helps me to stay in a helpful mood, heightening my awareness of what is lacking in a person's life.

Proverbs 19:17: *Whoever is kind to the poor lends to the Lord, and He will reward them for what they have done.*

Poverty can be obvious at times in a person's life. However, poverty can manifest itself in different forms. We can lack health emotionally, mentally, physically and spiritually. Even those who have the necessary provision to exist can suffer the poverty of having low self-esteem and positive relationships. They might be spiritually poor, experiencing crippling fear and anxiety. My conversation with others can discover a person's need when I am in a helpful mood based on a belief that if Christ is relevant, then so am I.

Unlock a relevant soul script through immersing yourself in God's word (the bible)

The belief that our voice will make a difference will increase when we immerse ourselves in these verses:

When I immerse myself in these verses I value myself as someone who has a voice:

I carry more inside of me than I think and others need me to know this

2 Cor 4:7: *But we have this treasure in jars of clay to show that this all-surpassing power is from God and not from us.*

I not only carry all I need to help others but I have all I need to step out and do it

2 Timothy 1:7: *For the Spirit God gave us does not make us timid, but gives us power, love and self-discipline.*

When I immerse myself in this verse I value others knowing my voice will make a difference to others

My life is about letting God reach others through me

2 Cor 5:20: *We are therefore Christ's ambassadors, as though God were making His appeal through us.*

My weakness becomes God's window of opportunity to show His wisdom and power

1 Cor 1:27-29: *God chose the foolish things of the world to shame the wise; God chose the weak things of the world to shame the strong. God chose the lowly things of this world and the despised things—and the things that are not—to nullify the things that are, so that no one may boast before Him.*

<u>When I immerse myself in this verse I value my future because my voice will make an even bigger difference</u>

I determine the limit of resource and influence that God entrusts me with

Luke 16:10-12: *Whoever can be trusted with very little can also be trusted with much, and whoever is dishonest with very little will also be dishonest with much. So if you have not been trustworthy in handling worldly wealth, who will trust you with true riches? And if you have not been trustworthy with someone else's property, who will give you property of your own?*

My aspiration and expectation bring the future into the now

James 1:6-7: *When you ask, you must believe and not doubt, because the one who doubts is like a wave of the sea, blown and tossed by the wind. That person should not expect to receive anything from the Lord.*

Conversation with God:

Father God, I choose to put aside the thoughts, feelings and impulses that do not fit with who you are because it is no longer I who you live but Christ who lives in me. I put off the old me and put on the new me. May my thoughts be your thoughts, my feelings your feelings and my impulses your impulses. I step into this day knowing that you are working through me to grow your Kingdom.

SECTION 6: BE MORE MEMORABLE

Day 36: The Winning Mindset of Sincerity

RELEVANCE unlocks a SINCERE mindset in me and this is HOW I approach my day

Kingdom Key: We are distinctive fruit

"No good tree bears bad fruit, nor does a bad tree bear good fruit. Each tree is recognised by its own fruit. People do not pick figs from thorn bushes, or grapes from briers (Luke 6:43-45).

Paul tells us in 1 Corinthians 2:16 that we have the mind of Christ. This is not about knowing all the thoughts of Jesus necessarily but our access to Christ's pattern of thinking. We have this when we build our lives around the commands of Christ in the Bible.

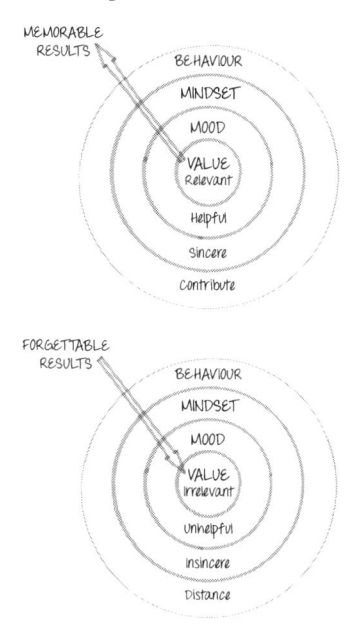

The winning conversation was demonstrated through the way Jesus lived his life. Jesus was relevant, lived from a helpful mood and had a sincere mindset. Because our identity is found in Christ we can adopt the mindset of Christ.

Col 3:2-4: *Since, then, you have been raised with Christ, set your hearts on things above, where Christ is, seated at the right hand of God. Set your minds on things above, not on earthly things. For you died, and your life is now hidden with Christ in God. When Christ, who is your life, appears, then you also will appear with Him in glory.*

1) Promote others through reinforcing value

Reinforcing value in a person reinforces your position in their minds

Jesus told a parable about a shrewd manager who lost his job but used the remainder of his working time to help the master's clients reduce their debts. By doing this he became memorable to those clients and secured their engagement in future dealings.

Kingdom Key: *Use worldly wealth to gain friends for yourselves, so that when it is gone, you will be welcomed into eternal dwellings* (Luke 16:9).

Jesus praised his shrewdness and also encouraged us to use the resource we have to build a platform with people because by doing so we become memorable.

2) Promote others through asking great questions

The quality of the question determines the quality of the answer

When we adopt a sincere mindset we show genuine interest in others by asking helpful questions. These questions can help to establish what Kingdom opportunity there is to help a person connect to the love of God through our actions.

When I ask sincere questions I cultivate humility in my life. Remember God elevates the humble and we become memorable (Psalm 147:6).

Kingdom Key: *Do nothing out of selfish ambition or vain conceit. Rather, in humility value others above yourselves, not looking to your own interests but each of you to the interests of the others* (Phil 2:3-4).

3) Promote others through quality listening

The longer I listen, the more valuable and memorable I become to someone

We become irrelevant and therefore forgettable when we demonstrate we are clearly not listening. Proverbs 18:13 in the Message version says, *Answering before listening is both stupid and rude.*

Some conversations are more challenging than others when it comes to staying relevant. The most challenging conversations are those that involve disagreement. Emotionally charged discussions often give way to two or more people communicating in an irrelevant fashion. When every person is simply focussing on being right, no one is listening and there is no room for resolution.

James encourages us to be quick to listen and slow to speak.

Kingdom Key: *My dear brothers and sisters, take note of this: Everyone should be quick to listen, slow to speak and slow to become angry, because human anger does not produce the righteousness that God desires* (James 1:19-20).

I think this principle alone, especially in situations where we could simply argue our point, shows us how to stay relevant even through disagreement. The more intense the situation and potential for disagreement is, the greater the opportunity for a Kingdom impression to be left. This takes self-control and a sincere humility.

Ask yourself the question, 'How can I make Jesus look good in this situation?' This helps establish a correct and sincere motive. God honours this regardless of how others take it.

4) Promote others by going beyond small talk

'Small talk' exists to lead us to 'big talk'

We can become lazy in our conversations. A sign of being lazy is when we do not progress beyond small talk. We distance ourselves from people when we do not seek to take our conversations any deeper.

Kingdom key: *Make sure you don't take things for granted and go slack in working for the common good; share what you have with others. God takes particular pleasure in acts of worship—a different kind of "sacrifice"—that take place in kitchen and workplace and on the streets* (Heb 13:16 Message).

When we are serving the good of others we are worshipping God. This means our conversations are part of our worship. Seek to give meaningful worship to God by learning to hold meaningful conversations. Sometimes, like me, you won't feel like it but remember we live from the inside-out. Feelings follow belief. Act your way into right feelings and be memorable through moving from small talk to big talk.

5) Promote others through unlocking doors

Feel for the key that they are looking for

Our actions validate our faith. We can cultivate a good talk within but unless we actively seek how our thoughts can inform actions then we will not prove our potential. God is looking to promote those who put their faith into action.

Kingdom principle: *They claim to know God, but by their actions they deny him. They are detestable, disobedient and unfit for doing anything good* (Titus 1:16).

The Kingdom economy works on the principle of sowing and reaping. The thought of sowing achieves nothing; only the act of sowing will yield results. Who knows what will result from you sowing the action of helping others today? My guess is if God showed you the potential, you would not hesitate.

You can trust God's principles without seeing the result up front so search for opportunities to help others today and let Him surprise you!

6) Promote others through finding the common ground

Every person has a point of engagement if I look hard enough

Jesus was a master of finding common ground in order to have influence. His calling of the fisherman as his disciples was a master class to us all.

Kingdom Key: *"Come, follow me," Jesus said, "and I will send you out to fish for people." At once they left their nets and followed Him* (Mathew 4:19-20).

While the analogy did not reveal everything, it revealed enough to 'hook' them. Decide today that you will get an understanding of what others know and build on that common ground so that your relationship grows. By doing this you are building a platform for the Kingdom message in you.

7) Promote others through connecting to WHO they are before WHAT they do

Engage with the identity before the capability of a person

Having a sincere approach is about caring for the WHO before the WHAT. In Luke 15 we have three parables where Jesus communicates his passion to rediscover what has been lost. Jesus did not come to recruit for a cause; first and foremost He came to restore lost people. Our passion has to be for the person.

Kingdom Key: *'Rejoice with me; I have found my lost coin.' In the same way, I tell you, there is rejoicing in the presence of the angels of God over one sinner who repents"* (Luke 15:9-10).

People are hungry for identity, and our focus has to be on caring sincerely for WHO they are. This genuine interest is pointing out the God-value in them. It also creates an openness to discover their lost identity which can only be found in Christ Jesus.

8) Promote others through attracting favour

You cannot fight for favour; you have to earn it

People will be attracted to the favour of God on your life. It is the 'X Factor' of heaven. Believing that you are favoured is a heightened awareness that the 'cause' of my choice will have an 'effect' that is shaped by God.

Kingdom Key: *My eyes will be on the faithful in the land that they may dwell with me; the one whose walk is blameless will minister to me* (Psalm 101:6).

Favour is an unknown quality and whilst our daily decisions feed into it, ultimately God determines how it is outplayed. Therefore, we simply have to remain faithful to God's process.

Kingdom Key: *Sow your seed in the morning, and at evening let your hands not be idle, for you do not know which will succeed, whether this or that, or whether both will do equally well* (Ecclesiastes 11:6).

Keep sowing through promoting others ahead of yourself through acts of kindness today and God will work with your investment.

9) Promote others through the strength of humility

Humility will create the permission to keep a conversation going

When facing conversations that feel difficult and arduous, the key is to stay patient and gently persist in order to see progress. There can be many reasons why people make it difficult for us to draw them into our conversation but if we keep our approach sincere we have the best chance of breaking through.

Kingdom Key: *Through patience a ruler can be persuaded, and a gentle tongue can break a bone* (Proverbs 25:15).

Regardless of how tough the conversation is to get going or to keep going, gentleness and patience creates a sincerity that opens people up. Remember the Kingdom is not always obvious but it will always be memorable. You do not have to look like the 'obvious' person to connect to, but your approach will leave a Kingdom impression.

Be intentional but not intense, be purposeful but not prying.

Remember you have the Holy Spirit as your partner working with you. He is the Master of conversation.

10) Promote others freely and end up rich

Meaningful relationships are worth their weight in gold

It is always important to remember that you are a tool in the hand of God and not the other way around. Sometimes we can try and do God's job for Him. He will make us memorable if we <u>stay faithful</u> in promoting others with sincerity. The more we do this with our relationships, the more we become the 'go-to' person ('the head') and not the forgettable person ('the tail').

Kingdom Key: *The Lord will make you the head, not the tail. If you pay attention to the commands of the Lord your God that I give you this day and carefully follow them, you will always be at the top, never at the bottom* (Deuteronomy 28:13).

Love Him and learn how to love people through relationships and over time let God amaze you with what He does.

Conversation with God:

SECTION 6: BE MORE MEMORABLE

Father God, I thank you for the truth of your Word. As I mediate on it may it unlock the winning mindset I need to see your Kingdom come and your will be done in my life today!

Day 37: The Winning Choices of Contributing Proactively

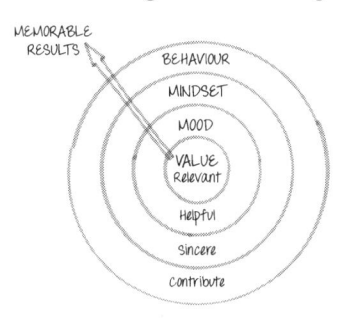

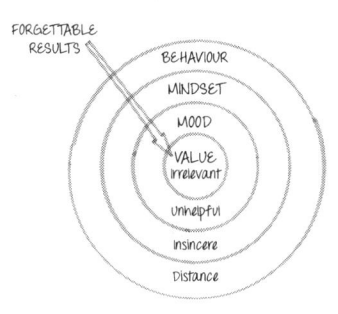

Today we look at some practical ways to develop the winning conversation that will make you MORE memorable. The more you inform the right choices, the more you activate the results. As well as adopting these practical methods it is vital to invite the Holy Spirit to lead our conversations with others. He can give us the words that unlock opportunities to help people. (John 16:13)

If you start a conversation with someone for the first time, you will want them to want the conversation to continue. When you do not have any relational credit with them, you have to start creating some in that first conversation. Your ultimate goal is to create an opportunity that allows you to contribute value to them and in turn establish credibility and trust.

Building that platform takes time. It requires you to become an intense listener who knows how to create relevant moments through asking great questions. To create a 'relevant moment' you must learn to shut everything else out of the conversation and focus solely on the person. This gives you the best opportunity for engaging your intuition, soul, mind and body in the conversation. Remember that the quality of your external conversation is determined by the quality of your internal conversation. If your mind is engaging with the distractions around the room, or another line of internal thought, then your focus will be sabotaged and the quality of your external conversation will plummet. We have all been on the receiving end of conversations with people we knew were not present to us. We feel demoted in value because something or someone else is clearly more important.

You need to listen intensely so that you can make statements that create a rapport with the other person. Here are some LISTEN statements that will lead you to make quality observations.

Stay RELEVANT by following this process:

Recall last time
Engage your whole self
Learn key facts
Echo their answers
Value through LISTENING
Avoid over-thinking
Next steps leave them lighter
Talk it back and see solutions

Let's look at these:

Recall *last time*

When someone picks up the last conversation you had with them and remembers what you talked about, you know that you mattered in those moments. You had their attention. Despite their busyness, they remembered you. The pause button was pressed; now 'play' is being pressed. Not only does the conversation carry on; the relational investment is reactivated. This will lead to positive results.

Engage *your whole self*

A conversation is more than just words. While people will rarely be aware of it, there are multiple conversations going on during one conversation. From the way a person stands, to their eye movements and even breathing, many messages are being communicated. A person's body language can put others at ease or on edge. It is futile to work on our words if our body language overrules it with an alternative message.

My relevant behaviour will mean I fully engage my WHOLE self. I become irrelevant when I allow my mind to drift off to something that happened thirty seconds ago, yesterday or something I am anticipating. When I am not in the NOW moment I am out of the game and I cannot produce a memorable conversation. I want my entire being to be focused on the person I am talking to so they feel the maximum value.

Learn *key facts*

Every person has a drawer full of valuables, a place where they put their most important things. As you talk with someone, imagine this drawer with their name on it. As you talk, recognise the things they are passionate about and visualise putting them in the valuables drawer. When you pull these things out of the imaginary drawer in future conversations, you will have their attention because you are valuing what they value. Now you have entered the top 1% of conversations.

There are four P's that help us look for these valuables:

People - those they love and care for

Pleasure - what they do with the precious spare time they have

Possessions - how they express themselves through what they own

Places - where they have been or are going that speaks of who they are.

Echo their answers

The challenge with conversations is that they can become a multitasking activity if we are not careful. We ask questions or make statements and then rehearse the next lines while the other person is answering. The reality is that it is impossible to multitask. As someone has said, 'to do two things at the same time is to do neither.' We can only focus on one thing at a time which is why it is good to have drummed into our subconscious those patterns that our conversations need to follow. This frees us up to engage wholeheartedly and not be stuck for what to talk about.

The best way to remember what is being said is for us to echo what is being said. When we put another's words in our own voice two things happen. Firstly, we can be corrected should we have heard incorrectly; secondly, we are more likely to remember what we parrot back to ourselves.

I am not advocating a weird kind of repetition of everything people say but the echoing of key facts which help us to remember what has been said. This takes data from short-term to mid-term memory.

Value *through* LISTEN

Here are key statements or questions you can ask that will set you apart from the 99% of other conversations:

LISTEN

'What I **LOVE** about you is…' Examples '…you never give up…you put others first…you bring the best out of me…you are consistent when others are not…'

'I can **IMAGINE** you…' Examples '…turning this story into a book one day…taking this product to market…writing songs from your experience…going for this career…teaching others through your experience.'

'I can **SEE** your strengths are…' Example '…empathising with those in need…motivating those on the periphery of life…breaking down a challenge and coming up with potential solutions…'

'**TELL** me about your challenges…' Example '…at work… achieving a long term goal…developing that skill to a new level.'

'You **ENCOURAGE** me when you…' Example … 'don't allow your challenges to change your attitude… when you do what you do day-in, day-out…you smile at people all the time even when you are going through challenges…'

'**NEVER** underestimate what… this means/does' … Example … 'your influence through what you do… how you encourage me.'

Avoid over-thinking

You need to keep as much clear thinking space as possible in order to stay in the now moment. Over-thinking how you are coming across and where this conversation could lead takes you out of the now moment. It is easy to switch from a producer who is trying to solve a problem to a consumer who is only concerned with how they are coming across. It is so easy to make the conversation about us; when we do this we become irrelevant.

Next steps *leave them lighter*

Ask yourself the question, 'What is the one thing I can do to help someone walk away with a greater lightness in their step?' It could be a commitment to go away and think of a solution or an offer to follow up the conversation. The old adage of 'a problem shared is a problem halved' has much truth; when you help others with their problems you ignite the law of sowing and reaping; those who sow generously will reap generously.

Talk it back *and see solutions*

When you leave a conversation, the information you have downloaded is in a time-critical phase; you need to talk it back soon in order to put it into the long-term memory box. This discipline may at times feel totally unnecessary. However, the champion lives from the inside-out and is not focussed on WHAT.

Talk it back *and identify solutions*

When you leave a conversation, the information you have downloaded is in a time-critical phase. You therefore need to talk it back soon in order to put it into the long-term memory box. When you talk it back, you will then be able to identify possible ways in which you can add value to that person. You might get back in touch with them and say something like, 'I was thinking about what we were talking about. Have you thought about X?'

Not every conversation will afford you the opportunity to go through the above mnemonic systematically. If you start to adopt the ideas in your conversation habits then over time you will start to reap the results of being memorable to those with whom you interact.

Conversation with God:

Father God I pray that you will help me to put some of what I have read into practice today. Help me to contribute proactively to others through my conversations. I invite you Holy Spirit to speak through me.

Day 38: The Winning Evaluation

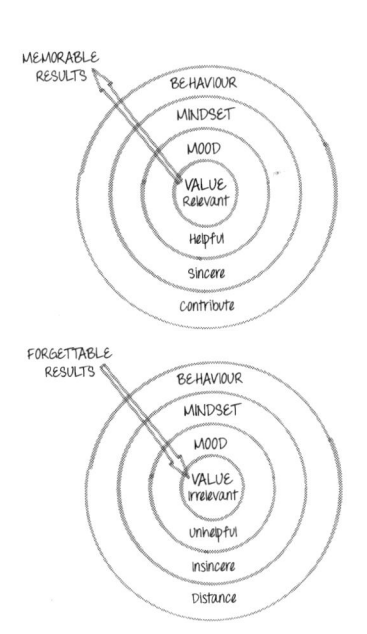

Benchmark which mindset you have when it comes to the MEMORABLE conversation.

The fruit of my actions will reveal the root of the conversations I host. Today we are looking at ten questions related to specific situations. I encourage you to be brutally honest as to which response most fits your nature. Tally up how many you answered according to which voice and make a decision to go back under the bonnet of your inner conversations to strengthen your foundation as a champion. If you feel frustrated then that is not a bad thing as long as you focus that frustration on making certain you commit to hosting the winning conversation.

1) Strategy: What do you do when you need a strategy in place to go after a goal?

Consumed – The effort needed to gain clarity demotivates me

Complacent – The lack of clarity can cause me to be distant from my purpose and disconnect from those

Competitor – I actively seek clarity in my conversations to find an answer

Champion – I involve myself in helping others with strategy knowing that in turn I will gain the clarity I need.

2) Change—What do you do in the midst of uncomfortable change?

Consumed - I become preoccupied with how I can matter in this new situation

Complacent - I lean back and wait for the dust to settle, not realising that I am disconnecting myself from my opportunity

Competitor - I actively seek the opportunities with a positive attitude and have as many conversations as possible to establish my new position

Champion - I seek to add strength to those who are carrying weight through the transition knowing that as I help the voice of others come through and add value to others so I am building a platform for the future.

3) Ideas—What do I do with a burning idea?

Consumed - Disconnect from facilitating others and focus solely on my idea and how I can make it happen

Complacent - Wait for other ideas to fail and then see if mine fits

Competitor - Persistently flag up my idea, keeping it present at every opportunity even if its connection is not obvious to the current challenges

Champion - Seek to add value to the ideas of others knowing that my ideas require connection points to be a solution to a problem.

4) Ownership—What do I do if I have responsibility for an area but little passion for it?

Consumed - Carry out the tasks to the bare minimum, often neglecting the things that appear of little significance

Complacent - Complete all tasks but have no desire to further the effectiveness of the responsibility

Competitor - Fulfil the responsibility but with one eye on where I want to get to.

Champion - I understand that the only way to be relevant to people is to be wholeheartedly committed to what they are committed to.

5) Big picture—How do I position myself in relation to the future?

Consumed - I lose heart by the distance between myself and my goals so I stop making them to avoid feelings of disappointment

Complacent - I periodically spend quality time looking at the bigger picture of my future and this usually takes place around events such as the turn of the year, birthdays or events that cause me to stop and think bigger

Competitor - I regularly visit the future and keep myself fully available for the opportunity to seize my goal

Champion - I view the time line of my NOT YET goal daily in the morning and the evening in order to keep it fresh and alive inside of me. This prepares me to take the daily steps toward its fulfilment.

6) Promotion—How I go about getting promotion?

Consumed - I can easily become disheartened by an apparent lack of progress so I lack presence with people in my current activity

Complacent - I can take my 'foot off the pedal' when there is little progress but then I will be inspired at times to pick up the pace, although this will come from an outside source

Competitor - I will position myself for opportunities that appear to have a direct correlation with where I want to go. My conversations will be based on how the other person can get me to where I need to go

Champion - Promotion finds me as I pursue my goal of helping others feel like they 'matter.' While I have a clear set of goals I make sure that I create a tension between this and a pure desire to help others by listening to them and connecting into them

7) Contentment—How do I stay content?

Consumed - I create a form of contentment that gets me through life but all I do is subdue my goal-setting to avoid disappointment

Complacent - I generally feel content but deep down I know that I am not being stretched and so my contentment is more a satisfaction with what I know than a contentment from being stretched and unlocking my potential

Competitor - I switch between contentment and frustration. When I see obvious wins I get a feeling of satisfaction but I am not sure if that is contentment. I certainly don't feel content when frustrated. I only feel as good as my last win

Champion - My wins lie in me pressing into people and adding value. Therefore my contentment is pretty constant as there are always opportunities to add value. I keep WHAT in my periphery vision and WHO in my line of sight

8) Legacy—What am I doing about legacy?

Consumed - I cannot see the point in building beyond my lifetime because I am not sure I have anything to contribute and because I will not be around to appreciate it

Complacent - I believe in the notion of legacy but I am not right now actively engaged in building something of significance that will outlive me, but one day I will

Competitor - I promote the notion that success lies in our successors and that legacy has to be at the heart of a worthy goal; I will do what I need to achieve first and then I will put my energy into my legacy

Champion – My life is about my legacy. If I build people I am sure to build beyond my lifetime because the seed I sow can become a forest in future generations

9) **Preparation—How do I view being prepared?**

Consumed - Preparation can be a waste of precious time. I only prepare for events that appear significant for my progress

Complacent - Preparation is seasonal. It is often down to how I feel. Sometimes I go through periods where preparation is enjoyable, even exciting. However, it does come down to how I feel about the task in question and what else is going on in my life at the time

Competitor - Preparation is crucial for the things I prioritise. If I do not prepare for the moments I know are significant, I prepare to fail

Champion - Preparation is a daily and weekly discipline that forms the bedrock of my life. I immerse myself in the principles that keep me in a state of being prepared. I still need specific preparation periods but these are like moving up a gear rather than moving from a standing start

10) **Relevant—How do I view being relevant?**

Consumed - I am irrelevant. There is nothing inside me that others would want. I do not look above my own lack

Complacent - I am relevant to very few people. Past rejection and lack of self-belief has created a low aspiration in me for wanting to connect. Sometimes the aspiration is snuffed out all together

Competitor - I can be relevant to many but not all, depending on the circumstances

Champion - I am relevant to all. Regardless of who stands before me - whether a homeless person or the Queen of England - I can find points of connection that can create a lasting impression. This is because my focus and commitment is WHO they are

PRACTICE V POTENTIAL in the MEMORABLE conversation:

Based on the answers to the above questions, how many times could you honestly say that your answer was 'champion'?

SECTION 6: BE MORE MEMORABLE

Consumer: 1-2 times
Complacent: 3-5 times
Competitor: 6-8 times
Champion: 9-10 times

My Overall POTENTIAL: I AM A CHAMPION

MY Overall PRACTICE: I HAVE BEEN A _____

In order for my practice to match my potential, I have identified the following three things I can do to unlock the champion in me:

1_____

2_____

3_____

Day 39: The Winning Accountability

By pulling this whole week under the title of 'building a platform not a soapbox,' we can quickly review this conversation. Utilising the dice in spare moments throughout the day, or in a small group session, we can focus on the inner conversation of relevance.

The Winning Dice—***Building a platform and not a soapbox***

We must never underestimate the strength of our defaults. We are naturally opinionated people who often believe our way is right and want others to subscribe to that opinion. Frustration can set in when we feel our voice falls on deaf ears. However if every opinion was aired and believed, there would be chaos. The way to get your voice heard is not to shout louder.

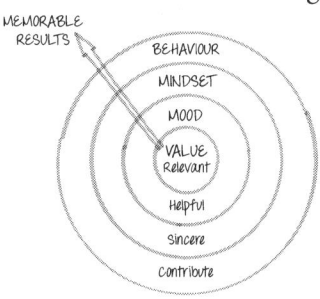

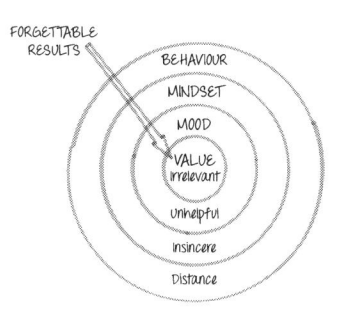

Those who stand on soap boxes are often ignored. People have to build credibility to be heard.

Devote yourself to **building a platform** of the credibility you receive for persistently being fruitful in what you do, even when it does not flow with your opinion.

Even at those times when you feel no one is giving you credit or appreciating all you do, refuse to stand on a soapbox. Focus your energy on building the platform of your credibility by keeping a right attitude and giving your very best. A voice will be heard better when spoken from a bigger platform, so keep building!

Commit to choosing to do the following:

Step 1: RECALL. Sometimes we need a quick review of what a platform builder and soapbox user look like so we can stay on the course of allowing RELEVANCE to have the loudest voice in our lives, in the process drowning out IRRELEVANCE. Here is a description based on what we have looked at this week:

What does a platform builder look like?

They avoid getting caught up in opinion-sharing conversations.
They are consistent in showing up and giving their best
Good reports follow them
They are patient but progressive
They focus energy on solutions rather than problems
They align what they do to the big picture
Their private life matches their public life
They carry humility and an attractive reluctance
Favour follows them
They understand that the process acts to protect them against an inability to handle future pressure
They decrease in self but increase in faith
They are willing to do freely what others require payment for

What does a soapbox builder look like?

They seek to align their opinion to others

Proving themselves in the eyes of others is their goal

Discord follows them

They attach the blame for their disappointment to their surroundings

They seek to elevate themselves by pointing out what others do not do/have

They use flattery to gain access

They ask for promotion

They seek to bypass process in order to get promotion

They are full of themselves and other people are a means to an end

There are always strings attached to what they offer

Step 2: REVIEW with others

Get together weekly with people who are committed to developing the winning conversations and discuss the following:

i) Why are we so prone to pulling out a soapbox and raising our voice?

ii) Why does the process of building a platform seem so unattractive?

iii) Give examples from this past week when you have used a soapbox?

iv) How have you been building your platform this week?

v) What challenge can you set yourself to take your platform building to the next level? (Make sure these challenges are reviewed next time you meet up so that accountability produces results and people are inspired by the stories shared.)

vi) What conversations are your relationships causing you to have?

Step 3: REFLECTION to be shared

Now create a reflection that you can share with someone in

your group or someone else that you are coaching to be a champion in life. Why not take the time with your children, loved one, friend over coffee and share what you have learnt? Simply sharing this reflection will accomplish much in your life and deepen relationships, enriching them with vulnerability and moments of movement.

Follow our basic structure:

i) What I realised for the first time/again this week is .... (share the thought)

ii) The change I need to make is...(share the action point)

iii) Can you help me make it...(invite help and create accountability)

Once you have got into the habit of doing this, why not decide to turn your thoughts into a blog or even take your coaching to another level? There is so much in you and it is directly connected to your commitment to stretch yourself.

Section 7: Be MORE influential

Day 40: The Winning Conversation makes you MORE influential

INCLUSIVENESS unlocks the door of INFLUENCE

Kingdom Key: You are the light of the world

You are the light of the world...put it on its stand, and it gives light to everyone in the house. (Matthew 5:14a-15)

When you get the revelation that Jesus Christ fully lives in you understand that you carry the ultimate influencer. There is a leader inside you that has not yet been fully seen. It does not come through manipulation or coercion but through learning to live from your Christ identity.

When I host the **influential** conversation I become...

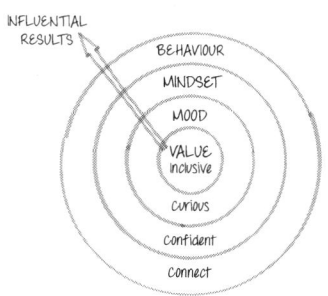

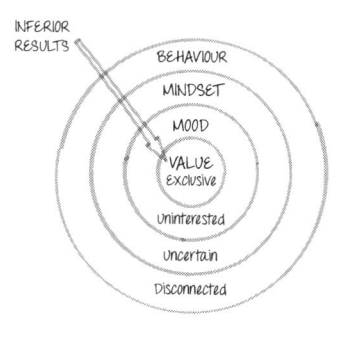

1) MORE interested in connecting the dots

The 'dot' of my life finds its significance when it is connected with others

As people who are carrying out a Kingdom assignment, we must understand the inclusive nature of the Kingdom. Paul reminds us that everyone can be included and we will not know the outcome until we reach out and 'pull' people into our world so that they may experience Jesus through the community of the Body of Christ (the Church).

Kingdom Key: *There is neither Jew nor Gentile, neither slave nor free, nor is there male and female, for you are all one in Christ Jesus* (Gal 3:28).

We are part of a connected Kingdom where we find our completeness in oneness. Inclusiveness is an essential key to the Kingdom.

2) MORE people focussed

Problems follow people but people are my purpose

We can see from the ministry of Jesus and the earliest Christians that the focus was clearly people. The Church was a living and vibrant organism. Over time man has become caught up with structure and organisation. While these make good servants, they make poor masters. We tend to prefer inanimate systems and structures because it means we do not have to deal with the problems that come with people.

Why is this? Dealing with a problem requires a conversation. The weakness of our internal conversation causes us to shy away from the more demanding conversations in life. The Church is meaningless when it loses the focus of people, and without conversations the Church is impotent because it cannot fulfil its mandate to disciple people.

God the Father did not send the Son to establish an impressive organisation, Jesus was sent for people and the mission focus has never and will never change.

Kingdom Key: *For God so loved the world that He gave His one and only Son, that whoever believes in Him shall not perish but have eternal life* (John 3:16).

If we struggle to be with people then we will struggle with our purpose because people are IT, they are the objective of God's

Kingdom! The more time we spend with Jesus the more we increase our desire to spend time with people.

3) MORE community centric

A healthy life cannot be grown without a community

Without a body to belong to a human organ is incomplete and dysfunctional. It has no meaning on its own and despite trying to adapt to 'bodiless' living, no meaning that is conjured up will meet its needs or bring the fit that brings fulfilment. This is why Jesus said that as people experience Christ-centred community they will find something that resonates with a deep longing they have. This is the longing for belonging - the longing to be connected.

Kingdom Key: *A new command I give you: Love one another. As I have loved you, so you must love one another. By this everyone will know that you are my disciples, if you love one another* (John 13:35:34-35).

4) MORE conscious of peoples' needs

True influence is determined by a person's ability to meet the needs of people

My need to find purpose and fulfilment is found when I include others in my world and help meet their needs. Paul helps us see that the revelation of God in our lives is given for the benefit of our role in the community. I would suggest that the more I sow into the community of Christ's followers, the deeper revelation I get of Him.

Kingdom Key: *Now to each one the manifestation of the Spirit is given for the common good* (1 Corinthians 12:7).

5) MORE engaging

The more value I add the more engaging I become

The more conversations I create that refresh people, the more I put a demand on the Christ potential in me to draw on heaven's resource. The more that flows through me, the more supply I draw on.

Sometimes we feel like we cannot afford the time or energy to engage with others. The truth is we cannot afford NOT to. What we desire lies in the connectedness of the body, not in isolation. As I cultivate the winning conversation I will see how my life is enriched as I broaden my conversations to include a greater quantity and quality.

Kingdom Key: *One person gives freely, yet gains even more; another withholds unduly, but comes to poverty. A generous person will prosper; whoever refreshes others will be refreshed* (Proverbs 11:24-25).

6) MORE aware of blind spots

HOW I present myself speaks louder than WHAT I present

The message is not encapsulated by simply words but by demonstration. In Romans 10:15 Paul quotes the prophet Isaiah with regards to the message of God not just sounding good but looking good in how it is presented.

Kingdom Key: *And how can anyone preach unless they are sent? As it is written: "How beautiful are the feet of those who bring good news!"*

But not all the Israelites accepted the good news. For Isaiah says, "Lord, who has believed our message?" Consequently, faith comes from hearing the message, and the message is heard through the word about Christ (Romans 10:15-17).

Whilst I am an advocate for effective communication the defining factor of the church or any organisation in communicating its message it through demonstration. The goal has to be incarnating the central message through an immersive experience that leaves the person convinced that we are what we preach.

The early church demonstrated that the message has to be caught. It is contagious when it is experienced (Acts 2:42-27).

7) MORE aware of the questions people carry

My influence lies in my ability to uncover and unlock the burning question a person carries

Only the power of God can bring a solution to the problem of sin in a person's life. While sin is the root problem, people right now are grappling in different ways with its impact on their lives. We are called to help bring heaven's solutions to earthly problems created by sin. We can only do this through the power of God's Spirit in our lives and with the wisdom of God.

In our humanity we can feel overwhelmed and underequipped. The Apostle Paul was aware of the limits within himself but simply saw this as a God-given opportunity for that power and wisdom to be displayed.

Kingdom key: *My message and my preaching were not with wise and persuasive words, but with a demonstration of the Spirit's power, so that your faith might not rest on human wisdom, but on God's power* (1 Corinthians 2:4-5).

Like others in the Bible, Paul was not the best public speaker, but it was his awareness of the need to be a channel of God's power that made him effective. Yes we must develop skills and talents; that is good stewardship, but ultimately it's the power of God flowing through us that makes ALL the difference. Let God work through your certain intention and determined action to unlock Kingdom results in your life today!

Conversation with God:

Father, I thank you that the light of the world, Jesus Christ, lives in me, and you have identified me as 'a light to the world.' I choose to focus on your ability rather than my inabilities and believe that I will help to bring light into the dark places of peoples' lives. Help me to see the people who are on the fringe and to believe that as I engage with them the Holy Spirit will give the words to say. My eyes are wide open and I choose to seek opportunities to include people in my world to help them experience the Kingdom of God through my life.

Day 41: The Winning Voice of Inclusiveness

INCLUSIVENESS that unlocks the door of INFLUENCE

Kingdom Key: You are the light of the world

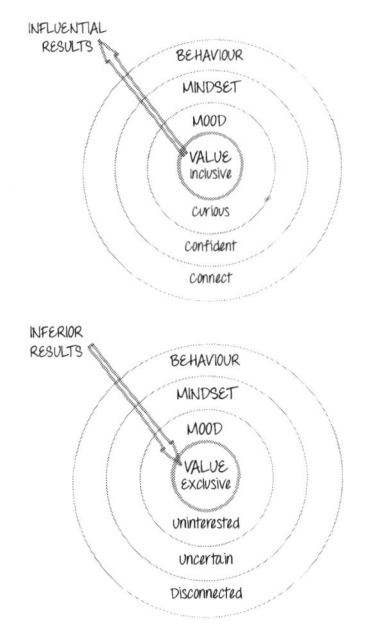

You are the light of the world... put it on its stand, and it gives light to everyone in the house. (Matthew 5:14a-15)

To be a person of INCLUSIVENESS I have to immerse myself in my new identity in Jesus Christ. This belief will lead me into the right feelings. The more I immerse myself in the belief that I am inclusive, the more influential I will become.

Now I have Christ in me I have to die daily to the old me and live from the new me.

Paul says in Galatians 2:20: *I have been crucified with Christ and I no longer live, but Christ lives in me. The life I now live in the body, I live by faith in the Son of God, who loved me and gave himself for me.*

This means WHO I am is WHO he is. I have adopted my new identity and I choose each day to live from the Christ core.

I am inclusive because Jesus is inclusive!

To unlock INCLUSIVENESS I have to believe that...

1) I AM built for discomfort

What I possess without pain is not worth possessing

Faith is not comfortable; it is a stretch. It places a demand on us that pulls our potential out of us. Champions are built for discomfort.

The Apostle Peter was up for such a faith challenge. Remember the time he walked on water? Whose idea was it? It was Peter's. The disciples were out at sea and in the boat at night when Jesus came walking on the water toward them; they thought He was a ghost.

Kingdom Key: *But Jesus immediately said to them: "Take courage! It is I. Don't be afraid."*

"Lord, if it's you," Peter replied, "tell me to come to you on the water." "Come," He said (Matthew 14:27-29).

Peter saw an opportunity to do what Jesus did and wanted in! Although Peter only managed a few steps, he was the only one who tried! Yes Peter failed, but that is because he tried.

When it comes to possessing new relationships with more people there will be failed attempts, but what the process does in you and the relationships that are added to you will make it worthwhile. Kingdom advancement relies on us getting out of the boat of comfort and taking some wild steps on the water.

Conversation with God:

Father God, help me to step out of the boat today and talk to people I do not normally speak to. Help me initiate a conversation and grow me through any discomfort I feel.

2) I AM invited

Always make the first move

Did Jesus go and find His disciples or wait for them to turn up to a church building? He went out there and found them. If Jesus can do it and He lives in you, then you can make the first move to start conversations.

Kingdom Key: *When Jesus was leaving that place, He saw a man sitting in a tax office. The man's name was Matthew. Jesus said to him, "Follow me!" So Matthew got up and followed Him* (Matthew 9:9).

Conversation with God:

Father, lead me to speak to people today. I choose to allow the excitement of where these conversations could go to inspire me to overcome my fear of doing it. I want you Jesus to call out to people through my life today.

3) I AM over myself

Move over and let the real you through

The real you is FULL of love, powerful and self-disciplined, not shy and timid. Choose to let Christ take over the old, shy, timid you because He has made His Spirit come alive in you.

Kingdom Key: *For the Spirit God gave us does not make us timid, but gives us power, love and self-discipline.* (2 Tim 1:7)

Conversation with God:

Father God, I choose to see the barriers of shyness and timidity broken down by initiating conversations with people I otherwise would not talk to. I believe that you can help me break this fear once and for all starting today.

4) I AM growing through relationships

The power of presence has no substitute

Remember we are first and foremost spiritual beings. When we are physically present with other people, the conversations are not just the ones we hear but ones we feel as well.

We all know how a personal and physical presence can create a positive or negative atmosphere. When someone has a mood it can almost become tangible. Why is that? It's the spiritual side of our nature manifesting itself.

This spiritual dimension is heightened when two or more Christians are present because God adds the extra dimension of His presence. This is why bringing people who do not know Jesus into a gathering of two or more faith filled Christians is powerful.

Kingdom Key: *Where two or three gather in my name, there am I with them* (Matthew 18:20).

Conversation with God:

Father, help me to realise that when I meet physically with someone you are present and that it's more than WHAT I say; it's more about WHO I carry. I carry Christ and I go into today with that as my confidence.

5) I AM indiscriminate

When I over think, I overlook

The losing voice of exclusiveness will always try and tempt you to recoil from networking and connecting more widely. Even as you start to connect with people you will tell yourself that there are certain people you CANNOT speak to, maybe because of who they are, or because of their intimidating presence. At this point stand firm in your Christ conviction, 'I am inclusive and this excludes no one, regardless how I think I will fail in my conversation with them.'

Kingdom Key: *Therefore, my dear brothers and sisters, stand firm. Let nothing move you. Always give yourselves fully to the work of the Lord, because you know that your labour in the Lord is not in vain* (1 Corinthians 15:58).

You have a Kingdom assignment and heaven is counting on you so give yourself FULLY to the work you have to do. God will work through you and it will not be *in vain*.

Conversation with God:

Father, help me to stand firm in the belief of who I am in you. When feelings of intimidation come, help me to take these thoughts captive and step out in my Christ identity.

6) I AM into addition

You are connected when you have added value

The early church did not simply attract people to meetings; they ADDED people to their number daily. Their goal was not merely attendance driven but addition driven. It is not simply about the amount of connections that I can create but the depth of those connections. Depth is created through the value that I add on a consistent basis to those connections.

Kingdom Keys: *And the Lord added to their number daily those who were being saved* (Acts 2:47b).

Nevertheless, more and more men and women believed in the Lord and were added to their number (Acts 5:14).

Conversation with God:

Father God, help me not just to create connections but to add people to my circle of influence by seeking to be a constant source of support and help with the goal of them being added to the Christian community.

7) I AM inclusive in crowds

To catch a new type of opportunity I have to fish in different waters

Jesus invited many people into His circle of concern when He was in a crowd. He did not get carried away with the vast numbers but focussed on individuals and sought to ADD them to His circle of influence.

On numerous occasions it was the people that were being ignored who Jesus included. He was in demand by the many but His internal conviction of inclusion made those on the fringe of the crowd His priority.

His conviction lives on inside of us through the Holy Spirit.

Kingdom Key: *He called out, "Jesus, Son of David, have mercy on me!"*

Those who led the way rebuked him and told him to be quiet, but he shouted all the more, "Son of David, have mercy on me!"

Jesus stopped and ordered the man to be brought to Him. When he came near, Jesus asked him, "What do you want me to do for you?" (Luke 18:38-41).

While we may not have people grabbing our attention by shouting, our awareness through the Holy Spirit can discern who is 'crying out' for someone to include them.

Conversation with God:

Father, help me to prioritise the excluded today. Turn my priorities upside-down when I start to go with the crowd rather than be drawn to the Kingdom appointments you have lined up for me.

8) I AM inclusive in small groups

Small environments breed the authenticity that crowds lack

Transitioning people between environments is a key part of discipleship.

Relationships develop in different environments. When Peter saw the 3000 people saved on the day of Pentecost it did not end there. The key to their growth was in how they transitioned these people into different environments in order to further their growth. They grew large by going small, encouraging development through interactive and more intimate environments.

Kingdom Key: *Every day they continued to meet together in the temple courts. They broke bread in their homes and ate together with glad and sincere hearts, praising God and enjoying the favour of all the people. And the Lord added to their number daily those who were being saved* (Acts 2:46-47).

Conversation with God:

Have I committed myself to a small group environment where I can grow? Father God, help me create different environments where I can facilitate the growth in other people, both believers and unbelievers.

9) I AM committed to close moments

Lasting impact lies in the close moment

Jesus took Zacchaeus from the crowd into his home environment.

He often pulled His disciples from the crowd into a small group situation because He knew their development required a different dynamic - one in which they could open up.

Kingdom Key: *When Jesus reached the spot, He looked up and said to him, "Zacchaeus, come down immediately. I must stay at your house today." So he came down at once and welcomed Him gladly* (Luke 19:5-6).

We will often be surprised by people's willingness to transition to an environment where a more purposeful and focussed conversation can take place.

There are many other examples of these kinds of conversations that Jesus had.

John 3:1-2:

Now there was a Pharisee, a man named Nicodemus who was a member of the Jewish ruling council. He came to Jesus at night and said, "Rabbi, we know that you are a teacher who has come from God. For no one could perform the signs you are doing if God were not with him."

We are not sure when Jesus first met Nicodemus but we know that it was at night that they met one-to-one. This was when Jesus shared with him about being 'born again' - about adopting the new identity needed for the Kingdom.

Conversation with God:

Father God, I pray that you will help me understand the right timing for transitioning my existing relationships with unbelievers into a different context in order to develop these further. Give me wisdom and courage I pray.

10) I AM committed to continued concern

Continued concern is continued influence

The Apostle Paul's letters are an inspiration and example to us of how we show our commitment to 'continued concern'. Despite the challenges of communicating across wide geographical areas, especially when he was in prison, Paul committed himself to developing relationships.

Kingdom Key: *I thank my God every time I remember you. In all my prayers for all of you, I always pray with joy because of your partnership in the gospel from the first day until now, being confident of this, that He who began a good work in you will carry it on to completion until the day of Christ Jesus* (Phil 1:3-6).

How influential was this continuation of concern?

The answer is "massively". Not only did he continue to build the Church through these communications but his writing also served to form a significant part of the New Testament.

We may not be an Apostle but the principle of showing love by continued communication is something immensely valuable.

Who knows what legacy our notes and messages may leave!

Conversation with God:

Father God, forgive me for the times when I have neglected relationships, when people have been out of sight and therefore I have allowed them to be out of mind. Help me to develop a discipline of continued concern, especially in today's technological age, when I have no excuse for not staying in touch.

Day 42: The Winning Mood of Curiosity

INCLUSIVENESS unlocks a CURIOUS mood in me

Kingdom Key: You are the light of the world

You are the light of the world… put it on its stand, and it gives light to everyone in the house. (Matthew 5:14a-15)

The Kingdom key of Inclusiveness unlocks my WHY which is my PURPOSE.

My purpose is the 'good work' which I was created to do (Eph 2:10).

The vision of my life was prepared by God before I was even born (Jeremiah 1:50).

I am having the INFLUENTIAL conversation led by the voice of inclusiveness which means I choose to put myself in a CURIOUS mood.

Curiosity is awareness of the unseen

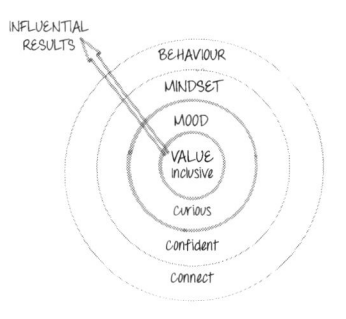

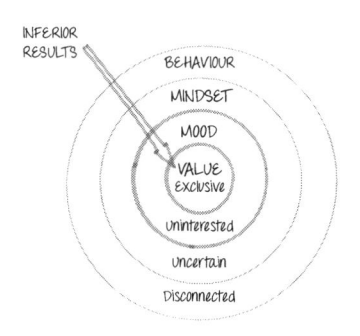

There is so much inside a person - experiences, potential, wounds, questions, perspectives, and so much more. Your Kingdom assignment makes you a curious person, desiring to know what lies inside of people. Loving people more means being more interested in them.

Proverbs 20:5: *The purposes of a person's heart are deep waters, but one who has insight draws them out.*

You have insight through the guidance of the Holy Spirit. As well as embracing the suggested techniques in my book The Winning Conversation, lean into the Holy Spirit and let Him drop questions into your mind that bring out what is inside people. Do it with Christ confidence. Influence others by being curious in conversation.

Curiosity communicates interest

We communicate that we are not interested in people when all we do is make statements as opposed to drawing out what is in them through questions. Be more interested in the opinions of others and they will become more interested in your opinions.

Proverbs 18:2: *Fools find no pleasure in understanding but delight in airing their own opinions.*

Curiosity creates access

The Holy Spirit is our partner and we can allow Him to prompt us in order to position us to access new relationships that can have Kingdom impact.

In Acts 8:29-31 we can see how Philip partnered with the Holy Spirit. Through Phillip's curiosity, the Good News of Jesus was shared.

The Spirit told Philip, "Go to that chariot and stay near it."

Then Philip ran up to the chariot and heard the man reading Isaiah the prophet. "Do you understand what you are reading?" Philip asked.

"How can I," he said, "unless someone explains it to me?" So he invited Philip to come up and sit with him.

While we may not bump into people reading Bibles every day, we can ask questions that help us understand what people think about key life questions. Our interest in them is building a platform for our message.

People carry many unresolved questions and while some of these are not at the forefront of their minds, they form the raw material for intriguing and hugely influential conversations.

Who knows where the conversation will go and what Kingdom influence will result?

Unlock an inclusive soul script through immersing yourself in the word of God (the Bible)

The belief that we can reach out to more people in order to make a difference will increase when we immerse ourselves in these verses:

When I immerse myself in this verse I value myself from an inclusive belief:

I value myself as someone who can reach out to others in order to make a difference

I have a heavenly position and share Christ's position on inclusion…that none should perish but that all should come to repentance

Ephesians 2:6: *And God raised us up with Christ and seated us with Him in the heavenly realms in Christ Jesus…*

I am valuable and useful when I reach out to others

Matthew 5:13: *You are the salt of the earth. But if the salt loses its saltiness, how can it be made salty again? It is no longer good for anything, except to be thrown out and trampled underfoot.*

When I immerse myself in this verse I value others from an inclusive belief:

I value other people and can reach out to others in order to make a difference

I have the mind of Christ therefore I can relate to others as He did.

Philippians 2:5: *In your relationships with one another, have the same mindset as Christ Jesus.*

I carry the wisdom and grace of Christ in my internal conversation that will make a difference in my everyday conversations

Colossians 4:5-6: *Be wise in the way you act toward outsiders; make the most of every opportunity. Let your conversation be always full of grace, seasoned with salt, so that you may know how to answer everyone.*

When I immerse myself in this verse I value my future from a inclusive belief:

I value my future because there are more people I can reach and therefore help

I am significant and will not shrink back from people.

Hebrews 10:39: *But we do not belong to those who shrink back and are destroyed, but to those who have faith and are saved.*

I will reach out to more people than ever through the time given to me in order to make God look good

1 Peter 2:9: *But you are a chosen people, a royal priesthood, a holy nation, God's special possession, that you may declare the praises of Him who called you out of darkness into His wonderful light.*

Conversation with God:

Father God, I choose to put aside the thoughts, feelings and impulses that do not fit with who you are because it is no longer I who live but Christ who lives in me. I put off the old me and put on the new me. May my thoughts be your thoughts, my feelings your feelings and my impulses your impulses. I step into this day knowing that you are working through me to grow your Kingdom.

Day 43: The Winning Mindset of CONFIDENCE

INCLUSIVENESS unlocks a CONFIDENT mindset and this is HOW I approach my day

Kingdom Key: You are the light of the world

You are the light of the world…put it on its stand, and it gives light to everyone in the house. (Matthew 5:14a-15).

The Kingdom key of Inclusiveness unlocks my HOW which is to have a CONFIDENT mindset.

Paul tells us in 1 Corinthians 2:16 that *we have the mind of Christ.* This is not about knowing all the thoughts of Jesus necessarily but our access to Christ's pattern of thinking. We have this when we build our lives around the commands of Christ in the Bible.

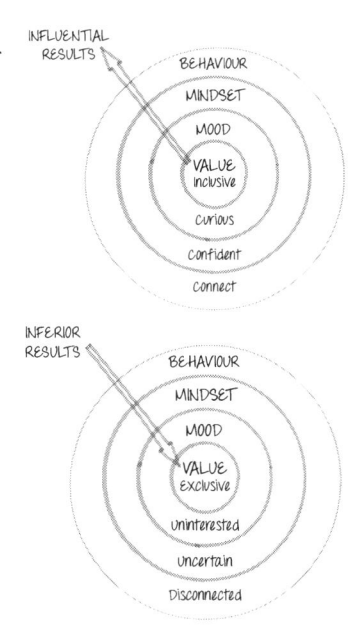

The winning conversation was demonstrated through the way Jesus lived his life. Jesus was inclusive, lived with a curious mood and had a confident mindset. Because our identity is found in Christ we can adopt the mindset of Christ.

Col 3:2-4: *Since, then, you have been raised with Christ, set your hearts on things above, where Christ is, seated at the right hand of God. Set your minds on things above, not on earthly things. For you died, and your life is now hidden with Christ in God. When Christ, who is your life, appears, then you also will appear with Him in glory.*

The winning mindset means I determine daily to:

1) Present confidently without fear of rejection

Rejection is no indicator of personal value

If I have God's approval, then who else can top that? I am accepted as an ambassador for the Kingdom and I go with His commendation.

Kingdom Key: *For it is not the one who commends himself who is approved, but the one whom the Lord commends* (2 Corinthians 10:18).

Even if I am rejected by people, I will not allow this to set my value. God's Word cannot be nullified so I present myself based on this truth.

2) Present confidently and embrace inconvenience

Anchor your life in the reality of people through making new connections

When I make a new connection with someone I have the opportunity to discover what life looks like through a different lens. While making new connections can come at 'inconvenient' times, it keeps me sharp and aware of my Kingdom assignment. We always need to be ready to be inconvenienced.

Kingdom Key: *Preach the word; be prepared in season and out of season; correct, rebuke and encourage—with great patience and careful instruction* (2 Tim 4:2).

There is no 'out of office' sign for someone who carries the inclusive belief and seeks to make an impact. Your potential for influence demands that you go beyond what many believe reasonable in order to include people in your world.

3) Present confidently and create an atmosphere of acceptance

Confidence attracts, arrogance repels

When a person carries authentic confidence they communicate an acceptance to others. Be confident enough to simply practice hospitality. Offering to serve someone else's need is something any one of us can do. Whether that is to buy a drink for someone or invite them for a meal. The practice of hospitality is a sign of acceptance. When we accept people outside of our established circles, we release heaven on earth. It is the simple acts of kindness that make the biggest difference in our world.

Kingdom Key: *Do not forget to show hospitality to strangers, for by so doing some people have shown hospitality to angels without knowing it* (Heb 13:2).

Who knows who will come into your circle of influence when

you go out each day and present yourself confidently letting Christ connect to the world through you?

4) Present confidently to create new seasons for your life

People define seasons before events

We can see from the Bible how new connections can start new and significant seasons in peoples' lives. Kingdom appointments initiate new seasons.

In the Old Testament Daniel was brought into the presence of the King to serve in the royal household.

This was a new connection that ushered in a new season.

Kingdom Key: *He changes times and seasons; He deposes kings and raises up others. He gives wisdom to the wise and knowledge to the discerning. He reveals deep and hidden things...* (Daniel 2:21-22a).

If you feel like you are in a 'dry' and 'barren' season, your new season always starts with someone, not something.

You can also help someone else into their new season.

Extend your circle of influence today!

5) Present confidently to reveal what is in you

With new introductions come new questions

Esther was introduced to the royal household via a beauty competition in which King Xerxes chose her as his queen. In the light of Haman's plot to wipe out the Jewish nation, Mordecai (Esther's adopted father) encouraged Esther to use her influence and present herself confidently in speaking up for her people. He suggested that this relationship with the King was a divinely appointed season in which she was to be an answer to the question 'who will speak out on behalf of Israel?'

Kingdom Key: *For if you remain silent at this time, relief and deliverance for the Jews will arise from another place, but you and your father's family will perish. And who knows but that you have come to your royal position for such a time as this?* (Esther 4:14).

Just like Esther, you have a sphere of influence that requires you to present yourself in your new identity as a Kingdom influencer. Your new identity is not trying to be someone you are not, it is actually learning to dig deep into God and be who you were always intended to be. Esther was made aware of the impact her decision to step into this influence would have. Know today that there is an impact beyond your understanding when you decide to step up to the plate as a Kingdom influencer.

Make a decision today to present yourself confidently, knowing whose you are!

6) Present confidently through asking great questions

Great questions have the ability to reveal gold in people

Questions have the ability to pull out of people what is in them.

Get someone to talk long enough and you will be able to discern what is going on inside them.

Kingdom Key: *A good man brings good things out of the good stored up in his heart, and an evil man brings evil things out of the evil stored up in his heart. For the mouth speaks what the heart is full of* (Luke 6:45).

Whilst our confidence comes from the fact that Jesus Christ is working through us, we cannot be lazy. We are partnering with Him, after all.

Kingdom Key: *Do your best to present yourself to God as one approved, a worker who does not need to be ashamed and who correctly handles the word of truth* (2Tim 2:15).

Whilst Paul was speaking here about being able to discern false teachers, the principle of preparation applies. When we prepare we unlock an internal confidence. You can be prepared with great questions before talking with people and have confidence in the questions you are asking.

7) Present confidently and unlock knowledge

SECTION 7: BE MORE INFLUENTIAL

Wisdom lies in the unlikeliest of places

Jesus helped us to see that greatness and great things come from the unlikeliest of people and places in the Kingdom of God. While the disciples were arguing over who was the greatest, Jesus picked out a child and gave them a Kingdom key.

Kingdom Key: *Then he said to them, "Whoever welcomes this little child in my name welcomes me; and whoever welcomes me welcomes the one who sent me. For it is the one who is least among you all who is the greatest"* (Luke 9:48).

Whether it is Saul hiding in the luggage, Gideon in the winepress, Moses in the back of the desert (I could go on), God's chosen people are in unlikely places ready to reveal 'unlikely' demonstrations of God's wisdom and power.

Never write any conversation off. Embrace the Kingdom adventure of discovering diamond conversations in the 'unlikeliest' of lives! Who knows what you are going to discover today if you spread the net of inclusivity?

8) Present confidently and position yourself for promotion

You are your own limit to the opportunity that lies in other people...have the conversation!

We can often complain to others and to God when opportunity does not afford itself and yet neglect the key Jesus revealed in his Kingdom sermon. He made it very clear that we set the limits for what we receive, what we find and the doors that open. We have to embrace the habit of ASK (**A**sk **S**eek **K**nock).

Kingdom Key: *Ask and it will be given to you; seek and you will find; knock and the door will be opened to you. For everyone who asks receives; the one who seeks finds; and to the one who knocks, the door will be opened* (Matthew 7:7-8).

There is no limit to how much or how often you ASK!

9) Present confidently and go one more conversation than you feel is possible

Believe your conversations are ready to convert into results

As we confidently and diligently give our all to connecting ourselves to people and cultivating relationships, we can rely on God to make the right relationships develop and grow to produce Kingdom results.

Kingdom Key: *The horse is made ready for the day of battle, but victory rests with the Lord* (Proverbs 21:31).

We are champions because of Christ and so He takes care of how and when the victories/results become obvious, as long as we show ourselves faithful to the process. Remember what we have said before, 'prize the process and the process will take care of the prize.'

Paul reminds us that results are in God's hands while commitment to the process is our responsibility.

Kingdom Key: *I planted the seed, Apollos watered it, but God has been making it grow. So neither the one who plants nor the one who waters is anything, but only God, who makes things grow* (1 Corinthians 3:6-7).

Keep showing up and He will keep showing up!

10) Present confidently and enjoy relational 'freedom'

Disciplined choices lead to great outcomes

The more we present with confidence, the more freedom we find in being ourselves with other people. True freedom in life produces relational freedom.

Every true breakthrough will bring a breakthrough in our ability to relate to others. Many people feel bound internally at the thought of presenting confidently to others. For some this bondage is so extreme that it even makes us feel physically sick.

Kingdom Keys: *It is for freedom that Christ has set us free. Stand firm, then, and do not let yourselves be burdened again by a yoke of slavery* (Gal 5:1).

While practicing techniques and preparing well will unlock this potential, sometimes we need a spiritual breakthrough.

Meditate on this passage. Perhaps ask someone to pray with you.

There is MORE influence in you than you think.

So let Jesus break the yoke!

Conversation with God:

Father God, I thank you for the truth of your word. As I meditate on it may it unlock the winning mindset I need to see your Kingdom come and your will be done in my life today!

Day 44: The Winning Choice of Connecting wider than you feel comfortable

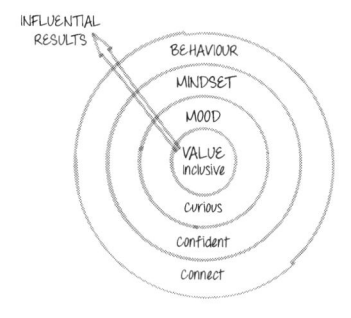

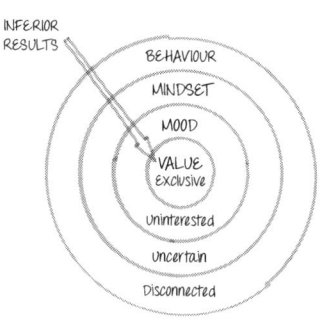

Today we look at some practical ways to develop the winning conversation that will make you MORE influential in life. The more you inform the right choices, the more you activate the results. As well as adopting these practical methods it is vital to invite the Holy Spirit to lead our conversations with others. He can give us the words that make us an influence to the people we meet. (John 16:13)

INFLUENTIAL RESULTS
BEHAVIOUR
MINDSET
MOOD
VALUE inclusive
Curious
Confident
Connect

INFERIOR RESULTS
BEHAVIOUR
MINDSET
MOOD
VALUE Exclusive
Uninterested
Uncertain
Disconnected

Go in search of questions

I have come to the realisation that if you do not carry any questions you are not thinking or dreaming big enough. If you have everything that you need then it is time to increase your personal challenge and create some need. If our answer is that we have everything then we are either thinking too small or do not have enough clarity on what is going to take us to where we are going.

Your cause should be big enough that it causes you to question, 'How am I going to make this happen?'

The size of the question you carry indicates the size of the person you are. Your question should be causing you to call on the help of other people. This indicates that the problem you are trying to solve is bigger than you but also that you are committed to collaborating in order to achieve the end result.

Once you have the question that is bigger than you, you will want to look for people who are able to contribute towards the cause. The steps to including people in on the cause are simple and yet often undervalued.

Daily learn to **A.S.K**:

Ask *to receive*

We all love to feel needed. Inclusiveness is not only about including new but also familiar people to greater degrees. One way of doing that is being clear on what you need. It is good to review constantly what it is we do need as this causes us to once again focus on our goals.

Seek *to find*

What is in a relationship that can unlock the next level? Have you ever played a computer game where you have had to find keys or items that unlock the next level and you cannot progress until you find them? I am a firm believer that much if not all we need lies in relationships but we either do not have the relationships or the level of relationship to uncover the keys that help us progress to the next level. Think about conversations you could start that could begin a journey of discovery.

Knock *to open doors*

What about starting those conversations? I would say this is one of the most daunting disciplines for people to master. However, having a strategy for a conversation can go a long way to removing our fears because fear is about the unknown. Having a plan helps to create a known path.

When meeting people, learn and practice to **KNOCK**:

Kick-start (Statement-Question)
Name
Occupation and/or obsession
Challenge
Knowledge

Kick-start

Do not just sit and wait for people to come to you. Remember, you are an answer not a question! A great way to start a conversation is to find someone who looks lost. They will be grateful that someone stopped them from drowning in embarrassing unfamiliarity.

Always kick-start your conversation with a statement followed by a question. A statement could be related to the weather, or the place you are in, or anything. People love to give their opinions and you just need to ask about something they value and you will be off to a great start.

Name

A great next step is to say, 'Hi I'm [NAME]. And your name is...?' It is so important that you know someone's name if you are going to discover how you can be an answer to them. When asking for someone's name, often we are thinking of the next question, which then means we are not actually paying attention to the person's name.

When you hear the name, repeat it back to them and include it as often as possible during your conversation. What we repeat, we learn and remember.

Occupation

The key to being an answer to someone is to truly value him or her. Remember that the key to valuing someone is to be more 'interested' than 'interesting'. We may be tempted to fill them in on how great our life is and how wonderful things are at the moment but we are an answer, not a question, looking for an audience.

Try to find out if they enjoy their job or a hobby. We should try to find out who the real person is rather than just rely on our perceptions.

Challenge

Every person has a current challenge, something they are trying to overcome or something they would love to take on. When we try and understand what someone is currently facing, it shows that we are not only interested in them but also interested in helping.

Know

Finally, ask yourself, "What does this person know from their background or experience that could really help me?" This is not a selfish question because we feel valued when we are adding value to others. By asking good questions about what they know you are helping them to know they are valuable.

So, wherever you are, remember there is a power when we learn to ASK!

Day 45: The Winning Evaluation

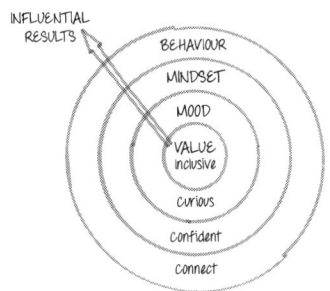

Benchmark which mindset you have when it comes to the INFLUENTIAL conversation.

The fruit of my actions will reveal the root of the conversations I host. Today we are looking at ten questions based on situations we find ourselves in and I encourage you to be brutally honest as to which response most fits your nature. Tally up how many you answered according to which voice and make a decision to go back under the bonnet of your inner conversations to strengthen your foundation as a champion. If you feel frustrated then that is not a bad thing as long as you focus that frustration on making certain your commitment to hosting the winning conversation.

1) Introducing yourself—How do you feel about introducing yourself?

Consumed - I will hold back until I am spoken to as I am not looking for connections. However, I am happy to talk if someone asks the questions.

Complacent - Depending on how I feel and the environment I am in determines how much effort I put into meeting people. If it's an environment where I feel at ease then I have no problem chatting to people.

Competitor - I know I need to make fresh connections and so will be open to the conversations that appear easiest and look like they could be fruitful.

Champion - I choose to enjoy the process even if it does not come naturally. The more I do it the more I see the importance. People need to feel included and that is my job wherever I am.

2) People's Names—What are you like with people's names?

Consumed - I am useless with names so I apologise up front that I am unlikely to remember.

Complacent - I am ad hoc when it comes to remembering. I always have a laugh with people about how bad I am with names. I guess you either have the ability or you do not.

Competitor - I need to try harder with names because I know when people remember mine and the names of those I care about it makes a difference.

Champion - I attempt to remember the names of everyone I meet by using a strategy. The excuse, 'I am not good with names,' is an excuse for not trying. I am always amazed how surprised people are when I remember their names. It is precious to them so it should matter to me.

3) Small talk—Are you good at small talk?

Consumed - I can hold a conversation about the usual things because it polite. However I keep myself to myself.

Complacent - I am good at small talk and keeping a conversation going. I am not very good at understanding or deciding where it could or should go.

Competitor - I can do small talk but I want to get past that to the real issues. After all I want to help people and fix their problems. If they do not want it, that is their problem.

Champion - Small talk is an important tool. It is a way of building a rapport with someone. I am comfortable with small talk but try and ask questions that steer the conversation to bigger talk. It has to feel natural and not forced.

4) Conversations—How do you view conversations?

Consumed - They are important but mainly to get to the point of what needs doing. I don't like wasting words.

Complacent - Relationships need conversations so if I am committed to relationships I have to be committed to conversations. I guess the more I do it the more I will just get better.

Competitor - They are really important and I choose to better myself at conversations, always trying to be more aware of how I come across

Champion - Conversations are everything. If there is one thing in life I should concentrate on it is the conversation I am having with myself that will spill over into my conversations with others

5) Questions—Do you ask meaningful questions in your conversations?

Consumed - I ask the questions that provide the answers for what I need.

Complacent - I will ask questions if I feel like having the conversation and if I think the relationship could go somewhere.

Competitor - I try to get to know someone by asking questions based on the information they offer me.

Champion - I have a set of questions that are like tools. I always try to be ready and armed with questions that can create momentum in a conversation and position myself as someone who could learn something from the person. When I position myself this way I rarely run out of something to say.

6) Acceptance—Does feeling wanted play a part in whether you enter into a conversation or not?

Consumed - I wait for conversations to come to me because I figure people will talk to me if they want to.

Complacent - This is the most important factor because if I do not feel wanted then I cannot enter a conversation.

Competitor - I find it easier speaking to the people who look 'less important' because I figure that they will always want a conversation. However I tend to excuse myself from conversations with more 'important' or 'exuberant' people because I fear I am not important enough. But I will talk with them if they address me.

Champion - I do have to deal with the feeling of needing to be wanted but I do not allow external permission to be the deciding factor. I am an answer and so I will speak to others because it's who I am; that is my choice.

7) Quiet and removed—Is remaining quiet and removed in public ever a good thing?

Consumed - I prefer to observe. I find it interesting to watch people so I am often quiet and removed. Not everyone can be a conversationalist.

Complacent - If I am having a bad day or not feeling like a conversation then I do remove myself from being open to conversations. I just get on with what I have to do.

Competitor - I always think it is important to engage even when I do not feel like it, although there are always exceptions.

Champion - Unless there are genuine reasons why I cannot engage, conversing with people is who I am. The best path to self-help is to help someone else. So I will always challenge any reason why I should not engage in conversation.

8) Learning from others—Is learning something you do through conversations?

Consumed - If I ask then I listen and I will learn. But I always try to figure things out on my own.

Complacent - I am always open to advice and will always listen if it's given. I usually have all that I need but am open to helping someone else if they ask.

Competitor - I am hungry to learn and will learn from people who are further on than me. However most of the time I try and help other people.

Champion - I take the position that I can learn something from anyone. I also find that I learn best when trying to see how I can be an answer to someone else's challenge.

9) Failed conversations—What happens when a conversation goes wrong?

Consumed - This is why I mainly communicate with those I know because I feel at ease talking to them. Most other conversations are small talk.

Complacent - I try not to push conversations with new people because I do not feel it is a major strength of mine. I do not like the embarrassment of when they go wrong.

Competitor - I walk away playing the conversation in my mind time and time again, thinking about what I should have said. I say it doesn't affect me, but it does. If it goes really wrong it can affect my mood and my willingness to engage further. I then get over it the next day so it does not hold me back in the long term.

Champion - Failure is part of progress and I do not believe people think about my mistakes as much I do. I am naturally critical so will try and channel my failure into improving for next time.

10) Confidence—How confident do you feel in conversation?

Consumed - I am comfortable in conversation with those I know but I do not push myself to start them with new people.

Complacent - I lack confidence with new people and so try and wait for the right situations to make themselves obvious.

Competitor - I feel confident with people I know and those who openly engage with me. Some people you just know are open to conversation and so I am confident in those situations.

Champion - Confidence is something that will grow through practice and so I choose to be confident even though at times I do not feel so.

PRACTICE V POTENTIAL of the INFLUENTIAL conversation

Based on the answers to the above questions, how many times can you honestly say that your answer was 'champion'?

Consumer: 1-2 times

Complacent: 3-5 times

Competitor: 6-8 times

Champion: 9-10 times

My Overall POTENTIAL: I AM A CHAMPION

MY Overall PRACTICE: I HAVE BEEN A _____

In order for my practice to match my potential I have identified the following three things I can do to unlock the champion in me:

1_____

2_____

3_____

Day 46: The Winning Accountability

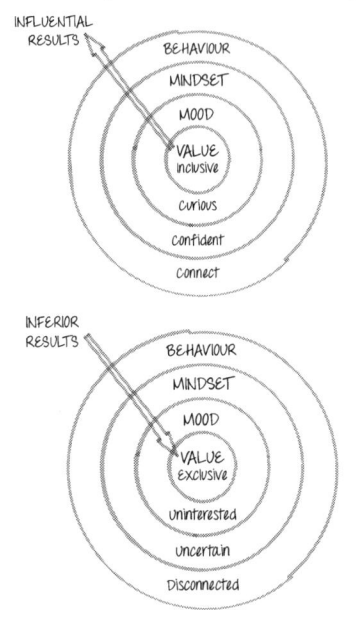

INFLUENTIAL RESULTS
- BEHAVIOUR
- MINDSET
- MOOD
- VALUE — Inclusive
- Curious
- Confident
- Connect

INFERIOR RESULTS
- BEHAVIOUR
- MINDSET
- MOOD
- VALUE — Exclusive
- Uninterested
- Uncertain
- Disconnected

Pulling this whole week under the title of 'be an answer and find a question' enables us to be able to review this conversation quickly. Using the dice in spare moments throughout the day, or in a small group, helps me to focus on the inner conversation of inclusiveness.

The Winning Dice—***Be an answer and find a question***

When we see someone on their own they are a 'question' and they become our responsibility because we are people called to be an 'answer'. Regardless of how 'irrelevant' I may feel I can always find common ground on which to connect and build a moment to touch their life.

When you include yourself in a conversation with someone else you have an opportunity to build on your mission to help people. Through seeking conversations through new connections you expose yourself to more opportunities to create answers. Be someone who includes themselves whenever a need becomes obvious. While you may not be the direct answer, you can help create options. You can create the anticipation for results and this is how you become influential. Influential people care enough to point to solutions!

We decide to be all about people as they are our greatest resource and have to be our highest priority. The WHO of people always comes before the WHAT of task. Opportunities come from unanswered questions and if people contain our greatest resource then we have to have an incessant drive to discover what is unanswered in people's lives. In doing so people feel valued because it's primarily about what we can do for them and not what they can do for us. People will sit up and take notice of everything I am about if I first centre who I am around what they currently need. A good listener will eventually get a good listen themselves.

'Being an answer' is about initiating, willing to be the last to be heard and elevating the needs of others above our own.

Step 1: RECALL together

Sometimes we need a quick review of what being an answer and finding a question looks like so we can stay on course to allow INCLUSIVENESS to have the loudest voice, drowning out EXCLUSIVENESS. Here is a description based on what we have looked at this week:

What does 'being an answer' look like?

Being the first to strike up a conversation

Having questions ready that will give you confidence to make conversation

Being among the first to befriend a stranger

Smiling and greeting indiscriminately even when in a crowd

Surveying a room full of people and seeing opportunities to start conversations, especially with strangers

Making a determined effort to learn people's names

Listening intently to the person rather than focussing on the next thing to talk about

Offering possible help when it hasn't been asked for

Anticipating need before need comes looking for you

Being interested rather than interesting

Thinking and planning ahead of meeting new people

Being excited about finding new ways of doing things

Having a healthy discontentment with the way things are

What does 'being a question' look like?

Being comfortable speaking to the same people

Being happy to let someone ask before being asked

Having a lack of confidence and security in how they are perceived in conversation

Being fearful and timid

Standing in closed groups that do not allow new people to join

Promoting in-jokes when those who do not yet belong are present

Allowing jargon to be used when people who are not conversant with it are present

Rarely offering suggestions of how to improve things

Always awaiting instruction

Step 2: REVIEW with others

Get together weekly with people who are committed to developing the winning conversations throughout the journey of this book and this week discuss the following:

i) Can you think of any barriers to conversations that you currently have?

ii) What plan could you put in place to overcome these?

iii) Can you think of significant connections that you have made that would never naturally have taken place?

iv) How do you feel about asking people for help? How do you feel when someone asks you for help?

v) What could you start to do daily that would create a greater experience of being inclusive, therefore driving

deeper the conviction inside you?

vi) Based on your winning purpose, how important is immersing yourself in this conversation going to be? What would be the result if you remained at the same level you are now?

SECTION 7: BE MORE INFLUENTIAL

Step 3: REFLECTION to be shared

Now create a reflection that you can share with someone in your group or someone else that you are coaching to be a champion in life. Why not take the time with your children, a loved one, a friend over coffee to share what you have learnt. Simply sharing this reflection will accomplish much in your life and deepen relationships, enriching them with vulnerability and moments of movement.

Follow our basic structure:

i) What I realised for the first time/again this week is …. (share the thought)

ii) The change I need to make is …. (share the action point)

iii) Can you help me make it? (invite help and create accountability)

Once you have got into the habit of doing this, why not decide to turn your thoughts into a blog or even take your coaching to another level? There is so much in you and it is directly connected to your commitment to stretch yourself.

THE WINNING KEYS

Section 8: Be MORE EXPANSIVE

Day 47: The Winning Conversation makes you MORE expansive

CREATIVITY unlocks the door of EXPANSIVENESS

Kingdom Key: I am unlimited potential.

Give, and it will be given to you. A good measure, pressed down, shaken together and running over, will be poured into your lap. For with the measure you use, it will be measured to you (Luke 6:38).

When I host the EXPANSIVE conversation I become:

1) MORE focussed

What I focus on I feed and what I feed I grow

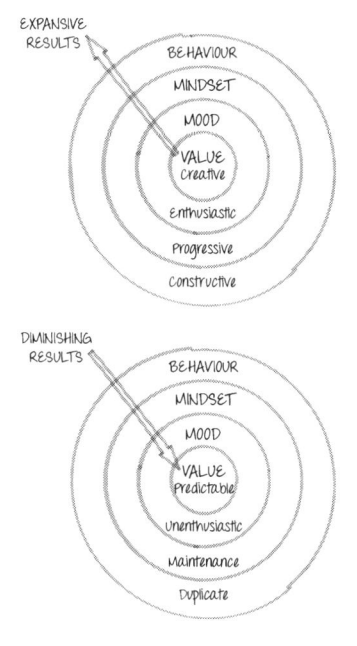

The quality and quantity of my results are directly linked to the intensity of my focus. The expansive conversation is about unlocking the creativity in our lives through focusing intently on the right things.

Kingdom Key: *Since, then, you have been raised with Christ, set your hearts on things above, where Christ is, seated at the right hand of God. Set your minds on things above, not on earthly things. For you died, and your life is now hidden with Christ in God* (Col 3:1-3).

Paul reminds us that focus involves setting our hearts after someone or something. If we want to produce Kingdom results then we need to set our hearts on the things above, the things of God which are unseen but drive everything that can be seen. The more we focus on the things above the less interested we become in that which feeds our old sinful nature and we feed on that which grows our new identity in Christ.

James in his letter reminds us that when we focus on a temptation it will grow a desire. When we feed this desire with more focus it then produces an act of sin and ultimately death.

Kingdom Key: *...but each person is tempted when they are dragged away by their own evil desire and enticed. Then, after desire has conceived, it gives birth to sin; and sin, when it is full-grown, gives birth to death* (James 1:14-15).

By adopting the practice of meditating on God's words we create the visible reality of the invisible and unlimited potential that lies inside us.

2) MORE desperate

It is only a true desire when it is desperation

Desperation produces results. In Luke 14 Jesus lays out the cost of following Him. Jesus was trying to communicate the depth of desire it takes to follow Him and live the Kingdom life.

Kingdom Key: *If anyone comes to me and does not hate father and mother, wife and children, brothers and sisters—yes, even their own life—such a person cannot be my disciple. And whoever does not carry their cross and follow me cannot be my disciple* (Luke 14:25-27).

Jesus was not advocating hating loved ones. He was asking for total commitment. He tapped into the deepest desires that people have - for the people we love. Just as we would do anything to help and protect them, our desire for Jesus and His Kingdom should be so great that it trumps every other desire we carry.

Verse 33: *In the same way, those of you who do not give up everything you have cannot be my disciples.*

Jesus knew that when we develop a deep desperation to see something happen this unlocks our potential to see extraordinary results. In the Kingdom of God this deep desire plus the power of Christ in us unlocks supernatural results.

3) MORE aware

The 'big' events in life are created by the thousands of 'little' daily choices we make

We often believe the biggest decisions we make are buying a house, choosing someone to marry, our career path. These are indeed big decisions. However the breadth of options we have is actually created through the small decisions we make daily in our faith, finances, relationships and development. Our small, apparently 'insignificant' choices are the platform for the 'bigger' choices we can make in life. The expansive conversation heightens our awareness of how ordinary choices can lead to extraordinary results.

Kingdom Key: *I went past the field of a sluggard, past the vineyard of someone who has no sense; thorns had come up everywhere, the ground was covered with weeds, and the stone wall was in ruins. I applied my heart to what I observed and learned a lesson from what I saw: A little sleep, a little slumber, a little folding of the hands to rest and poverty will come on you like a thief and scarcity like an armed man* (Proverbs 24:30-34).

Poverty does not just suddenly happen; it grows through the process of daily choices. In contrast, success does not just happen; it comes as a result of our commitment to a process.

The more we align our daily choices with the principles of God's Word, the greater and more effective platform we create to unlock expansive Kingdom results.

4) MORE empowering

The results of collaboration far exceed the extended effort of working with others

We are empowered to live expansive lives when we work and pray in agreement with one another. Creating a rhythm of prayer and agreement takes our collaboration into the heavenly realms where we can unlock God's resource.

Kingdom Key: *Again, truly I tell you that if two of you on earth agree about anything they ask for, it will be done for them by my Father in heaven. For where two or three gather in my name, there am I with them* (Matthew 18:19-20).

5) MORE youthful

The expansiveness of your life will not exceed the expansiveness of your imagination

Kingdom living requires us to give more space to the inner child that longs to get out.

Kingdom Key: *Truly I tell you, unless you change and become like little children, you will never enter the kingdom of heaven. Therefore, whoever takes the lowly position of this child is the greatest in the kingdom of heaven. And whoever welcomes one such child in my name welcomes me* (Matthew 18:3-5).

Why does Jesus showcase the attitude of the child here?

Children are more trusting and less cynical than adults. The older we get, the more risk averse we become. Our 'been there, done that' attitude rules us out of living adventurous lives in the Kingdom. It turns us into caretakers when we are called to be risk-takers!

Unlocking the Kingdom child in us is the key to us believing once again that the impossible can become possible.

According to Paul, God can do more than even our most youthful imaginings.

Kingdom Key: *Now to Him who is able to do **immeasurably more** than all we ask or imagine, according to His power that is at* *work within us, to Him be glory in the church and in Christ Jesus throughout all generations, forever and ever! Amen* (Ephesians 3:20-21).

Expand your imagination today by unlocking the Kingdom child in you and see how God supersedes all you can ask or imagine.

You cannot out imagine God!

6) MORE moment-conscious

Momentum is never created in a moment but is created from moments

Worship God through your choices. Do everything as if you were doing it directly for Him. Every moment will matter more when you make it matter for Him.

Kingdom Key: *Whatever you do, work at it with all your heart, as working for the Lord, not for human masters* (Col 3:23).

Make the ordinary decisions with an extraordinary awareness of God's involvement. Awareness of God's involvement leads to limitless thinking. You don't do anything ordinary when you do it for Him!

7) MORE deliberate

Results are often unpredictable but they are always the result of being deliberate

Lean into God and put the weight of your faith behind your choices. Make your choices flow out of your winning conversation with God.

The more you pray without ceasing (1 Thess 5:17), the more awareness you have of heaven's extraordinary involvement in the apparently 'ordinary' moments of your life.

Praying without ceasing is not about being locked away in a tower praying; it is simply keeping God involved in your internal conversation.

When my internal conversation is centred upon the straight

talking of Jesus, I walk a straight path in life. Whilst He did not promise an easy path, it is an effective and expansive path.

Kingdom Key: *Trust in the Lord with all your heart and lean not on your own understanding; in all your ways submit to Him, and He will make your paths straight* (Proverbs 3:5-6).

While you may not see immediate results, you will ultimately see extraordinary results and over time God will astound you. Don't always try and figure it out because you won't. God has the right to remain mysterious; He is God and mystery is one of His distinctive characteristics. As one of the earliest Christian theologians once said, "A comprehended God is no God at all" (St John of Chrysostom).

We are called to have faith for the result; let God figure out the process.

Kingdom Key: *"Have faith in God," Jesus answered. "Truly I tell you, if anyone says to this mountain, 'Go, throw yourself into the sea,' and does not doubt in their heart but believes that what they say will happen, it will be done for them. Therefore I tell you, whatever you ask for in prayer, believe that you have received it, and it will be yours"* (Mark 11:23-24).

Day 48: The Winning Voice of Creativity

CREATIVITY unlocks the door of EXPANSIVENESS

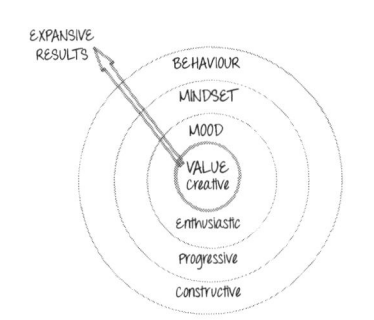

Kingdom Key: I am unlimited potential

Give and it will be given to you. A good measure, pressed down, shaken together and running over, will be poured into your lap. For with the measure you use, it will be measured to you (Luke 6:38).

To be a person of CREATIVITY I have to immerse myself in my new identity in Jesus Christ. This belief will lead me into the right feelings. The more I immerse myself in the belief that I am creative, the more expansive I will become.

Since I have Christ in me then daily I have to die to the old me and live in the new me. This is why Paul says in Galatians 2:20: *I have been crucified with Christ and I no longer live, but Christ lives in me. The life I now live in the body, I live by faith in the Son of God, who loved me and gave Himself for me.*

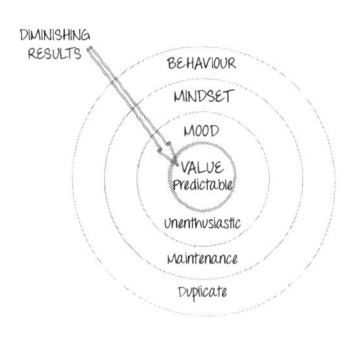

This means WHO I am is WHO He is. I have adopted my new identity and I choose each day to live from the Christ core.

I am creative because Jesus is creative!

To unlock my EXPANSIVENESS I have to believe that…

i) I AM positively fearful

Fear has to be present for courage to breathe

Positive fear can bring focus. It can lead us to ask the bigger questions in life which in turn cause us to prioritise. A new perspective with a process of prioritisation means we can run with fewer tasks and therefore put extra energy behind the few things that bring expansive results.

The fear of God is a positive fear. It awakens us from the predictable patterns we fall into and unlocks a strong desire in us that will bring freshness and order to our lives.

Kingdom Key: *The fear of the Lord is the beginning of wisdom; all who follow His precepts have good understanding. To Him belongs eternal praise* (Psalm 111:10).

The fear of God takes us from working IN our lives to working ON our lives. We are able to capture God's perspective and align ourselves to His principles in order to be prepared for His best. High awareness of God's commands and how they work contextually in our lives unlocks joy and delight.

Kingdom Key: *Blessed are those who fear the Lord, who find great delight in His commands* (Psalm 112:1).

Conversation with God:

Father God, help me to be aware today of your expectations for my life. I exchange my expectations for yours. I know when I find delight in what makes you pleased I will unlock divine joy inside me.

ii) I AM exclusive when it comes to goals

Focus is a clear choice about what I include and exclude

Prayer is our best focusing tool. When I have my conversation with God and allow Him to speak through His Word He is able to go deeper than just my rational thinking. He delves into the engine room of my life where everything that makes anything happen can be examined and corrected.

Kingdom Key: *All a person's ways seem pure to them, but motives are weighed by the Lord. Commit to the Lord whatever you do, and He will establish your plans* (Proverbs 16:2-3).

Bringing the planning of my activities into my conversation with God helps me to learn what He wants me to focus on. If I walk right with Him then my desires align with His. What I then see as important or not important can be dealt with.

The establishing of anything that lasts in this world starts in a place of prayer. If we establish our plans in prayer then we know that anything that seeks to prevent those plans coming to fruition will not succeed because everything that is seen is established in the unseen realm.

Prayer keeps me aware of heaven's involvement in my day-to-day life and is the key to keeping the right pace in running the race in the lane that God has marked out for me.

The writer to the Hebrews reminds us that we are being cheered on by all those who have gone before us. This eternal perspective inspires you to '**L**et **E**ternity **G**uide **A**ll the **C**hoices **Y**ou make' (L.E.G.A.C.Y).

Kingdom Key: *Therefore, since we are surrounded by such a great cloud of witnesses, let us throw off everything that hinders and the sin that so easily entangles. And let us run with perseverance the race marked out for us* (Heb 12:1).

My conversation with God helps to identify the things that are going to slow the pace of my progress in my Kingdom pursuit.

Conversation with God:

Father, I bring all that I have to do before you and ask that you align my heart to yours so I know what I need to prioritise and what I have to put aside. I want to see Kingdom results from my efforts today for your glory.

iii) I AM free from the fear of failure

The more I distance myself from failure, the greater distance I put between myself and success

Unlocking the potential of Christ in us is not for the faint hearted. Paul describes the process in brutal terms:

Kingdom Key: *We are hard pressed on every side, but not crushed; perplexed, but not in despair; persecuted, but not abandoned; struck down, but not destroyed. We always carry around in our body the death of Jesus, so that the life of Jesus may also be revealed in our body* (2 Corinthians 4:8-10).

Some of the words Paul uses are words akin to how it feels when we fail. Failure is a key part of the intense process of letting Christ break through our sinful nature so that the Spirit of God can break out.

Paul says we carry around the death of Jesus which unlocks the revelation of Jesus and his resurrection power. In my own words, the process of me being made like Christ will be like carrying the contradiction of death and life - scary and exciting - and the sense of losing while winning. Fixing my eyes on the NOT YET goal, His winning purpose in my life gives me a focus and helps to pull me through.

Conversation with God:

Father, I thank you that I carry both the death and life of Christ in me. I am humbled that you see me as worthy to be worked on. I thank you that the diamond of Christ in me is being brought out of the rough of my sin and when things get challenging I keep fixed on you and what you are producing for eternity.

iv) I AM certain

My creativity is my certain path to my goal

There is no doubt that I have everything I need to grow the future I believe God has for me; it is stored up in the all-sufficiency of Christ in me. The more I look at the challenge and size of my purpose through Jesus, the more I get to discover more of who He is and this brings my potential to the surface. Ultimately knowing Jesus and becoming like Him is THE goal.

Kingdom Key: *His divine power has given us everything we need for a godly life through our knowledge of Him who called us by His own glory and goodness* (2 Peter 1:3).

Conversation with God:

I bring the challenges of pursuing the winning goal before you, Father God. I want to fix my eyes on Jesus and see my obstacles through Him. I have confidence that through my devotion and focus, what I need is in me and will rise to the surface.

v) I AM what I imagine

Your imagination forms your declaration

My imagination is powered by the words I carry in my internal conversation. It I want to unlock a positive imagination that powers a creative life then my internal conversation needs to be united to the words I mediate on in my heart and the words I utter from my mouth. A disunited conversation becomes a destructive force in my life.

The Psalmist helps us see that we need the consistency and strength of God 'my rock' to bring strength and consistency to our meditation and declaration.

Kingdom Key: *May these words of my mouth and this meditation of my heart be pleasing in your sight, Lord, my Rock and my Redeemer* (Psalm 19:14).

Conversation with God:

Father God, I thank you for your consistent nature. I thank you that you are the same yesterday, today and forever. May my meditation and declaration be in alignment with you today.

vi) I AM original

I have everything I need to achieve the unique cause for which I am alive

When God created us He did so from His own likeness. Gen 1:26 reminds us that God said, Let us make man in our image. He called you out of himself. This means that already in you is all you need to be who God has made you to be, and to do what He wants you to do. We are not waiting for further instalments of what we need in order to get going on the cause; we already have all we need.

Kingdom Key: *Yet you, Lord, are our Father. We are the clay, you are the potter; we are all the work of your hand* (Isaiah 64:8).

The image of the potter and the clay is important. It is impossible for human hands to produce exact replicas of a clay pot. While to the human eye many pots will look the same, they are not identical. God's hands produce 'difference.' They specialize in uniqueness.

We discover our difference when we work according to the pattern with which we were made, from the inside-out.

Kingdom Key: *Oh yes, you shaped me first inside, then out; you formed me in my mother's womb. I thank you, High God—you're breathtaking! Body and soul, I am marvellously made! I worship in adoration—what a creation! You know me inside and out, you know every bone in my body; you know exactly how I was made, bit by bit, how I was sculpted from nothing into something. Like an open book, you watched me grow from conception to birth; all the stages of my life were spread out before you, the days of my life all prepared before I'd even lived one day* (Psalm 139:13-16, The Message).

Conversation with God:

Father, I thank you that you shaped me from the inside-out. I choose to follow the pattern of unlocking my potential from the inside-out, from WHO I was made to be. The more I focus on you, Jesus, the more I look in the divine mirror of WHO you have called me to be.

vii) I AM a constituent part

A lonely victory is no victory at all

My significance lies in what I am apart of not the 'part' that I am. My cause supports the whole Body of Christ; the whole is not designed to support my part. This is such an important principle to remember because my expansiveness cannot happen in isolation; it needs to be connected to the expansion of the Body, otherwise I become disillusioned and ultimately disconnected.

Kingdom Key: *But I also want you to think about how this keeps your significance from getting blown up into self-importance. For no matter how significant you are, it is only because of what you are a part of* (1 Corinthians 12:19-24, The Message).

Paul did what Apostles do best as master architects and builders; he kept the bigger picture before God's people, the framework of Christ's Kingdom principles. The role of the Apostle is given to the Church by Jesus to prevent the constituent parts running off and doing their own thing. Apostles are big-picture thinkers.

Paul exemplifies this thinking through 1 Corinthians 12.

Conversations with God:

Father, forgive me for the times I have had an isolation mindset. Deal with any hurts, pride or ignorance preventing me from connecting to what is bigger than me. Help me expand what I do by helping expand what you are doing through your Kingdom. 'YOUR Kingdom come, YOUR will be done, on earth as it is in heaven.'

viii) I AM designed to blend

SECTION 8: BE MORE EXPANSIVE

I start life as an ingredient but I want to become a blend

The body has many parts but it's the blend of parts that unlocks its potential.

We may have many contacts with people but expansiveness happens when we move from a collection of names to connection with people. Unlocking Kingdom results is about getting with the strategy of heaven which is always based upon us taking a collaborative approach. How the body connects makes ALL the difference.

Paul encourages connected thinking

Kingdom Key: *I want you to think about how all this makes you more significant, not less. A body isn't just a single part blown up into something huge. It's all the different-but-similar parts arranged and functioning together. If Foot said, "I'm not elegant like Hand, embellished with rings; I guess I don't belong to this body," would that make it so? If Ear said, "I'm not beautiful like Eye, limpid and expressive; I don't deserve a place on the head," would you want to remove it from the body? If the body was all eye, how could it hear? If all ear, how could it smell? As it is, we see that God has carefully placed each part of the body right where He wanted it* (1 Corinthians 12:14-18, The Message).

The Prophet Ezekiel was told by God to prophesy to a heap of dry bones so that the many parts that lay before him would be reconnected and live again. This collaboration brought about a multiplication of influence because these bones became an army - a strategic threat to the enemy.

Kingdom Key: *I will make breath enter you, and you will come to life. I will attach tendons to you and make flesh come upon you and cover you with skin; I will put breath in you, and you will come to life. Then you will know that I am the Lord…So I prophesied as he commanded me, and breath entered them; they came to life and stood up on their feet—a vast army* (Ezekiel 3:4-6, 10).

Conversation with God:

Father, help me to discern your strategy. May my conversations today lead me to understand more of how I can support the expansion of your Kingdom. Use me to breathe new life today into peoples' lives, especially those that have lost life and hope.

xi) I AM optimistic

Optimism is a discipline not a feeling

We can take inspiration from Caleb who maintained his expansive expectation for forty years and did not give up or give in. From a creative belief, he saw that the people of God could take the land they went to spy (Numbers 13). Ten of the spies hosted a losing conversation, allowing the external to squash any aspiration they had on the inside, but Caleb and Joshua were different. They had a winning conversation because they knew WHO they were in God. Maintaining this high aspiration and optimism for forty years was no small thing.

Kingdom Key: *I was forty years old when Moses the servant of the Lord sent me from Kadesh Barnea to explore the land. And I brought him back a report according to my convictions, but my fellow Israelites who went up with me made the hearts of the people melt in fear. I, however, followed the Lord my God wholeheartedly. Now then, just as the Lord promised, He has kept me alive for forty-five years since the time He said this to Moses, while Israel moved about in the wilderness. So here I am today, eighty-five years old!*

Then Joshua blessed Caleb son of Jephunneh and gave him Hebron as his inheritance (Joshua 14:7-10, 13).

Timing is God's job; staying faithful to my convictions is mine. While the longer it takes for a dream to come about carries an internal pressure, this time and pressure produces the diamond of heaven in you, Christ's glory.

God has not failed to be faithful yet and He is not going to break the habit of eternity with you!

Conversation with God:

Father, I galvanise my convictions once again in your presence, I refuse to give up and quit on what I know to be true. Like Caleb

SECTION 8: BE MORE EXPANSIVE

I declare that I will certainly see the fulfilment of my winning goal. Whilst I have yet to see it, I thank you for the gift of this day, that it is a tool to be used to chip away at unlocking the expansive work you want to do through me.

x) I AM controlled by my future

Maturity is delayed gratification

You cannot get more expansive than eternity. There are no borders to eternity and God has set eternity in our hearts (Ecclesiastes 3:11). The desire for expansion that I have is my God-given attraction towards my heavenly home and I must not mistake it as a desire for the things of this world. While there is nothing wrong with being blessed in this world with possessions, position and power they must never become our WHY. God may bless us so that it becomes part of HOW we outwork our potential but my desire should be for what lasts and these are eternal matters.

Eternity needs to be my WHY. The more I stay eternity-focused the more quality decisions I make in my life. The key to unlocking a fruitful life is to stay eternity-focused. The more eternity-focused I become the higher the quality of decisions I will make. The moment I get caught up in the now is the moment I lose clarity on where I am headed in this life.

Kingdom Key: *Do not store up for yourselves treasures on earth, where moths and vermin destroy, and where thieves break in and steal. But store up for yourselves treasures in heaven, where moths and vermin do not destroy, and where thieves do not break in and steal. For where your treasure is, there your heart will be also* (Matthew 6:19-21).

Build life for eternity; align everything you have now with eternity. Who do you know that does not yet know Jesus? Do you want to see them in heaven? Start to pray for opportunities to share your faith.

Conversation with God:

Father, I thank you that you have set eternity in my heart and

I choose not to get caught up and pulled back by the things of this world. I am building for an expansive eternity and I want as many people to experience this as possible. I make everything I do follow that goal because this is WHY I am alive.

Day 49: The Winning Mood of Enthusiasm

CREATIVITY unlocks an ENTHUSIASTIC mood in me

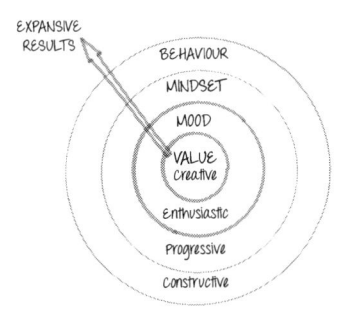

Kingdom Key: I am unlimited potential.

Give and it will be given to you. A good measure, pressed down, shaken together and running over, will be poured into your lap. For with the measure you use, it will be measured to you (Luke 6:38)

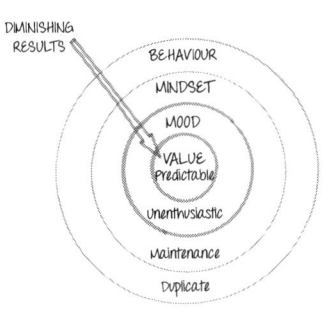

The Kingdom key of Creativity unlocks my WHY which is my PURPOSE.

My purpose is the 'good work' which I was created to do (Eph 2:10).

The vision of my life was prepared by God before I was even born (Jeremiah 1:50).

I am having the EXPANSIVE conversation led by the voice of creativity which means I choose to put myself in an enthusiastic mood.

Enthusiasm is about intense enjoyment.

Enthusiasm does not require the absence of problems or challenge. Our challenges can create a positive demand on our lives that cause us to stir up a greater enthusiasm in order to face the problem.

Creativity brings intense enjoyment for Christians when we take the challenge we face to God in order to get his divine perspective. We can innovate alongside God and this process causes us to draw even closer to Him. This proximity increases our confidence in Him as we get to see Him close at work; through partnering with Him, we see the problems and challenges overcome.

Kingdom Key: *In all this you greatly rejoice, though now for a little while you may have had to suffer grief in all kinds of trials. These have come so that the proven genuineness of your faith — of greater worth than gold, which perishes even though refined by fire — may result in praise, glory and honour when Jesus Christ is revealed. Though you have not seen Him, you love Him; and even though you do not see Him now, you believe in Him and are filled with an inexpressible and glorious joy, for you are receiving the end result of your faith, the salvation of your souls* (1 Peter 1:6-9).

Peter speaks of the inexpressible and glorious joy that is unlocked in us as we work with God through obstacles and challenges. When there appears to be no way past a problem we have to dig deep into the creativity of Christ in us, which unlocks genuine faith causing divine joy (enthusiasm) to flow.

Enthusiasm is about clarifying the WHY

David experienced the highs and lows of life, the failures and the successes. An interesting period of his life was when he started to distance himself from God's presence because he witnessed the death of Uzzah (2 Samuel 6) and became afraid. During this time David was angry and started to lose connection to his WHY through doubt (2 Sam 6:9-10). He sent the Ark of the Covenant to the house of Obed-Edom, the Hittite.

However, after three months David made the decision to bring the Ark back. He made a choice and created an atmosphere of worship and praise.

We see the level of detail he observed the following verses.

Every six steps he made a sacrifice.

David was serious about his WHY again - retaining the presence of God.

Kingdom Key: *When those who were carrying the ark of the Lord had taken six steps, he sacrificed a bull and a fattened calf. Wearing a linen ephod, David was dancing before the Lord with all his might, while he and all Israel were bringing up the ark of the Lord with shouts and the sound of trumpets* (2 Samuel 6:13-15).

David's creative and costly sacrifice unlocked deep enthusiasm inside him. He lacked no fear of what others thought; he was 100% focused on the presence of God in which he was a champion, a winner.

When we choose obediently to centre ourselves in God's presence we clarify our WHY, our purpose, which is to make Him look good and feel good. This allows enthusiasm to rise within and it pumps through our veins.

An enthusiastic life causes us to lift our heads with renewed vigour and be determined to lead an expansive life.

Enthusiasm is about believing in the mosaic of your life

There are times when we feel weak, like we could go to pieces, and we struggle to try and give the impression we have it all together. Enthusiasm drains from our veins and we return to predictable patterns that take little effort and in which we derive a level of comfort. However, we need to know that we work with One who not only has it all together but puts it all together (Col 1:17).

Enthusiasm should not follow things going right; it should be a mood that we cultivate regardless of how things are going. Our enthusiasm should be based on the fact that Jesus is praying for us and the Father is working through the Holy Spirit in us to pull all things together for the good.

Kingdom Key: *In the same way, the Spirit helps us in our weakness. We do not know what we ought to pray for, but the Spirit himself intercedes for us through wordless groans. And he who searches our hearts knows the mind of the Spirit, because the Spirit intercedes for God's people in accordance with the will of God. And we know that in all things God works for the good of those who love Him, who have been called according to His purpose* (Romans 8:26-28).

Our broken moments can become building moments when we use God's tools. You may not see how all the pieces will come together but meditate on and declare the words of God and your creative belief will release enthusiasm. God will build you if you simply remain committed to His creative process.

Unlock a creative soul script through immersing yourself in the bible (God's word):

The aspiration and belief that I can unlock limitless increase and progress in my life to help others comes when we immerse ourselves in verses such as these:

When I immerse myself in this verse I value myself from a creative belief:

I value myself as someone who can progress and grow

I am made in the likeness of God and I put on the new me

Eph 4:24: *Put on the new self, created to be like God in true righteousness and holiness.*

I will reject the predictable sameness of my old identity because I house the creative God

Romans 12:2: *Do not conform to the pattern of this world, but be transformed by the renewing of your mind. Then you will be able to test and approve what God's will is—His good, pleasing and perfect will.*

When I immerse myself in this verse I value others from a creative belief:

I value others knowing my growth will bring progress to others

I can create ways to reach others with the love of Christ despite the obstacles because I called to do GREATER things.

John 14:12: *Very truly I tell you, whoever believes in me will do the works I have been doing, and they will do even greater things than these, because I am going to the Father.*

I choose to grow people by building them up using the gifts that God has given to me.

1 Cor 14:26: *What then shall we say, brothers and sisters? When you come together, each of you has a hymn, or a word of instruction, a revelation, a tongue or an interpretation. Everything must be done so that the church may be built up.*

When I immerse myself in this verse I value my future from a creative belief:

I value my future because my progress will lead to me making an even bigger difference

I am a joint-heir with Christ therefore I will create the expansive future that is my inheritance in Christ for His glory.

Romans 8:17: *Now if we are children, then we are heirs – heirs of God and co-heirs with Christ, if indeed we share in his sufferings in order that we may also share in His glory.*

I am not fenced in; I have a big God in me who is growing me to grow others!

2 Corinthians 6:11-18 (The Message): *I can't tell you how much I long for you to enter this wide-open, spacious life. We didn't fence you in. The smallness you feel comes from within you. Your lives aren't small, but you're living them in a small way. I'm speaking as plainly as I can and with great affection. Open up your lives. Live openly and expansively!*

Conversation with God:

Father God, I choose to put aside the thoughts, feelings and impulses that do not fit with who you are because it is no longer I who you live but Christ who lives in me. I put off the old me and put on the new me. May my thoughts be your thoughts, my feelings your feelings and my impulses your impulses. I step into this day knowing that you are working through me to grow your kingdom.

Day 50: The Winning Progressive Mindset

CREATIVITY unlocks a PROGRESSIVE mindset in me and this is HOW I approach my day

Kingdom Key: I am unlimited potential.

Give and it will be given to you. A good measure, pressed down, shaken together and running over, will be poured into your lap. For with the measure you use, it will be measured to you (Luke 6:38).

Paul tells us in 1 Corinthians 2:16 that we have the mind of Christ. This is not about knowing all the thoughts of Jesus necessarily but our access to Christ's pattern of thinking. We have this when we build our lives around the commands of Christ in the Bible.

The winning conversation was demonstrated through the way Jesus lived his life. Jesus was creative, lived with enthusiasm and had a progressive mindset. Because our identity is found in Christ we can adopt the mindset of Christ.

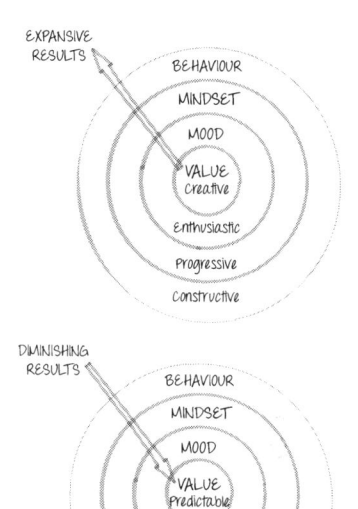

Col 3:2-4: *Since, then, you have been raised with Christ, set your hearts on things above, where Christ is, seated at the right hand of God. Set your minds on things above, not on earthly things. For you died, and your life is now hidden with Christ in God. When Christ, who is your life, appears, then you also will appear with Him in glory.*

1) Think of different ways of achieving greater levels of effectiveness

There is <u>always</u> another approach!

Whatever the obstacle that stands in front of you, there is a way past it! God may have brought Moses to the Red Sea, to a trapped situation between the sea and Pharaohs army, but He also told Moses by faith to use what he had in his hand which was his staff and God would work His miracle power.

God has put everything in your possession that you need today and through your creative faith in Christ you can carve a path through the ocean of your 'impossible' obstacles. Get ready to tell your story to others about Him when you are on the other side!

Don't seek God through the problem; seek God for who He is and then look at the problem. Take time to get your 'Christ' glasses on and then look again at the obstacles through the eyes of faith.

Kingdom Key: *This is what the Lord says— He who made a way through the sea, a path through the mighty waters, who drew out the chariots and horses, the army and reinforcements together, and they lay there, never to rise again, extinguished, snuffed out like a wick: "Forget the former things; do not dwell on the past. See, I am doing a new thing! Now it springs up; do you not perceive it? I am making a way in the wilderness and streams in the wasteland* (Isaiah 43:16-19).

2) Keep my attitude flexible, like soft clay in the hands of a potter

My ability to adapt determines my ability to grow

God has new opportunities that He wants to expose you to. The new opportunity and provision that it will unlock is like the 'new wine' that Jesus spoke of in Matthew's Gospel.

Kingdom Key: *No one sews a patch of unshrunk cloth on an old garment, for the patch will pull away from the garment, making the tear worse. Neither do people pour new wine into old wineskins. If they do, the skins will burst; the wine will run out and the wineskins will be ruined. No, they pour new wine into new wineskins, and both are preserved* (Matthew 9:16-17).

Jesus uses the imagery of the wineskin which is like the container of our lives (2 Cor 4:7). Our lives need to be capable of carrying the new opportunity (new wine) that lies waiting for us. Once a wineskin has been used it becomes tough and brittle. Therefore when new wine is poured in and its properties begin to force the wineskin to expand, it can't contain it so it breaks and ruins both the wine and the wineskin.

Spending time with God, keeping our hearts soft and in the place of being a living sacrifice (Romans 12:1-2), means that we are ready to adapt and change in order to expand with the opportunities that God is bringing our way.

In what way have you become inflexible? How might new

opportunities be wasted because the 'vessel' of your life cannot handle it? It's time to prepare for the expansive opportunities God is bringing your way.

3) Protect the creative space in which expansive possibilities come

The margin for success is created through protecting your margin for creativity

God is the creative being at work inside us. God introduced us to the principle of the Sabbath rest by himself resting after creating the world in six days. This is not just about setting aside at least one day to rest from labour. This is about maintaining our creative rhythm.

Creativity works best from a place of rest. A lack of margin in our time, finances and energy kills our creativity.

Read the words of Isaiah and see how the imagery of the eagle soaring into the expansiveness of the skies comes from a posture of rest.

Kingdom Key: *Do you not know? Have you not heard? The Lord is the everlasting God, the Creator of the ends of the earth. He will not grow tired or weary, and His understanding no one can fathom. He gives strength to the weary and increases the power of the weak. Even youths grow tired and weary, and young men stumble and fall; but those who hope in the Lord will renew their strength. They will soar on wings like eagles; they will run and not grow weary, they will walk and not be faint* (Isaiah 40:28-31).

Learn to work from rest rather than labouring in order to earn a rest. The fruit of working from rest is an expansive life. Our lives are shrunk when trying to produce fruit under constant pressure, striving for results.

4) Combine desperate determination with strategic planning

My desperation ignites my determination to follow the direction of my plan

Remember the winning conversation formula:

Certain intention x determined action = Extraordinary results.

We need to combine our desperation for results with a focused plan. Jesus encouraged people not to follow Him out of their impulsive desire in the moment because He knew that feelings come and feelings go. He wanted them to think through the full impact on their homes, businesses and future.

Kingdom Key: *Suppose one of you wants to build a tower. Won't you first sit down and estimate the cost to see if you have enough money to complete it? For if you lay the foundation and are not able to finish it, everyone who sees it will ridicule you, saying, 'This person began to build and wasn't able to finish'* (Luke 14:28-30).

Jesus wanted them to plan ahead, to fully understand and outwork what this decision meant not just in the now but in the future.

Expansiveness comes through the desire of our hearts and the planning using our heads.

God is not asking you to leave your brains behind. He has given them to you for a reason.

5) Embody the change I want to see as I shape a new culture

A change embodied is easier to emulate

Do I exemplify expansive thinking in every area of my life? Am I speaking as though I am expansive but actually thinking and living small? If I want others to live an expansive life then I need to model what I want others to achieve.

Kingdom Key: Whatever you have learned or received or heard from me, or seen in me—put it into practice. And the God of peace will be with you (Phil 4:9).

If you were someone who had chosen to follow you, would you be inspired to live big?

If not then ask what areas of your life need to change in order to expand.

6) Feed my focus in order to frame my goals with clarity

Focus management is more effective than time management.

When I see the possibility of what can be and allow that to stir my desire, I am challenged to get focused in the now.

Hebrews 11 is the hall of fame where many of the Bible's faith heroes are celebrated.

Read what it says about Moses' parents.

Kingdom Key: *By faith Moses' parents hid him for three months after he was born, because they saw he was no ordinary child, and they were not afraid of the king's edict* (Hebrews 11:23).

What they saw ahead for Moses caused them to prioritise ruthlessly in the now moment.

The cost for our future has to be paid in the present. What cost do you need to pay now in order get the future that you can see God has in store for you?

Moses' parents paid a high cost. They sacrificed their direct involvement in their child's life in order to unlock God's plans and purposes for their son and ultimately for the people of God. Visions and goals for our future cost but when we allow our decisions to be inspired by our love for God and others, we can follow through with the sacrifice.

7) Create the environment for growth from small beginnings

The quality of your attention to a goal is like the quality of the soil for a seed to grow

The miracle of the feeding of the 5000 helps us understand the power of the creative belief in the Kingdom of God and how to handle the small beginnings when believing for an expansive miracle.

Kingdom Key: *He said to his disciples, "Have them sit down in groups of about fifty each." The disciples did so, and everyone sat down. Taking the five loaves and the two fish and looking up to heaven, He gave thanks and broke them. Then He gave them to the disciples to distribute to the people. They all ate and were satisfied, and the disciples picked up twelve basketfuls of broken pieces that were left over* (Luke 9:14-17).

Jesus had clarity:

Clarity on the overall goal = feed the 5000

Clarity on resource = Five loaves and two fish

Clarity on HOW = Sit the crowd down in smaller groups of 50 people

Clarity on WHAT = Disciples to have some each and hand it out

Jesus created the environment for the miracle and managed the creative process. Breaking down a task is not about doing God's job for Him; it is about us having clarity on what we can do and then understanding what only God can do.

Sometimes we do not see the miracle goal reached because we still have not exhausted what we can actually do. It is only when we come to the end of ourselves that God takes over.

Get clarity on what only God can do and then what you have faith to receive from Him!

8) Carve an original path through obstacles and problems

Problems are stepping stones along your path to fulfilling your potential

Your progressive mindset understands that problems are simply portals through which God's grace can unlock the uniqueness that is in you. Taking these challenges into an atmosphere of prayer and praise is vital. Joshua understood this when leading the people of Israel.

Kingdom Key: *When you see the ark of the covenant of the Lord your God, and the Levitical priests carrying it, you are to move out from your positions and follow it. Then you will know which way to go, since you have never been this way before* (Joshua 3:3-4).

The Ark of the Covenant represented the presence of God. When moving into uncharted territory, His presence is paramount. It prepares us for the unknown and allows the network of heaven to work the **S**pirit **I**n **M**e (SIM).

9) Give time to unlearn what is preventing the winning approach

Creativity is a rhythm of positive deconstruction and construction of ideas and methods.

The three major creative tools God used to create the world were His Wisdom, Knowledge and Understanding.

Kingdom Key: *By wisdom the Lord laid the earth's foundations, by understanding He set the heavens in place* (Proverbs 3:19).

How do we get to use these tools to create our lives and futures? We have these tools already; they just need sharpening. We sharpen our wisdom, knowledge and understanding by evaluating our performance against the principles in the Bible.

Evaluation means simply taking something apart and comparing it against a chosen standard. The more we learn to take apart our decision-making process and analyse it, regardless of how painful or ashamed it makes us feel, the more we have insight into how we really are. When we do this against the backdrop of God's principles we see what needs to change in order to grow in wisdom and win.

Wisdom wins in life, that's why God was pleased with Solomon's request for wisdom when he could have chosen anything (1 Kings 3:9). Solomon went on to build the most beautiful Temple, one of the wonders of the world.

We have access to unlimited wisdom and creativity because God lives in us. We unlock it through placing the demand of evaluation on ourselves. This creates a positive pressure to learn, develop and seek help from others which in turn produces progress.

Kingdom Key: Let the wise listen and add to their learning, and let the discerning get guidance (Proverbs 1:5).

10) Operate from a simple not an overcrowded environment

Overcrowding my life with commitments will kill my potential

Simplicity and creativity are intrinsically linked. As human beings we drift naturally towards complication and away from simplicity. Therefore if we do not place a restraint on ourselves we will complicate.

For the early Church the restraint of persecution challenged them to keep things simple. Persecution refined them and helped them to keep the main thing the main thing. Without persecution we have to create self-imposed demands and constraints to make sure we don't over-reach and end up in mediocrity.

Kingdom Key: *Our boasting is this: the testimony of our conscience that we conducted ourselves in the world in simplicity and godly sincerity, not with fleshly wisdom but by the grace of God, and more abundantly toward you* (2 Cor 1:12, NKJV).

When we become enticed by the lure of outward 'success' our lives end up becoming overcrowded. We overcompensate for our lack of internal satisfaction by striving and not living from our grace filled being. God won't give us grace for what He hasn't asked us to do. Feelings of being busy and wanted by people feed our pride; this kind of outside-in living diminishes our Kingdom results.

If you want to stay small and limited then get overcrowded. If you want to allow Kingdom expansion to come through you then get back to simplicity and operating in the grace God has given you. Then you will be able to 'let it grow' rather than trying to 'make it grow.'

Conversation with God:

Father God, I thank you for the truth of your word. As I meditate on it may it unlock the winning mindset I need to see your Kingdom come and your will be done in my life today!

Day 51: The Winning Choice to Construct Imaginatively

Today we look at some practical ways to look at how you can develop the winning conversation that will make you MORE

SECTION 8: BE MORE EXPANSIVE

expansive in life. The more you inform the right choices, the more you activate the results.

It is a myth to believe that the more I do the more results I will see in my life. When the voice of creativity is at the table then the choice I make is to get better not busier. When we buy into the lie that busy is best then we usually rob resource from other more important areas of our lives, believing it's a loan that one day we can repay. However, time is a currency against which we cannot borrow. For instance, when we take from our family time and invest in our work lives we can never have that time back.

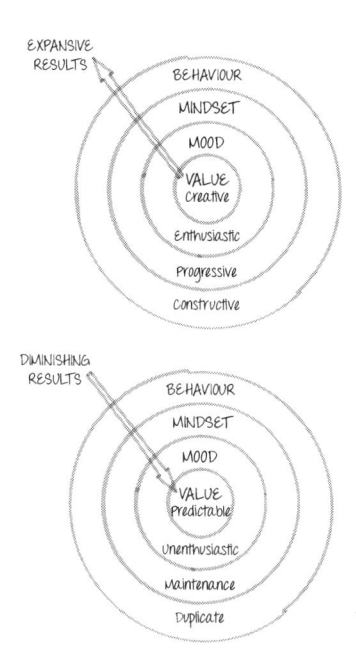

If we are going to win in every area of our lives then we need to learn to construct imaginatively.

The quality of a creative process is determined by the quality of the questions we ask. A question can disturb and frustrate the voice of predictability that tries to perpetuate more of the same in your life. The more we embrace questioning the more airtime we give to the voice of creativity.

To get better we have to become more SKILL-full.

S.K.I.L.L means that I

SHARPEN THE AXE
KILL THE FOXES
INNOVATE WITH OBSTACLES
LEAD THROUGH OTHERS
LEARN FROM THE BEST

SHARPEN THE AXE

Kingdom Key: ECC 10:10 *If the ax is dull and its edge unsharpened, more strength is needed, but skill will bring success.*

A woodcutter knows that his optimum results are not based on effort alone. He has to learn when it is the right time to stop chopping down trees and to sharpen his axe. If he sharpens his axe, less effort is needed to cut through the wood. He has to learn the rhythm of applying effort and sharpening his tool. Getting the right combination and rhythm sets the level of results he will achieve.

The belief that I AM CREATIVE comes when we understand that it's not 100% chopping trees; there have to be strategic pauses in the cutting in order to rest, develop skill and have space to question everything in order to find new ways of doing things and halt any unproductive and inefficient approaches.

During periods of evaluation and rest a helpful question to sharpen our thinking is to ask the question, 'What can produce more results with less effort?'

We can unlock creativity in our rest, development as well as our work lives. All of this will work towards keeping us sharp in living out our lives and pursuing our goals.

KILL THE FOXES

Kingdom Key: Song of songs 2:15 *Catch for us the foxes, the little foxes that ruin the vineyards, our vineyards that are in bloom.* In ancient Biblical wisdom we are told, 'Catch for us the foxes, the little foxes that ruin the vineyards, our vineyards that are in bloom.' Cute little foxes are out to rob from your vineyard. There are lots of little activities in our daily lives that look harmless, just like the foxes. However, in reality they are eating our grapes. In other words, they are stealing the time and energy needed to produce the results we long to see.

What are the little foxes that are robbing our potential?

Procrastination
Distraction
Excuses
Escapism
Laziness
Over-promising

Negativity
Sarcasm
Lying
Poor Body Language
Disorganisation
Bad Manners
Poor comments
Independence
Lateness
Busyness

Identify and kill these foxes!

INNOVATE WITH OBSTACLES

Whenever you're confronted by a major hurdle, ask, 'Is this obstacle supposed to be my mountain to climb?' Just because we are faced with an obstacle does not mean we are supposed to climb it. If it is, then conquer it! The challenge is what will unlock the potential inside you.

Here are three statements that help us see that our obstacles are opportunities for innovation. With each statement there is an expansive question to ask.

i) My limitation is my direction

There are times when obvious limitations seem to deny us progress towards a goal. The person who truly believes that creativity is part of WHO they are enlists the use of their imaginations and resources to create motion in the direction of their goal. They know that limitations lead them to dig deep and mine the creative genius that is only unlocked through challenges.

Question: *Where is my limitation leading me?*

ii) My hindrance is my help

Sometimes a hindrance actually buys us creative time. We will live frustrated lives if we attribute a negative meaning to every challenge we face. I look back and see hindrances that in hindsight were positive because they prevented us moving too quickly in a particular direction and kept us from over-committing to people or projects.

If we let frustration creep in when we experience hindrances we can make poor choices out of desperation. Sometimes a hindrance is simply a 'pause' button being pressed.

I have heard it said that it's important not to make a permanent decision in a temporary situation. Frustration stemming from uncertainty can cause us sometimes to force decisions in order to get a feeling of assurance. However this could potentially create longer term damage.

Question: *In what way could this hindrance be helping me?*

iii) My disadvantage is my advantage

Advantage is about having favour in a certain area or with certain people. Disadvantage is about lacking favour in these areas.

We are naturally prone to identifying what we lack and what others have. This can cause us to want to give up and not pursue our goal. However, our disadvantage is simply an opportunity to focus.

Innovation is about progress. What disadvantage does is prevent us continuing in the wrong direction. For every wrong direction there is a right direction. I need to ask in what way my disadvantage can actually become my advantage. Creativity will always find a way.

Question: *When is my disadvantage my advantage?*

LEAD THROUGH OTHERS

If we are building a legacy that will positively impact the world then the most effective way of doing that is through our investment in others. There are people connected to us who are strategically placed to work through and multiply the results we want to see. It is important that we do not see this as simply using people to get what we want. Our approach has to be to put them first and seek to unlock their potential and uniqueness while giving them opportunity through which to develop.

This can be as simple as giving responsibilities to our children to work with a close team on a community or work project to achieve a shared goal. The sooner we realise that we are a cog in the wheel and not the wheel itself the more we get to play at being ourselves and also have the enjoyment of seeing others flourish. We create opportunity in life through creating opportunity for others. The winning life is all about the right order. If we put others first and we will not be short changed; in fact, we will experience extraordinary increase in the most important areas of life.

So regularly ask, 'Who am I connected to with whom I and they could achieve more?'

LEARN FROM THE BEST

The way we create skilfully is by keeping ourselves in the position of a learner. We must become hungry to learn. Learning is not simply acquiring greater knowledge and understanding to increase skills; it is the environment where we have permission to do things differently. We often carry a subconscious block to trying to do things differently. This comes from a default belief that 'I am predictable.' However, learning from others challenges that belief and causes us to reinforce the belief that I am creative and I can challenge everything I do in order to get better.

The expansive question is, 'Is there someone I can learn from that would cause me to look at what I do differently?'

Day 52: The Winning Evaluation

Benchmark which mindset you have when it comes to the EXPANSIVE conversation.

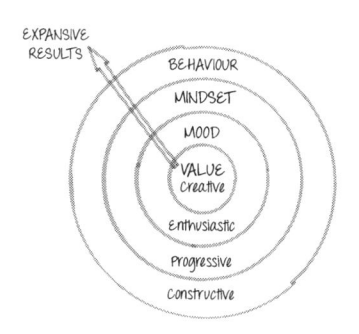

The fruit of my actions will reveal the root of the conversations I host. Today we are looking at ten questions based on situations we find ourselves in and I encourage you to be brutally honest as to which response most fits your nature. Tally up how many you answered according to which voice and make a decision to go back under the bonnet of your inner conversations to strengthen your foundation as a champion. If you feel frustrated then that is not a bad thing as long as you focus that frustration on making certain your commitment to hosting the winning conversation.

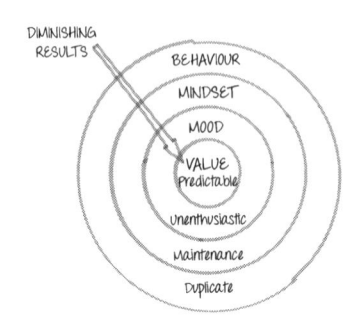

1) Frustration—How do you deal with frustration in your life?

Consumed - I allow the frustration to take the wind out of my sails. Frustration feeds a 'why bother attitude'

Complacent - How I feel and the environment I am in dictates how much effort I put into meeting people. If it's an environment in which I feel at ease I have no problem chatting to people; in fact it's a pleasant way to pass away the time

Competitor - I release frustration through quick wins to improve efficiency. I feed off increased busyness to give 'feeling of progress'

Champion - I step back and look at how the change in landscape could steer me onto a more effective path to achieving the goal. I allow the frustration to refocus me and sharpen my priorities

2) Distraction—How do you deal with distraction in your day?

Consumed - Distraction is an innocent trait that has no significant bearing on the future

Complacent - I get frustrated when I realise I have become distracted over a period of time and pressure starts to build because of deadlines and time pressures. I forget about the frustration once the pressure is off and then tend to allow it to happen again

Competitor - Distraction must be managed when it becomes a noticeable pattern

Champion - Distraction is a time terrorist out to kill potential and I am on high alert to prevent it from happening

3) Excuses—How do you view your excuses?

Consumed - Excuses are a personality trait that I have come to accept. They are part of my makeup

Complacent - The excuses I tend to deal with are those that others challenge me about. I live with other excuses because they seem valid to me

Competitor - Dealing with my excuses is important but because I do not seek accountability it is all down to how I feel. I am making some progress though

Champion - My excuses reveal a hidden trait that is eating away at my future. They need exposing and hitting hard. No mercy!

4) Goals—How important are goals to you?

Consumed - Goals make us mechanical and usually set us up to fail. Why waste your life feeling bad about what you haven't achieved?

Complacent - I tend to have points in my year when I am reminded by others how important goals are and when that happens I totally agree. I then tend to run out of steam and return to living in the moment

Competitor - Goals are good because they create tick-lists we can mark on our way to a well ordered life

Champion - When followed intensely, goals cause us continuously to dismantle and reassemble what we do

5) Creativity—How do you view creativity?

Consumed - Creativity is for people of a certain disposition

Complacent - When I have time on my hands I like to think how I can be creative with what I have

Competitor - Creativity is something I do in the extra time I may have when everything else is ordered

Champion - Creativity is the lens through which I view everything; it enables me to form my future piece by piece

6) Scheduling—What do you think about scheduling?

Consumed - I don't waste time on details like scheduling

Complacent - I have control of my schedule for a while but then I tend to just 'go with the flow' and do what feels right to do

Competitor - I get everything that can be done into a neat order. I like to feel in control of my time and that everything gets enough time. I am efficient

Champion - I build my time around a single focus and work hard to simplify. My aim is to do more by doing less, to be effective not just efficient

7) Busyness—Is busyness a good thing?

Consumed - I prefer to stay busy as it helps me keep my focus off deeper issues that surface when I have time on my hands

Complacent - Sometimes it feels good because things are getting done and I do see progress. However at other times I can get overwhelmed and tend to be more reactive than proactive

Competitor - Busyness is what gets my juices flowing. Being 'on the edge' gives me an adrenaline rush. However I do get frustrated that I am not progressing as far as I think I should

Champion - Busyness is a form of laziness. Sometimes life can get full when circumstances happen beyond my control but through planning and focus and building my life around a single focus I make any form of busyness work for me

8) Time—How do you view time?

Consumed - I never have enough of it and I would create another 24 hours in the week if I could

Complacent - I have just come to accept that I only have a certain amount of time to achieve certain tasks and whatever does not get done rolls over to the following day or week. This can mean that pressure mounts but I address that when it happens

Competitor - Time is important and needs to be managed. However, sometimes my desperation to hit goals means I am not in a rhythm and I waste time through lack of order and discipline

Champion - Time is the most precious resource. It is far more precious than money. Therefore I am strict about what I give it to as I will never get it back again

9) Achievement—How do you view achievement?

Consumed - Achievement is looking back at points and highlighting what has been positive and being thankful for it

Complacent - Achievement is for the driven and those who need it. As long as I enjoy life then that is what achievement looks like for me

Competitor - Achievement is about unlocking my potential and is something for which I strive. I have to be careful that I do not attach my self-worth to it

Champions - Achievement has happened because I have the potential. Therefore life is about actualizing what already lies within me

10) Investment—How do you view investment?

Consumed - I do not have enough patience for investment. Life is for living so enjoy the now and let tomorrow take care of itself

Complacent - When possible I try to invest but I tend to allow the demands of now to override any goals into which I am investing. I lose focus and therefore drive

Competitor - I am passionate about investment but can often lack focus about why I am investing. Therefore, deep down I know my levels of investment are not what they should be

Champion - Investment is the pathway to obtaining extraordinary goals. The key is to sharpen the clarity of the goal and stay passionate about the WHY. This helps me to avoid the temptation of trading the ultimate for the immediate.

PRACTICE V POTENTIAL of the EXPANSIVE conversation

Based on the answers to the above questions, how many times could you honestly say that your answer was 'champion'?

Consumer: 1-2 times

Complacent: 3-5 times

Competitor: 6-8 times

Champion: 9-10 times

My Overall POTENTIAL: I AM A CHAMPION

MY Overall PRACTICE: I HAVE BEEN A _____

In order for my practice to match my potential I have identified the following three things I can do to unlock the champion in me:

1_____

2_____

3_____

Day 53: The Winning Accountability

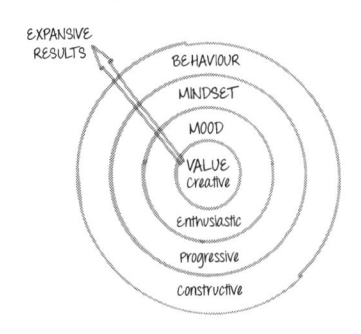

By pulling this whole week under the title of 'multiply and do not subtract', we are able quickly to review this conversation. Utilising the dice in spare moments throughout the day, or in a small group it helps to focus on the inner conversation of relevance.

The Winning Dice—**Be a Multiplier and not a <u>subtractor</u>**

Our attitude which is driven by our values and desires will

add, multiply, subtract or divide a community, group or even family. A champion is in the business of building. Our focus should always be on adding and multiplying so as to keep on helping others build bigger lives. A wrong attitude subtracts from a productive and creative environment and a divided belief system can divide a group of people.

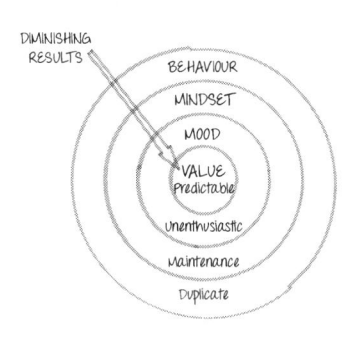

The winning conversation creates the expectation that every person **aims to multiply** and demand from themselves **addition at the very least** as they work on the principles that bring multiplication. When a group of people all work hard to bring a lift to what they are doing the level of synergy results in extraordinary wins for the team and a better environment for every individual.

When as a team we are all devoted to one another and a common cause then the result is synergy which has a multiplying effect. Synergy is the belief that the sum total of the potential in two or more people is greater than the sum total of the individual parts.

Creativity is ultimately a belief that moves us from independence to interdependence. At the very least we are creating something for someone. At the very best we are creating something for someone with someone.

We will always get what we have always had unless we try alternative ways of achieving the common goal. Multiplication requires new methods to be discovered to achieve established goals.

There is more in you than you think. You have an expansive life to grow into and this comes as you embrace the stretch created by goals that require an intense focus and a resolute effort every day.

Step 1: RECALL together

Sometimes we need a quick review of what a multiplier not a subtractor looks like so we can stay on course to allow CREATIVITY to have the loudest voice drowning out PREDICTABILITY.

What does a multiplier look like?

- They are a big picture thinker who do not despise the 'little' things because they can see how they can become a lot through creative investment
- They believe their significance is in the bigger picture and not in the single part
- They always look to find a win-win because agreement has an exponential effect on what they do
- They look to find new ways of doing something in order to achieve greater results
- They process challenges with patience and passion
- They embrace challenge in order to bring stretch
- They welcome change because they understand you cannot do what you have always done and expect different results
- They understand that celebrating the success of others is a win for the team
- They exhibit the principle of giving their first and best to their legacy
- They recognise that multiplication happens through people not tasks
- They seek to understand and learn how to delegate and empower others properly

What does a subtractor look like?

- Their main concern is protecting themselves
- They abdicate responsibility and seek to distance themselves from decisions that have been collectively taken
- They do not push themselves to contribute beyond a predictable point
- They seek personal recognition and promotion and are impatient when asked to simply carry on doing what they have been entrusted with

- They stay within expectations rather than pushing themselves to supersede expectations
- They allow personal issues to get in the way of the team spirit
- They do not deal with relational issues correctly
- They lack an appetite to learn
- They fail to learn from failure
- They respond negatively when challenged on their results
- They do not assume the best of others

Step 2: REVIEW with others

Get together weekly with people who are committed to developing the winning conversations through the journey of this book and ask the following:

i) Looking at the environment I was brought up in, can I identify

what has contributed to my philosophy on this conversation?

ii) How do I feel when I am brutally honest about how I am doing with this conversation?

iii) How can I use that feeling to create momentum?

iv) What goals can I put in place to start creating quick wins that will produce a sense of hope that I am winning in the long-term?

v) Are there any relational alignments that need to happen to help me achieve my goals in this conversation?

Step 3: REFLECTION to be shared

Now create a reflection that you can share with someone in your group or someone else that you are coaching to be a champion in life. Why not take the time with your children, loved one, or a friend over coffee, and share what you have learnt. Simply sharing this reflection will accomplish much in your life and deepen relationships, enriching them with vulnerability and moments of movement.

Follow our basic structure:

i) What I realised for the first time/again this week is ... (share the thought)

ii) The change I need to make is ... (share the action point)

iii) Can you help me make it? ... (invite help and create accountability)

Once you have got into the habit of doing this, why not decide to turn your thoughts into a blog or even take your coaching to another level? There is so much in you and it is directly connected to your commitment to stretch yourself.

Section 9: Be MORE valuable

Day 54: The Winning Conversation makes you MORE valuable

EXCELLENCE unlocks the door of being **VALUABLE**

Kingdom Key: I am the salt of the earth.

You are the salt of the earth; but if the salt loses its flavour, how shall it be seasoned? It is then good for nothing but to be thrown out and trampled underfoot by men (Matthew 5:13).

When I host the **VALUABLE** conversation I become...

1) MORE aware of my intrinsic value

What I do grows in value when I invest time in valuing who I am

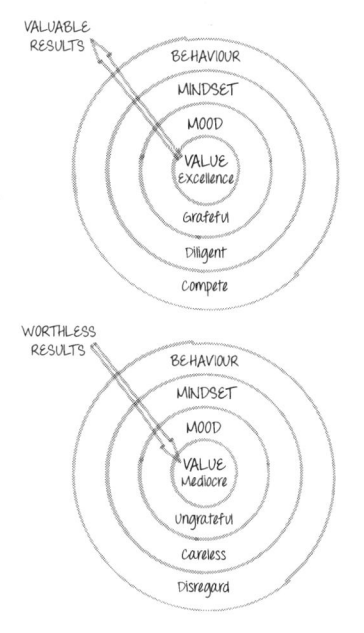

The Apostle Paul was passionate in his letters about the cross of Christ because it was this revelation from which he drew his greatest value. The cross became the point of exchange where Paul could deal with the pain, guilt and shame of his old life with the revelation and understanding of his new identity.

His letter challenged the church at Galatia to view life through the cross in order to enter into the freedom of Christ. This freedom was not earned through behaviour but came freely through believing in Christ Jesus.

Kingdom Key: *Make a careful exploration of who you are and the work you have been given, and then sink yourself into that. Don't be impressed with yourself. Don't compare yourself with others. Each of you must take responsibility for doing the creative best you can with your own life* (Gal 6:4-5: The Message).

Our intrinsic value is discovered when we learn to let Christ live His life through our lives. The crossover point that Christ made from death to life becomes the internal process that I undergo as His follower, from a devalued and sinful state to a prized and righteous state. The value we unlock in WHO we are in Christ establishes a genuine conviction of excellence that influences everything we do. Everything we do is an <u>extension</u> of who we are.

2) MORE in demand

We create a greater demand for what we have when we demonstrate an appreciation of what people really need

When we meet a human need we are expressing our appreciation for their life and therefore communicate true value. The greater the need we meet the more appreciated people feel. It should be our Kingdom aspiration to discern the needs we are shaped to meet so that we can communicate our appreciation of people through answering their needs. The greater the awareness of these needs, the more valuable we become in our impact on peoples' lives. According to Titus our productivity is linked to the level of need we meet.

Kingdom Key: *Our people must learn to devote themselves to doing what is good, in order to provide for urgent needs and not live unproductive lives* (Titus 3:14).

3) MORE uncommon in our care

Excellence is doing a common thing in an uncommon way (Booker T. Washington)

The value in the *root* makes its way to the *fruit*. Jesus is irresistible which means that if I am 'feeding' on Christ then everything I do will become irresistible to others as though Jesus himself were doing it. Excellence has its root in love. The verse that precedes the Apostle Paul's famous discourse on love in 1 Corinthians 13 teaches us this. *And yet I will show you the most excellent way* (1 Corinthians 12:31b).

We demonstrate our love for someone or something by the level of excellence we apply to it. A lack of excellence is a lack of love. Our excellence in one area will positively influence the standard of the rest of our lives.

4) MORE commanding

Let your excellence command the attention of others

Excellence is not a given simply because a person has more resource. Excellence is doing the best with what you have; it is making something or someone the object of your love and bringing massive emphasis to them by using all available resource to you.

Becoming MORE valuable is not about becoming richer; it is about distinction, being set apart because of the strength of your excellent belief which informs your excellent behaviour.

In 1 Kings 10 we read about the time when the Queen of Sheba visited King Solomon. We should bear in mind the Queen of Sheba was among the richest people in the world and was not easily impressed by material wealth.

Kingdom Key: *When the queen of Sheba saw all the wisdom of Solomon and the palace he had built, the food on his table, the seating of his officials, the attending servants in their robes, his cupbearers, and the burnt offerings he made at the temple of the LORD, she was overwhelmed* (1 Kings 10:4-5).

The excellence of Solomon flowed from his belief not from his belongings. The "wow" for the Queen of Sheba was the wisdom of Solomon which was his distinctive belief about how to use what he had. As one who has the Saviour of the world living in you, you have the edge when you follow Christ. You do not simply possess wisdom but carry Him by His Spirit. The more you seek to work that wisdom through gaining knowledge and applied understanding, the more valuable you will become. This will make you distinctive and give you the "wow" factor.

5) MORE aware of what you sign off

Become a signature of worth

When we are asked to sign off on a job that has been carried out for us, or sign for a delivery, we are being asked to give our approval to what has taken place. We are declaring what we believe to be acceptable.

While we do not physically do this, one way to create awareness of our true standards is to imagine that we sign off everything that we do. Would you be happy to put your signature, the symbol of your identity, on the conversations you had yesterday, or the work you carried out, the way you treated your family member or even the time you spent in conversation with God?

The prophet Malachi had to make God's people aware that many were signing off on sacrifices that were substandard; they not only communicated a devalued interest in God but were also a reflection of their own internal value. After all, the two are intrinsically linked.

Kingdom Key: *"Cursed is the cheat who has an acceptable male in his flock and vows to give it, but then sacrifices a blemished animal to the Lord. For I am a great king," says the Lord Almighty, "and my name is to be feared among the nations"* (Mal 1:14).

If my children mean the world to me and yet I do not give my best energy and attention to them when with them, I am saying one thing but communicating something else. If I do not give the best offering that I can, then I may sing a love song to God but my life is painting a very different picture.

So how do I govern the quality of what I sign off? I govern the quality of my life from the beliefs I store in my heart.

Kingdom Key: *Above all else, guard your heart, for everything you do flows from it* (Proverbs 4:23).

The more I value God, others and myself, the greater expectation I put on myself to give my best.

As an ambassador of Christ (2 Corinthians 5:20) my goal should be to be confident in signing my work off with the name of Jesus because He is the one I represent in His Kingdom.

6) MORE fragrant

Become a fragrance that produces a smile

The Pharisees and Sadducees were renowned in Jesus' day for projecting one thing through external behaviour while carrying quite another - self-glorification and self-gratification - in their internal beliefs.

Jesus often shone a light that exposed this cheap imitation of faith. He revealed the disconnection between how they behaved and what they really believed. On one occasion this division between external behaviour and internal beliefs was showcased through the example of a woman who had lived a sinful life but who repented and chose to worship Jesus.

Kingdom Key: *Then He turned toward the woman and said to Simon, "Do you see this woman? I came into your house. You did not give me any water for my feet, but she wet my feet with her tears and wiped them with her hair. You did not give me a kiss, but this woman, from the time I entered, has not stopped kissing my feet. You did not put oil on my head, but she has poured perfume on my feet. Therefore, I tell you, her many sins have been forgiven—as her great love has shown. But whoever has been forgiven little loves little"* (Luke 7:44-47).

The depth of the woman's appreciation for Jesus was demonstrated by her level of service toward Him and the cost of her worship. Our revelation of Christ has to impact the resolution we make to show uncommon care. It is only as we compete differently from the crowd that people will see Christ in us. Determine to trade in any cheap imitation of religious bravado for genuine, heartfelt appreciation for God and others through a pursuit of excellence.

7) MORE popular

Excellence is the amplification for your story

When I have the conviction of excellence in my belief system, I do not have to rely on my words to tell the story of my life.

In the Sermon on the Mount, Jesus casts the vision of his Kingdom and calls for a new depth of showing love. He calls on Kingdom people to practice loving the 'unlovely,' in the context of loving our enemies.

Kingdom Key: *If you love those who love you, what reward will you get? Are not even the tax collectors doing that? And if you greet only your own people, what are you doing more than others? Do not even pagans do that?* (Matt 5:46-47)

Jesus calls on us to depart from a life that blends in and to be set apart through competing differently otherwise we will have no right to claim that we belong to a different Kingdom, His Kingdom. The way we demonstrate Christ's value and love for other people will determine how loud and distinctive our story is.

Day 55: The Winning Voice of Excellence

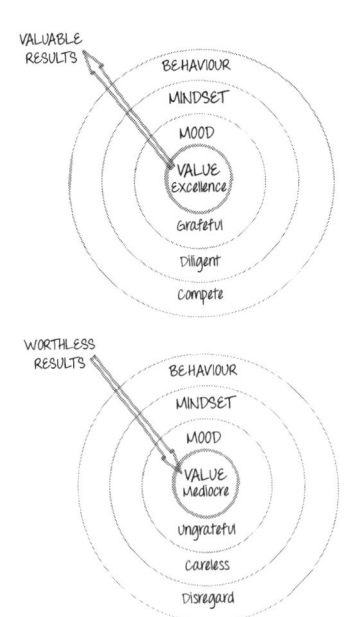

Excellence that unlocks the door of being **VALUABLE**

Kingdom Key: I am the salt of the earth.

"You are the salt of the earth; but if the salt loses its flavour, how shall it be seasoned? It is then good for nothing but to be thrown out and trampled underfoot by men" (Matthew 5:13).

To be a person of EXCELLENCE I have to immerse myself in my new identity in Jesus Christ. This belief will lead me into the right feelings. The more I immerse myself in the belief that I am excellent, the more valuable I will become in my world.

Since I have Christ in me then daily I

have to die to the old me and live in the new me.

Paul says in Galatians 2:20: *I have been crucified with Christ and I no longer live, but Christ lives in me. The life I now live in the body, I live by faith in the Son of God, who loved me and gave Himself for me.*

This means WHO I am is WHO He is. I have adopted my new identity and I choose each day to let Christ live through me. I am excellent because Jesus is excellent!

To unlock my being more VALUABLE I have to believe that…

i) I AM not my limits

Limits reflect the size of a task; solutions reflect the size of a person

The size of the task puts a demand on my potential. No demand can out-muscle Jesus Christ who lives in me.

Kingdom Key: *The one who is in you is greater than the one who is in the world* (1 John 4:4b).

I become valuable in my world because I am a person who brings solutions. Regardless of the limiting problem I can call upon God in conversation to give me the grace to beat the opposing obstacle.

Conversation with God:

Help me to grow in awareness of Christ in me and the hope that I carry. When I feel like I have hit my limits, help me to draw on hope Himself, Jesus Christ. I am limitless in Him.

ii) I AM extraordinary

A lack of distinction will result in extinction

The theme of God's people being set apart (consecrated) runs throughout the Bible. God wanted to demonstrate to the world what they were missing in opting out of a relationship with their Creator. Jesus continued this theme when He came to launch the Kingdom of God.

Kingdom Key: *As it is, you do not belong to the world, but I have* chosen you <u>out of the world</u> (John 15:19).

The Kingdom value of excellence is one way in which we help the world see God's distinctive nature. Our goal should be to show the world what they are missing through our behaviour. We should aim to live a life that is 'out of this world', demonstrating what happens when His kingdom is established in our lives. While not everyone will communicate to you how they really feel about the value you bring, make every effort to find ways of getting better. If your belief of excellence is genuine then you should not need prompting to increase the quality of your activity.

Conversation with God:

Father, I thank you that you, the all-knowing and all-powerful God, have chosen me. This means you know more about me and my potential than I do. I desire to unlock what you have invested in me in order to show my appreciation to you, my Lord and my God.

iii) I AM a success

Success is the pursuit of your legacy before your lifestyle

True success for the believer is something gifted by Christ not something we can attain in our own strength. Our achievement came through Christ defeating death and hell and rising again. This is an eternal achievement that can manifest itself through our earthly assignment.

I am committed to learning how to use the eternal investment for earthly use. I want to maximise the impact of what lies within so that others can experience eternity with Jesus.

Kingdom Key: *For you created my inmost being; you knit me together in my mother's womb. I praise you because I am fearfully and wonderfully made; your works are wonderful, I know that full well* (Psalm 139:13-14).

We do not work in this life to gain value and appreciation because who can add a greater value than the author of life Himself? When I read, 'I am fearfully and wonderfully made,' I am inspired to relearn how to live my life in order for the world to experience the wonderful and awesome love of God. If I believe that all His works are wonderful then I know I have the potential to be wonderful in all I do.

Conversation with God:

Father, you satisfy my need for appreciation when I accept the value you placed on me before the beginning of time. I am an act of God and a miracle and I desire to fulfil the purpose for which you have put me on this earth at this time.

iv) I AM valuable

My value is raised as I raise my value of others

Have you ever had a feeling of value and worth when you have worn a new suit or driven that new car? It is interesting how external things can produce an internal feeling of worth.

What we put on and surround ourselves with really does impact our feelings. However, these are momentary feelings stimulated from the outside-in. We often rely on our sense of importance and worth to be determined by the tangible and yet this only creates a feeling and does not reveal truth to us.

What if that feeling could be translated into a belief that did not go away? What if the conviction of self-worth and self-belief could flow from the inside-out and existed regardless of the quality of what surrounded me?

Kingdom Key: *Paul says But we have this treasure in jars of clay to show that this <u>all-surpassing power</u> is from God and not from us* (2 Cor 4:7).

Jesus Christ, who is a priceless treasure, a jewel that cannot be bought, dwells inside us. He became an inseparable part of us when we chose to receive Him as Lord and Saviour of our lives. While our lives may look and feel rough at times, we carry a diamond of potential that needs to be realized and brought out into the open for the world to experience. This diamond has no glory in and of itself but it has the extraordinary ability to refract light. To refract light means to direct beams of light in multiple directions. The purpose of the diamond is to show the all surpassing power of God in our lives. As long as we have the light of Christ we can refract His glory.

Conversation with God:

As I draw upon the value of being your child today I do so in order to place greater value on others. I want others to experience what I receive from you. Help me discern today those who are malnourished when it comes to value. Help me to be a channel of your grace today.

v) I AM my potential

Results are temporary; my potential is permanent

When results are good we take pride in them. We don't mind answering the question, 'How are things going?' However, we recoil from that question when results are poor for fear how it makes us look.

Paul learned that to win in life as believers we must boast about the place from which our success comes…the cross!

Kingdom Key: *May I never boast except in the cross of our Lord Jesus Christ, through which the world has been crucified to me, and I to the world* (Galatians 6:14).

Kingdom results come from Jesus. Therefore whilst evaluating results and aiming to see better results are encouraged in this book, we draw our value from the only success that ultimately matters, that Jesus defeated death and therefore I glory in His victory over death when He rose again. When I live from His victory my soul is never hungry for appreciation. His act of love for me is all the appreciation and worth I need.

Conversation with God:

Whilst I pray for great results today, Father, I realise that this does not define me. I am defined by the potential of Christ in me.

vi) I AM a mirror

My behaviour reveals my beliefs

Excellence is when the practice of what I produce mirrors the potential of Christ in me.

Kingdom Key: *...what are you doing more than others? Do not even pagans do that?* (Matthew 5:46-47).

When Jesus made this statement He was not advocating a life of reducing our value through comparison. Jesus was calling for our behaviour to be measured against what God has put inside us not around us.

Jesus knew the level of potential placed inside those who would hear His sermon. He also knew that once He had died and rose again every believer would carry inside them the same power that conquered the grave.

The apostle Paul grasped this blueprint and he was passionate about others getting it.

Kingdom Key: *I also pray that you will understand the incredible greatness of God's power for us who believe him. This is the same mighty power that raised Christ from the dead and seated him in the place of honour at God's right hand in the heavenly realms* (Eph 1:19-20).

If I have Christ in me and I am not setting higher standards in all areas of life than those who do not have Christ, I have to question my level of revelation, understanding or desire to live the winning life. This is a process that has to display progress over time and cause me to stand out. If I am not standing out then I am not stepping up to the plate when it comes to who I am called to be.

As we live from Christ's victory, we can bounce off failure rather than be consumed by it because we are focused on what the process is producing. We know that the ultimate result of being perfect sits the other side of this life in heaven.

Conversation with God:

Father, I desire progress today in living for you. I know my works do not determine my value but I truly want to be the best I can be so that others get to experience the Kingdom of God.

vii) I AM a bar-setter not a bar-settler

We will never rise beyond the bar of our expectations

The calling on a follower of Jesus Christ is to be light in a dark world and salt in an unsavoury place. We are called to be standard-setters and not standard-settlers. A standard-setter stands out through the way they live. Their life challenges the status quo of what everyone else sees as acceptable. This is why it is a lot easier to be a standard-settler. A standard-settler camps around the standards of the crowd.

When Jesus stepped onto the world stage over 2000 years ago He came to raise the bar.

The Sermon on the Mount is a bar-setting message.

The standard that the Jewish people were used to was the law and Jesus quite clearly stated His intention in that regard:

Kingdom Key: *Do not think that I have come to abolish the Law or the Prophets; I have not come to abolish them but to fulfil them* (Matthew 5:17).

In Matthew chapter 5 he uses the phrase *You have heard that it was said*. This is a reference point to where the bar had been set up to this point. For example in verse 21 we read:

You have heard that it was said to the people long ago, "You shall not murder, and anyone who murders will be subject to judgment."

In typical fashion Jesus inserts a 'BUT'.

But I tell you that anyone who is angry with a brother or sister will be subject to judgment. Again, anyone who says to a brother or sister, "Raca," is answerable to the court. And anyone who says, "You fool!" will be in danger of the fire of hell.

Jesus identified where the bar was set but then raised the level to a new benchmark. In fact He set it at an impossible level for man's sinful condition. He did this to show that only He could meet this standard. He came to make a way for us to become acceptable to a Holy God by dying for our sins and rising again so that we could share in the new life He has for us. With Christ in us we live from what He already accomplished. The potential for perfection is in us but it is going to take a lifetime to process and will climax when we are glorified like Him in heaven.

When a new culture is introduced into a person's life, or into an organisation, it will either compel people to rise to the new benchmark or repel them because they are bar-settlers. Bar-settlers are comfortable with where the bar is set; it is a fence in their life, a boundary that they are happy to paint and maintain.

However, the new you is a bar-setter because of Christ!

Conversation with God:

I thank you, Father, that I can live from Christ's accomplishment and so I will not settle for mediocrity but supersede expectations so that you look good through my life.

viii) I AM responsible for my own sense of value

No one can touch or tamper with your value and promise

In John 10:10 Jesus reminds us that the enemy comes to steal and kill and destroy. We are in a war and our enemy knows that a key to preventing his opponent Jesus from winning is causing God's people to devalue WHO they are. If he can do this then he renders the power of the cross impotent in our lives.

As believers excellence is about maintaining our awareness of our value. We protect this through adhering to the words of Paul in Ephesians 6.

Kingdom Key: *Therefore put on the full armour of God, so that when the day of evil comes, you may be able to stand your ground, and after you have done everything, to stand* (Eph 6:13).

To 'stand' in WHO we are is our responsibility; only we can make the choice to do this. Choose today to stand in the value of Christ and view everything through the lens of this value. See how you become increasingly valuable in WHAT you do in and to the world around you.

Conversation with God:

Father, today I choose to put on the full armour of God. I realise that there is an enemy who wants to devalue me but I choose to stand in my new identity, the excellence of Christ Jesus. I thank you that my day is full of promise because my life is too.

ix) I AM the King's speech

Mediocrity is an impediment that hijacks your message

The mouth is the overflow of the heart (Matthew 12:34) and, as James reminds in his letter (James 3). it is the rudder of our lives.

Kingdom Key: *Let your conversation be always full of grace, seasoned with salt, so that you may know how to answer everyone* (Col 4:6).

Our speech should and can reflect our position in Christ as co-heirs with Him (Romans 8:17).

Unlike King George, we do not require a speech therapist in order to know what to say. We can simply draw on grace - **G**od's **R**esource **A**t **C**hrist's **E**xpense - found in WHO we are in Christ, then speak life-giving words as a mouthpiece for God.

Excellence is an accent that identifies those who are truly after God's own heart. Let the God of excellence who is in you influence every part of your life, especially the most influential part of you, which is your tongue. Let your voice be identified as one that has an excellent tone through the quality of your words and how you utter them.

Conversation with God:

Father, help my conversation with you today to shape my conversation with those I meet. I want heaven to fill every word with life and grace. May I build value today in the lives of those I meet as I seek to impact my world for you.

x) I AM care-FULL

The proof of my value is in the care I give

A succinct explanation of excellence is to treat others as we would like to be treated. This is the golden rule of Jesus.

Kingdom Key: *So in everything, do to others what you would have them do to you, for this sums up the Law and the Prophets* (Matthew 7:12; Luke 6:31).

What has this to do with excellence?

Standards are not consistent in our world because every individual will automatically set the standard according to their own perspective. Quality is often subjective. A key way of raising standards is to help people break out of their own perspective and look through a different lens.

The most powerful way to change the way we think is to take ourselves out of the most comfortable position of our own perspective and put ourselves in someone else's shoes. This immediately causes us to challenge our default settings because we start to journey on a new route of understanding.

Jesus encouraged His followers to grow their emotional intelligence through the powerful tool of empathy. Empathy is the ability to step into the feelings of someone else.

Conversation with God:

Father, help me to be aware of others around me today. Help me to be empathetic and show an uncommon level of care. I thank you that you can help me treat others as I would want to be treated. Deepen and develop my emotional capacity so I can be effective for you in communicating and demonstrating my appreciation for others.

Day 56 - The Winning Mood of Gratitude

EXCELLENCE unlocks a GRATEFUL mood in me

Kingdom Key: I am the salt of the earth.

You are the salt of the earth; but if the salt loses its flavour, how shall it be seasoned? It is then good for nothing but to be thrown out and trampled underfoot by men (Matthew 5:13).

THE WINNING KEYS

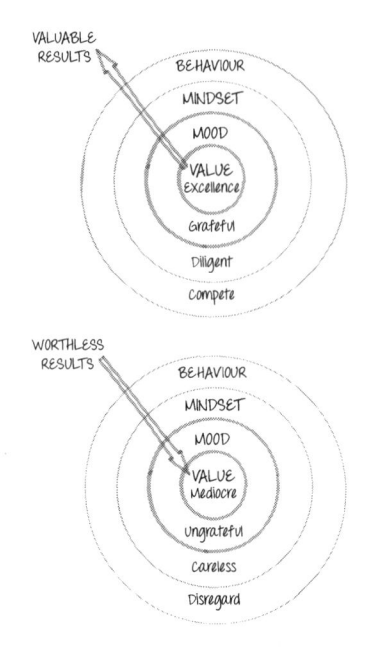

The Kingdom key of Excellence unlocks my WHY which is my PURPOSE.

My purpose is the good work which I was created to do (Eph 2:10).

The vision for my life was prepared by God before I was even born (Jeremiah 1:50).

I am having the VALUABLE conversation led by the voice of excellence which means I choose to put myself in a grateful mood. Gratitude flows when I use the power of remembrance.

Throughout the Bible we see the link between gratitude for what has taken place and faith for what will happen. God taught the Israelites to look back and remember what God had done in order to build faith toward what He could do. Gratitude unlocks our emotions and stirs our soul. It's like the oil that works its way through the engine, enabling it to kick into motion.

God reminded Israel how He had provided for them through the wilderness years...

Kingdom Key: *Your clothes did not wear out and your feet did not swell during these forty years. Know then in your heart that as a man disciplines his son, so the Lord your God disciplines you. Observe the commands of the Lord your God, walking in obedience to him and revering him. For the Lord your God is bringing you into a good land—a land with brooks, streams, and deep springs gushing out into the valleys and hills; a land with wheat and barley, vines and fig trees, pomegranates, olive oil and honey; a land where bread will not be scarce and you will lack nothing; a land where the rocks are iron and you can dig copper out of the hills* (Deut 8:4-9).

The goal of galvanising gratitude was to create a diligence toward the commands He had given them so that they could unlock their promise and be distinctive from the rest of the world.

There is so much in our past that can be used to fuel a grateful heart and stir an excellent spirit.

Take time to be thankful today and see the impact of gratitude on your attitude.

Gratitude clarifies true value

Mediocrity creeps in when we adopt a 'why bother' attitude. Our lack of personal value means we have little or no value to add to anything or anyone. Like a car that runs an engine with no oil, it eventually blows and becomes unusable. So it is with us. We reduce our emotional capacity when we run a long time without being grateful.

When I put myself in a grateful mood my perspective starts to shift and so do my priorities. If we do this we can win in life. Failure to do so will mean working from a faulty internal map; we will constantly find ourselves at dead ends wondering how we got there. Had Saul been grateful for having David as a servant he could have avoided the dead end of jealousy and been one of the most successful kings in history (1 Samuel 18ff).

Gratitude is a platform for possibility

Gratitude puts emotional currency at our disposal that we can use for other people. When our emotions are stirred our internal eyes are opened. We stop walking around with a glazed look or staring into nothing and become aware at the possibilities around us.

Kingdom Key: *But whatever were gains to me I now consider loss for the sake of Christ. What is more, I consider everything a loss because of the surpassing worth of knowing Christ Jesus my Lord, for whose sake I have lost all things* (Phil 3:7-8).

Paul's choice to follow Christ was costly and yet he maintained a mood of gratitude which stirred him to step up and push into the fullness of what God had for him.

Kingdom Key: *Not that I have already obtained all this, or have already arrived at my goal, but I press on to take hold of that for which Christ Jesus took hold of me* (Phil 3:12).

Open up your emotional potential today and be grateful.

Unlock an excellent soul script through immersing yourself in God's word (the bible)

We become convinced that we have an internal value that can and will make a difference when we immerse ourselves in these verses:

When I immerse myself in this verse I value myself from an excellent belief:

I value myself as someone who can add immense value to the world around me

My identity is Christ in me and this affects the value I place on my life

1 Corinthians 15:10: *By the grace of God I am what I am, and His grace to me was not without effect. No, I worked harder than all of them—yet not I, but the grace of God that was with me.*

My value is tamperproof and I have a new heritage in Christ Jesus

1 Peter 1:18-21: *You know that it was not with perishable things such as silver or gold that you were redeemed from the empty way of life handed down to you from your ancestors, but with the precious blood of Christ, a lamb without blemish or defect. He was chosen before the creation of the world, but was revealed in these last times for your sake. Through Him you believe in God, who raised Him from the dead and glorified Him, and so your faith and hope are in God.*

When I immerse myself in this verse I value others from an excellent belief:

I value other people and want to increase the value of their lives

I choose to serve others as my worship to you today

Heb 13:15 -16: *Through Jesus, therefore, let us continually offer to God a sacrifice of praise—the fruit of lips that openly profess His name. And do not forget to do good and to share with others, for with such sacrifices God is pleased.*

My anticipation of others' needs, and acting on that impulse, validates my excellence conviction

James 2:14-17: *What good is it, my brothers and sisters, if someone claims to have faith but has no deeds? Can such faith save them? Suppose a brother or a sister is without clothes and daily food. If one of you says to them, "Go in peace; keep warm and well fed," but does nothing about their physical needs, what good is it? In the same way, faith by itself, if it is not accompanied by action, is dead.*

<u>When I immerse myself in this verse I value my future from an excellent belief:</u>

I value my future because my internal value will make an even bigger difference to the world around me

I am chosen, royal, holy and special and my future will create value for God's Kingdom

1 Peter 2:9: *You are a chosen people, a royal priesthood, a holy nation, God's special possession, that you may declare the praises of Him who called you out of darkness into His wonderful light.*

I value others in faith of what will be, not based on how they currently are

Gal 6:9-10: *Let us not become weary in doing good, for at the proper time we will reap a harvest if we do not give up. Therefore, as we have opportunity, let us do good to all people, especially to those who belong to the family of believers.*

Conversation with God:

Father God, I choose to put aside the thoughts, feelings and impulses that do not fit with who you are because it is no longer I who live but Christ who lives in me. I put off the old me and put on the new me. May my thoughts be your thoughts, my feelings your feelings and my impulses your impulses. I step into this day knowing that you are working through me to grow your Kingdom.

Day 57: The Winning Mindset of Diligence

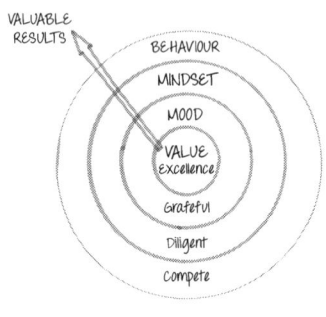

High level focus through practicing relentlessly

EXCELLENCE unlocks a DILIGENT mindset and this is HOW I will approach my day.

Kingdom Key: *I am the salt of the earth.*

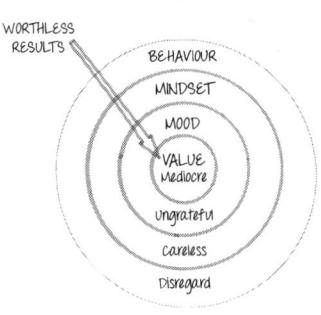

You are the salt of the earth; but if the salt loses its flavour, how shall it be seasoned? It is then good for nothing but to be thrown out and trampled underfoot by men (Matthew 5:13).

Paul tells us in 1 Corinthians 2:16 that *we have the mind of Christ.* This is not about knowing all the thoughts of Jesus necessarily but our access to Christ's pattern of thinking. We have this when we build our lives around the commands of Christ in the Bible.

The winning conversation was demonstrated through the way Jesus lived His life. Jesus was excellent, lived with gratitude and had a diligent mindset. Because our identity is found in Christ we can adopt the mindset of Christ.

Col 3:2-4: *Since, then, you have been raised with Christ, set your hearts on things above, where Christ is, seated at the right hand of God. Set your minds on things above, not on earthly things. For you died, and your life is now hidden with Christ in God. When Christ, who is your life, appears, then you also will appear with Him in glory.*

The winning mindset will determine daily to:

1) Go one more step than I feel like going

My pain zone is my growth zone

Kingdom growth will take an uncomfortable and 'unreasonable' route.

If you want to become MORE valuable to your world then unlocking your internal value comes when you put the 'unreasonable' demands of the Kingdom on yourself. Jesus helped us to see this in His Sermon on the Mount:

Kingdom Key: *I tell you, do not resist an evil person. If anyone slaps you on the right cheek, turn to them the other cheek also. And if anyone wants to sue you and take your shirt, hand over your coat as well. If anyone forces you to go one mile, go with them two miles. Give to the one who asks you, and do not turn away from the one who wants to borrow from you* (Matt 5:39-42).

Striking someone is one of the most provocative things a human being can do. Jesus used examples such as this to describe how we can grow through the most extreme situations. Refusing to retaliate is not a natural human response but one which we can harness when Christ lives in us. He himself practiced what He preached during the beatings that led to his crucifixion.

While the demands on you currently may not be as extreme as the examples given by Jesus, know that you can go further than you feel like going. There is one who you can enable you to push through. Respond in His strength!

2) Pursue perfection without losing heart

My goal is my chase and not my prize

Kingdom Key: *Be perfect, therefore, as your heavenly Father is perfect* (Matthew 5:48).

Did Jesus set before his disciples an unachievable goal? The meaning of the Greek word "perfect" actually has a wider meaning than what we might imagine. The word used here is *teleios* which actually means mature and complete. Through the complete work of Christ we can exchange our old incomplete nature for the completeness of His nature. Jesus was in fact pointing to the fact that by living from our new nature, His design, you are empowered to live a strong and effective Kingdom life for Him.

Living in completeness or perfection in the Kingdom of God is not an event, it is a process. Whilst I can choose to draw upon the design I have in Christ, there are times when the old me will get in the way and I fail or make wrong choices. Jesus knew this when He spoke these words but He still expects a wholehearted commitment to the journey until His perfect nature is fully formed in us.

Jesus did not come to intensify our potential to fail. He knows that we fail, mess up, take wrong turns and find ourselves at dead ends. In fact He uses these as opportunities to refine us. Our responsibility is to keep heading for perfection and our wholehearted commitment will mean that we will cultivate excellence along the way. We must celebrate excellence because it is a sign that God's glory is seeping through the cracks of the vessel that is our life.

3) Acquire a new taste for the process

I can learn to do what I least like to do in order to achieve what I have always wanted to achieve.

When we create order in one part of our lives we suddenly acquire a taste for bringing order to any disordered part of our lives. The diligent mindset creates momentum across the whole of our life.

Kingdom Key: *A sluggard's appetite is never filled, but the desires of the diligent are fully satisfied* (Proverbs 13:4).

This Kingdom key helps us to realise that laziness and disorder will never harvest true and lasting satisfaction in our lives. Why? Because we are made in the image of a God who is ordered. Whilst laziness at first looks like a form of freedom, it actually results in consequences that force us to do what we won't want to do.

Kingdom Key: *Diligent hands will rule, but laziness ends in forced labour* (Proverbs 12:24).

It is better to force yourself to do something than have someone else force you to do something you do not want to do as a consequence of laziness.

Once you use the Kingdom key of excellence you unlock a desire to bring greater standards to every area. Diligence is a Kingdom mindset that unlocks success in our lives. You are called to have dominion/rule on this earth, to have success harnessing the resource that you have, and you do this by putting on the Kingdom mindset of diligence.

4) Exceed rather than maintain my best work

Your 'next best' can always be found

My best will only get better if I make the process of unlocking my new identity my priority.

Kingdom Key: *And we all, with unveiled face, beholding the glory of the Lord, are being transformed into the same image from* **one degree of glory** *to another* (2 Corinthians 3:18, ESV).

If daily I choose to invest time in understanding and knowing who I am in Christ then as I progress, my life has the potential to get better and better. This includes my relationships, finances, career and opportunities. Your best days and work are ahead if you pursue the goal of being more like Jesus.

5) Long to learn what I do not yet know

You learn about what you truly love

Kingdom Key: *For this very reason, make every effort to add to your faith goodness; and to goodness, knowledge; and to knowledge, self-control; and to self-control, perseverance; and to perseverance, godliness; and to godliness, mutual affection; and to mutual affection, love* (2 Peter 1:5-7).

Winning in life is about passionately pursuing what you have yet to understand, especially about God's Word and your cause. The more you learn, the more you can compete differently. Is your life different today from what it was a year ago or five years ago? The level to which you have engaged with the process of learning will determine the difference you will see in your progress.

God is looking for those who are hungry for MORE and have the cutting edge of the Kingdom.

Do you want more from God? He wants to give you more. Jesus said:

Kingdom Key: *Whoever has will be given more, and they will have an abundance. Whoever does not have, even what they have will be taken from them* (Matt 13:12).

6) Love life with the simple wonder of a child

Simplify your life until intrigue has space to move

The sensitivity of your senses dissipates over time. I notice that noises that make no difference to me are exceedingly loud for my son. My ears have lost a level of sensitivity that he still has. The same can be true for the things that excite us; the older we get the more it takes to get us excited about opportunity and adventure.

When our heart and soul ages we begin to lose sensitivity to what God is doing. We start to settle for less than God's best for our lives and we stop expecting the best from ourselves.

Paul talks about losing our 'sensitivity' toward sin and the way to counteract this internal ageing of spirit; he tells us to keep putting off our 'old self' which is being corrupted by its deceitful desires and to be made new in the attitude of our hearts.

Kingdom Key: *Having lost all sensitivity, they have given themselves over to sensuality so as to indulge in every kind of impurity, and they are full of greed. That, however, is not the way of life you learned when you heard about Christ and were taught in Him in accordance with the truth that is in Jesus. You were taught, with regard to your former way of life, to put off your old self, which is being corrupted by its deceitful desires; to be made new in the attitude of your minds; and to put on the new self, created to be like God in true righteousness and holiness* (Eph 4:19).

Actively putting off our old self is about making a choice to do the opposite of what we feel.

What can you do today to bring out your inner child? Remember what you do in one area of your life will challenge the others areas. Do something for the first time!

7) Go frequently beyond the expected norm

Create the response you want to see by planning to do something you don't normally do

It is God's grace in our lives that enables us to give in a way that wows the world around us. The Apostle Paul was wowed by the Macedonian church who despite every reason not to give, gave.

Kingdom Key: *In the midst of a very severe trial, their overflowing joy and their extreme poverty welled up in rich generosity. For I testify that they gave as much as they were able, and even beyond their ability. Entirely on their own, they urgently pleaded with us for the privilege of sharing in this service to the Lord's people. And they exceeded our expectations: <u>They gave themselves first of all to the Lord, and then by the will of God also to us</u>* (2 Corinthians 8:2-5).

When the grace of God flows in our lives it enables us to exceed the expectations of those around us. So how did the Macedonian church do it? The key is in verse 5. By giving themselves to Christ, in other words starting with WHO they were in Him, then giving themselves to the 'will of God', they unlocked their Kingdom potential (the WHY) and the results are still being talked about hundreds of years later.

Give your best today based on your WHO and WHY and you will become increasingly valuable to your world.

8) Make an extraordinary and demanding promise

Our quality of life is determined through the promises we choose to keep

A diligent mindset understands that excellence is about making extraordinary agreements that are difficult to keep and that this tension makes a demand on our potential and draws the best out of us.

Kingdom Key: *All you need to say is simply 'Yes' or 'No' anything beyond this comes from the evil one* (Matt 5:37).

Cultivating the valuable conversation inside us is about practicing diligence. We need to practice keeping the small agreements consistently in order for the Kingdom of God to flow through our lives. When we learn to keep the small agreements we can increase the size of those agreements and unlock our potential. This means learning to diligently say NO if saying YES means we are going to break that agreement. Our value is diminished when we over-commit and therefore under-deliver on our promises. Momentum is created when we build on completed agreements. The longer road of building up momentum is the more sustainable and fruitful path to building kingdom value in our world.

9) Appreciate those who are unappreciative

Quality is increased by practicing through resistance

Worship is about adding worth to someone or something. When we add worth to others as believers we are adding worth to God. The more that action costs us, the greater the sacrifice of praise we give to God. Showing appreciation to the unappreciative can be extremely difficult. However as Christ's representatives we give to add value not to get value.

Kingdom Key: *And I pray that you, being rooted and established in love, may have power, together with all the Lord's holy people, to grasp how wide and long and high and deep is the love of Christ, and to know this love that surpasses knowledge— that you may be filled to the measure of all the fullness of God* (Eph 3:17-19).

Keep on giving out regardless of the response because God will never leave you without reward. It is God who ultimately promotes you so do everything as if you were doing it for Him.

We can stay appreciated if we keep our roots deep in Jesus, drawing our appreciation from Him. Our supply for appreciating others will never dry up.

10) Perfect the art of surprising other people

Exceeding expectations communicates my value for others

David consecrated himself (set himself apart for God) and was given the epitaph, 'a man after God's own heart' (Acts 13:22). His life proved he carried a conviction of excellence. In 1 Samuel 18 Saul starts to become jealous of David and when he discovers that David wants to marry Michal his daughter he puts a hefty price tag on her.

Kingdom Key: *The king wants no other price for the bride than a hundred Philistine foreskins, to take revenge on his enemies* (1 Sam 18:25).

Saul's intention was that this audacious and somewhat delicate task would mean certain death for David. However, David demonstrated an excellent spirit! Not only did he achieve the challenge of 100 foreskins but he brought back 200! What did Saul's face look like when David brought them to him? Once again David superseded expectations. This made Saul even angrier.

David was not led by the reaction of others but a conviction to do everything as if he were doing it in worship to God.

Choose today to worship through your work and supersede expectations.

Regularly take time to imagine what that looks like for you and see yourself doing it.

This prepares you to be diligent and means you compete differently, you stand out through 'uncommon' behaviour.

Day 58: The Winning Choices of Competing Differently

They say actions speak louder than words. This means that our actions and what they produce are part of our external conversation driven by our internal conversation. If we are committed to improving all we do based on an inner drive to express value and appreciation for others then we have to become strong on evaluation. The definition of the word evaluation means to 'make a judgement as to the amount, number or value of something.'19 Unless we evaluate then we cannot measure the fruit that comes from the root of excellence.

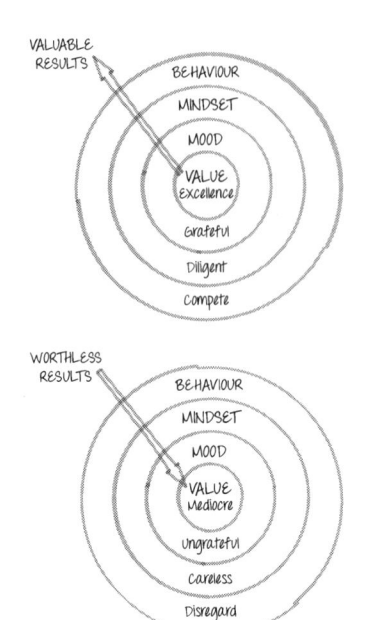

You increase your value based upon evaluation. For example:

There are two restaurants you like to visit. They both produce your favourite meal, Spaghetti Bolognese. Restaurant A is consistent and produces the same result every time. This is not a problem because at least you know what you are getting. Restaurant B greets you by saying, 'We cannot wait for you to order Spaghetti Bolognese today. We've tirelessly been working on the ingredients and presentation since we asked how we could make it better the last time you were here.'

While you like both restaurants and both have a good record, which one gets your custom? Which will you champion in conversations?

Restaurant B! They have operated from a belief that they are EXCELLENT which means that they APPRECIATE you so much that they ask you how they can improve your experience with them. This exhibits their desire to improve what they do regardless of what anyone else is doing.

The areas of your life you EVALUATE are the areas you truly value. Here is a simple tool to evaluate what you do:

Expectation *exceeded*
Value *added*
Alternative *approach*
Limits *identified*
Understand *perspectives*
Adjust *immediately*

Teach to *improve*
Explore *imaginatively*

Expectation *exceeded*

Did I exceed expectation? Feedback is priceless. While it is possible to try and anticipate what was in the mind of the other person, there is nothing like hearing direct feedback. Not only does this help them improve but it increases the value that person feels because everyone loves an opportunity to be heard.

Value *added*

Would I have felt valued if I were them? Putting yourself in the position of the other person or someone you love is a great way of challenging our actions. It follows the golden rule to treat others as we would like to be treated.

Alternative *approach*

What or how could I have done it differently? Sometimes we can simply perpetuate the same activity and expect different results. Looking at alternative approaches helps to lift our thinking and keep us fresh in our thought process. It also gives permission to think outside the box.

Limits *identified*

Where were my limits and how could I push past these in future? It is important to be honest and identify limits. No one enjoys looking at limitations but it is vital to identify them to create a way past them now and to form a longer term strategy to overcome them in the future. If there is a financial limit to our action then it might not be something we can immediately rectify but we can use this information to feed our goal-setting.

Understand *perspectives*

What did I understand about the other person and/or myself through this action? Our actions help reveal a lot about ourselves and others and unless we take time to look at this then we do not best inform our future actions. If we are committed to improvement then gaining understanding is vital for building wisdom.

Adjust *immediately*

What would I adjust next time to increase the value of what I communicate? Future plans are good and vital but momentum is about consistent improvements. It is amazing to see the impact of accumulative improvements.

Teach *to improve*

Who could teach me and who could I teach to improve what I do? Learning is about being the pupil and the teacher. Placing ourselves in these two roles multiplies the rate of what we learn. Trending what someone else who is ahead of us does on the journey is vital. Find success and tap into that person's wisdom. Creating a teaching moment where you share what you are learning helps you to focus on what you do from a new angle. It also creates accountability because you have publicly committed to an expected standard.

Explore *imaginatively*

While incremental improvements are essential, it is important to keep approaching your desired result with a blank sheet of paper. Ask yourself, 'If I had no prior knowledge of achieving my objective, how would I go about doing it for the first time?' You cannot truly eradicate all knowledge but you can uncover hidden possibilities. Remember there is MORE in you than you think and there are different ways of drawing out the potential that has been locked up in you. You imagination is a powerful tool; it is like a dog pulling at the leash. Sometimes you have to unhook it and let it burn off some energy!

If we are not growing, we are dying. There is no middle ground. The way we keep any part of our lives growing is to keep investing fresh thought and ideas. This is innovation and we innovate what we truly appreciate.

SECTION 9: BE MORE VALUABLE

Day 59: The Winning Evaluation

Benchmark which mindset you have when it comes to the VALUABLE conversation.

The fruit of my actions will reveal the root of the conversations I host. Today we are looking at ten questions based on situations we find ourselves in and I encourage you to be brutally honest as to which response most fits your nature.

1) Satisfaction—When do you feel a sense of satisfaction in something you do?

Consumed - My satisfaction comes from completion rather than the quality of what has been produced

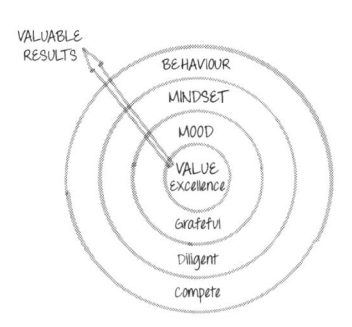

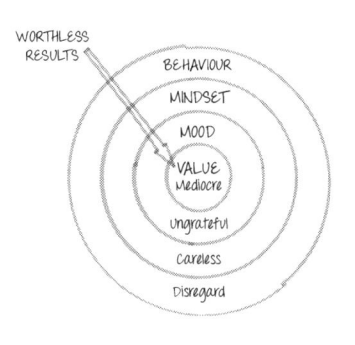

Complacent - Ticking an activity off a to-do list is more important than how my activity represents and reflects on me

Competitor - I will sign off with 'That'll do' but will make a mental note to do better next time. Any loss in quality will be put down to factors outside of my immediate control

Champion - I will never sign off with the words, 'That'll do'. Whenever this phrase is thought or spoken, I either need to spend more time on it or shouldn't be doing it at all.

2) Perfection - What do you feel about aiming for perfection?

Consumed - Perfection is an unobtainable goal and therefore should never be an aspiration

Complacent - Perfection is an admirable yet unrealistic goal

Competitor - Perfection is a valid goal that produces my personal best

Champion - Perfection requires the narrowing of a goal to a size where all my energy and effort can produce exceptional results - the wider the goal the lower the quality of results.

3) Average—What is your view of an average approach to an activity?

Consumed - Average feels good. The feeling of not standing out is actually one that satisfies

Complacent - The avoidance of the bad is my overriding aspiration rather than the pull of the best

Competitor - Average is a point through which I grow and a baseline from which to work

Champion - Average is an attitude not a result. 'Could I have done better?' The answer is always 'yes.' Average is distasteful and jars against my belief system. It is better not to have done something than to be represented by average

4) Evaluation—What is you feeling toward evaluation?

Consumed - Evaluation involves unnecessary paperwork and creates a negative feeling. Ignorance on the other hand is bliss

Complacent - Evaluation is an aspiration and should always be attempted

Competitor - Evaluation is a deal breaker. Evaluation should be the Siamese twin of the activity

Champion - If there is no evaluation, there should have been no activity. Evaluation expresses value. What you evaluate you appreciate.

5) Comparison—What are my thoughts on comparison? Is it valid?

Consumed - Comparison is a valid activity because it gives me confidence that I'm not doing that badly.

Complacent - Comparison is something I struggle with when

I occasionally raise my level of expectation. In fact it is one of the reasons why I revert back to having low aspirations. I do not like how it makes me feel

Competitor - Comparison is something I disapprove of but secretly do when I feel low. While it's not verbalised, it is internalised.

Champion - The only comparison involves how I am doing compared to how I know I can do. All other comparison is poison.

6) Innovation—What are my thoughts about innovation?

Consumed - Innovation is for the entrepreneurs of this world. It's not for me

Complacent - Innovation is an event not a process. It occurs sporadically when I want to achieve something special

Competitor - I wait for a crisis in order to be forced to innovate

Champion - Innovation is a key tool for personal progress. If any part of my life is not innovating, it is dying. Innovation is a discipline that releases fresh life into the day-to-day

7) Mistakes—What do I think when I make mistakes?

Consumed - It helps me to remember why I do not attempt to stretch myself too much

Complacent - Mistakes are a part of a life; I just have to pick myself up and move on when I make them

Competitor - Mistakes are a part of life and should be lessons. However, the lessons I learn are generic and not very specific. The potential of the mistake is not fully realised

Champion - Mistakes are diamonds in the rough. My mistakes reveal a lot about me. Evaluating my mistakes may feel painful but they can create a pain-free future

8) Failure—How does failure effect me?

Consumed - My failure becomes my reason for not trying. Raising the bar raises hopes only to be disappointed

Complacent - Failure makes me sad but after a few weeks the feeling wears off and I keep going

Competitor - While failure is not a goal, it is part of life. I brush myself down and press on toward a better outcome with renewed vigour

Champion - Failure becomes a strategic moment that can become as valuable, possibly more valuable, than a successful moment. I decide to use it rather than lose it

9) Feedback—How do I incorporate feedback into my life?

Consumed - What I do is connected to who I am. When someone criticises what I do, regardless of how constructive, it hurts

Complacent - If it is given to me I do listen and take it on board and try to remember the key points for the future

Competitor - I will receive feedback and use it to make me better. I only get defensive when I feel the criticism is given in the wrong spirit. However, I do not actively seek out feedback

Champion - I actively seek feedback because what I do needs to improve and is not connected to my self-worth. I can even use negative criticism given in a wrong way to improve what I do

10) Unappreciated—How do I act towards those who show a distinct lack of appreciation?

Consumed - When no one shows me appreciation it causes me to lose an appetite for trying. I cannot deal with the absence of value this creates in me

Complacent - It does affect me and it causes me to lose momentum. I can get bitter and the wind goes from my sails. However, that feeling will wear off but it does regulate the effort I put into something from that moment on. In fact, if I am honest, the level of appreciation I get sets the level of expectation I place on myself

Competitor - I can shake off a lack of appreciation quickly and

I will still compete to do well but will disregard the person who does not appreciate me

Champion - My internal belief of excellence provides the stimulus to value even the unappreciative. I believe that it can have an effect on the person who shows a lack of appreciation even if they do not show it. Sometimes people have become the product of a value-starved upbringing

PRACTICE V POTENTIAL of the VALUABLE conversation

Based on the answers to the above questions, how many times could you honestly say that your answer was 'champion'?

Consumer: 1-2 times

Complacent: 3-5 times

Competitor: 6-8 times

Champion: 9-10 times

My Overall POTENTIAL: I AM A CHAMPION

My Overall PRACTICE: I HAVE BEEN A _____

In order for my practice to match my potential I have identified the following three things I can do to unlock the champion in me:

1_____

2_____

3_____

Day 60: The Winning Accountability

Pulling this whole week under the title of 'uncommon care not unchecked choices' enables us to be able to review this conversation quickly. Using the dice in spare moments throughout the day, or in a small group, helps me to focus on the inner conversation of excellence.

The Winning Dice—*Uncommon care not unchecked choices*

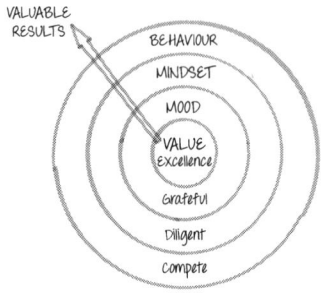

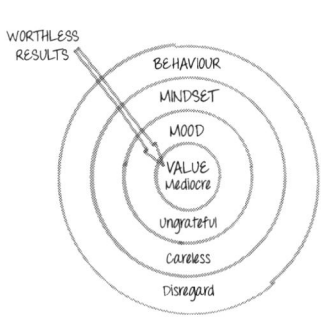

Create a personal culture that says, 'I make it my aim always to be care-ful and never care-less because I need to increase the value I place on people through my conversations with them in both word and action.' If the saying *'people do not care how much we know until they know how much we care'* is true, and I am all about people, then this is a non-negotiable axiom.

I want to be described as having an **uncommon care** in the transactions of my life. Credibility and reputation take a long time to build but can be pulled down in a moment with an **unchecked choice.** Maintaining an awareness of my 'care levels' is critical so I can make the most of every opportunity. How I maximise the potential of an opportunity is in my care-full handling of it.

Being care-full is about focus on detail. Failing to pay attention and being unfocussed has a wider impact than I will first realise. Constant neglect may not reveal obvious damage at first but its accumulative effect when not dealt with will become significant. The words, 'I couldn't care less,' are off limits. Regardless of how I feel I **choose to be care-full** with my words because they have immense shaping power. They create my future and potentially shape the future of others.

Excellence is a conversation I have beyond my spoken words; my body language, facial expressions and my response to situations and people all exhibit my true value of self and others. Even when people irritate me and treat me badly, I care-fully take every opportunity to better myself and ask how I can do them good. When I feel forced, I force my feelings to do what is right. I am care-full because what I do impacts the people around me and everything I do reflects on those who back me.

I choose to be uncommonly care-full in my fun so as to be considerate of how others feel. I choose to check my choices to an uncommon standard because I am valuable and others need my potential value to be realised.

This chapter is shorter as it is designed to be more reflective so that key commitments and decisions can be made during a full review of the week.

Step 1: RECALL together

Here is a quick review of what a person with uncommon care and unchecked choices looks like so we can stay on course to allow EXCELLENCE to have the loudest voice, drowning out MEDIOCRITY. Here is a description based on what we have looked at this week:

What does uncommon care look like?

I respond rather than react in a situation in which most people would react
I refuse to allow a 'that will do' attitude to exist
What I do stands out; it becomes 'outstanding'
I show great consideration
I always seek to understand before being understood
I continually seek to do what I always do in new and improved ways
I carry out my commitments on time and beyond the expected standard
I learn to anticipate need rather than wait for a request for help
When I fail, I seek to learn why and use what I find as a lesson to improve
I am friendly in all forms of communication
I sign off well from conversations leaving others with a smile
I smile and am pleasant at all times
I smell good, look good and generally seek to present the very best that I have

What does an unchecked choice look like?

I will generally be disorganised
My desk and area of work will look cluttered
I procrastinate on jobs that need doing
I gravitate towards what I enjoy most but will leave undesirable jobs till last even if they then impact negatively on others
I lack awareness of how I come across
My work displays a lack of care which then communicates a lack of love (spelling mistakes, bad grammar, things thrown together etc...)
I am quick to comment but do not realise how it makes the other person feel
I am hit and miss on following through what I have committed to do
I fail to follow processes that are set in place
My work starts to be picked up by others and I continually lean on others to get things done
I am quick to acknowledge my own rights but will cause the rights of others to be compromised through my poor performance
I neglect to recognise context and talk about sensitive issues in the wrong places in front of the wrong people
I fail to respond to communications within a reasonable amount of time

Step 2: REVIEW with others

Get together weekly with people who are committed to developing the winning conversations throughout the journey of this book and this week discuss the following:

i) Why is excellence uncommon?

ii) What examples can you think of that demonstrate the potential impact of unchecked choices left unaddressed over prolonged periods of time?

iii) Where could uncommon care potential take a person if it becomes a daily discipline?

iv) What goals could you set to raise the bar on uncommon care in your relationships, finances, health and vocation?

v) Can you think of a recent situation when uncommon care and/or an unchecked choice created a noticeable result? How did it make you feel?

vi) What relationships inspire me to have uncommon care? Which ones do I have to be aware of that influence me to make unchecked choices? Do I have to make relational re-alignments?

Step 3: REFLECTION to be shared

Now create a reflection that you can share with someone in your group or someone else that you are coaching to be a champion in life. Why not take the time with your children, a loved one, a friend over coffee to share what you have learnt. Simply sharing this reflection will accomplish much in your life and deepen relationships, enriching them with vulnerability and moments of movement.

Follow our basic structure:

i) What I realised for the first time/again this week is ... (share the thought)

ii) The change I need to make is ... (share the action point)

iii) Can you help me make it? ... (invite help and create accountability)

Once you have got into the habit of doing this, why not decide to turn your thoughts into a blog or even take your coaching to another level? There is so much in you and it is directly connected to your commitment to stretch yourself.

THE WINNING KEYS

Section 10: The Winning Momentum

Day 61: Winning Gears 1

The early Church turned from the small and somewhat 'insignificant' looking twelve men into a world shaping force. Through the process of discipleship, Jesus unlocked an unstoppable momentum in them.

While the early Church had no structure, funding or track record, Acts 2:42 shows us that they chose to centre their lives around:

Christ's **PRINCIPLES**: The apostles communicated these through their teaching and this built a deep awareness of God.

Christ's **PURPOSE**: The discipline of prayer kept the passion of the purpose alive inside them and raised their level of aspiration - what they were believing for.

Christ's **PRIORITY**: The sharing of bread and wine, otherwise known as Communion, kept their focus on the work of the cross and resurrection. This sharpened their priorities, reducing distraction.

Christ's **PRACTICE**: Fellowship with one another created oneness. Living life-on-life cultivated an interdependent environment.

While they, like us, would have been tempted to veer off course through self-centred and independent living, they led lives driven by principles that produced consistent choices. The level of their commitment to practicing these principles meant that they unlocked extraordinary results. Thus we read in Acts 2:47 *that the Lord added to their number daily those who were being saved.*

As I took the pattern above and put it into the context of my daily life I immediately saw my challenge. These practices fall into the 'non-urgent' category which means they get superseded by the things I feel and think are more important. If I am honest I prioritise the quick wins rather than the tried and tested principles of the Kingdom. I am then surprised when the results I desire do not materialise. I have bypassed the pattern of the Kingdom, which is inside-out.

The early Christians were different. They learned how to build momentum by 'moving through the gears.'

Gear 1: IMMERSE - get in an environment

The early Church created an immersive experience through a community that founded itself on the principles of God's Word. Whilst I guess there were many days when they did not feel like pulling out the scrolls and manuscripts that they had, or listening to the teaching of the apostles, they carried an awareness that these principles were the keys of the Kingdom that Jesus had given (Matt 16:19). If they wanted to see Kingdom results they needed to immerse themselves in the principles of God's Word which gave them their authority.

How is this done? You create an immersive environment through continual conversation. The process of asking questions and the sharing of experiences based upon principles causes people to invest in their conscious minds but also the deeper levels of soul and spirit.

A key is a sign of authority. If I gave you the key to my car it is a sign that I give you authority to use it. The principles of God's Word are our authority and without them we end up being slaves to our circumstances rather than making our circumstances slaves to God's Word.

Immersion creates the awareness you need

Awareness is about belief. Let's say that we had a conversation in which I told you how proud I was of my wife's compassion towards other people. The moment you meet her you are consciously and subconsciously looking for signs that validate or invalidate the belief that I have shared. If you trust me as a person then you are positively looking to validate that belief. Likewise if you do not trust me you look to validate your own suspicions.

Our beliefs seek to validate themselves through experience. This means that you have subconsciously already determined the day you want to have through your belief system, regardless of what you are thinking right now.

Such is the power of belief.

The key importance of God's Word for us as believers is that when we centre our lives on the principles it carries it heightens our awareness of God and makes it possible for others to have an experience of Him because His word infuses our internal conversation. Our internal conversation is the lens through which we view the world around us. Our core belief system is taken off sleep mode and we both consciously and subconsciously look for God in the everyday situations and conversations that we have.

Kingdom Key: *The point is: Before you trust, you have to listen. But unless Christ's Word is preached, there's nothing to listen to* (Romans 10:17, The Message).

Going back to my analogy, if you never met my wife Leanne then you would have no opportunity to know her for yourself. You would simply know about her which is different from actually knowing her. If you were able to hear her speak then suddenly you would have opportunity to own the belief that she is compassionate.

Many Christians know about God but the belief is not deep enough to bring about an actual experience of Him. Immersion helps us to transition from possessing a concept into the establishing of a conviction.

Immersion creates clarity

The early Church created a community that continued Christ's ministry and demonstrated His presence on earth as his Body (1

Corinthians 12:27). The only way this small collective could unlock their Kingdom potential was by committing themselves to an immersion that would produce Christ-likeness in them. People find clarity about who Jesus is when we commit ourselves to immersing ourselves in the principles of His Word.

Kingdom Key: *Cultivate these things. Immerse yourself in them. The people will all see you mature right before their eyes! Keep a firm grasp on both your character and your teaching. Don't be diverted. Just keep at it. Both you and those who hear you will experience salvation* (1 Tim 4:15-16, The Message).

What we cultivate we create and what we create we commission. From the beliefs we mull over in our internal conversation we create mindsets and actions that form our world. What we form in our world we commission in the lives of those we have influence over, such as our families and friends and those we lead.

Immersion creates a new predictability

Growth in the early Church became the rhythm of the Church. As the first Christians continued to immerse themselves in the principles of God's Word they unlocked the principles of the Kingdom. They became a group of people who were:

Prominent to the world around them

Resilient through persecution

Memorable through their love for one another

Influential in their reach

Expansive in their growth and spread

Valuable in their contribution to the world

The following Bible passages from The Book of Acts exemplify the predictable, positive trajectory of the church: Acts 5:14; 6:1; 6:7; 9:31; 11:21; 16:5.

Our growth and results can become predictable if we focus on the process ahead of the prize. The process creates health and the reason we should focus on health is because healthy things grow.

What you delight in, you drive deeper

The word discipline can often make us lose excitement. And yet because the early Church created momentum with their disciplines, they rode on the waves of extraordinary favour.

Kingdom Key: *They followed a daily discipline of worship in the Temple followed by meals at home, every meal a celebration, exuberant and joyful, as they praised God. People in general liked what they saw. Every day their number grew as God added those who were saved* (Acts 2:46-47, The Message).

Discipline was the key here. The first Christians exercised discipline in order to get these principle-driven practices moving. We are often turned off the idea of discipline because we see it has to great an effort. However the effort it takes to create momentum in our regular disciplines whilst high at first, will reduce over time as we find a rhythm that becomes our new normal.

I find the first five minutes of a long distance run to be the hardest because establishing rhythm takes more energy than keeping a rhythm. After a while the benefit of the process becomes your new pattern of behaviour. As soon as the benefits of our new behaviour are witnessed we perpetuate the desire to keep pressing on with the behaviour that produces the results we love.

Conversation with God:

Father, I thank you that you have made a way so that I can immerse myself in your presence (Heb 10:19). Your presence realigns my desires and my thoughts to you and I choose this day to seek after you with all my heart knowing that in doing so I will be moved to action for your Kingdom purposes. I want to experience you through the way I live my life today.

Day 62: Winning Gears 2

Gear 2: MAP- Make A Plan

Create tension

King Solomon penned proverbs, which are wisdom keys that

help us to unlock the potential of our lives. He recognized that God built creation with His wisdom (Proverbs 3:19) and that if we look close enough we can see the principles of God in action. In one of his proverbs he encouraged his listeners to take a look at one of life's apparently 'insignificant' creatures and to make notes.

Kingdom Key: *Go to the ant, you sluggard; consider its ways and be wise! It has no commander, no overseer or ruler, yet it stores its provisions in summer and gathers its food at harvest. How long will you lie there, you sluggard? When will you get up from your sleep? A little sleep, a little slumber, a little folding of the hands to rest- and poverty will come on you like a thief and scarcity like an armed man* (Proverbs 6:6).

God has wired the ant with an internal map causing it to build up a stock of provision in the harvest time ready for the wintertime when the supply runs dry. This insect is self-motivated and self-led to follow a plan that works for building a life of supply.

God has given us everything we could possibly need for a winning life but we must tap into the mapping ability He has given to us. The difference between humans and ants is that sin has tapped into our hardwiring and we live for the NOW rather than being led by the NOT YET.

Due to our unreliable hardwiring - which Solomon here describes as being 'sluggish' - we regularly have to go through a planning process to bring out the potential in us. In this we have to be diligent. Decisions to put off the seemingly unimportant planning process will result in a loss of supply and in poverty. Alternatively we can be like the ant, self-motivated and self-led to check our life maps and stay on course for a life of supply that feeds our winning purpose in life.

Conversation with God:

Forgive me, Father God, for my sluggish ways. Help me to construct a plan in partnership with the Holy Spirit that puts the demand on me that will unlock my Kingdom potential.

Gear 3: SHARE your plan with a coach

The only way of achieving our God-given purpose is to be willing to fail our way to achieving it. Our willingness to be open about our failings will have a great bearing upon our ability to gain wisdom in order to get better.

Kingdom Key: *Therefore confess your sins to each other and pray for each other so that you may be healed. The prayer of a righteous person is powerful and effective* (James 5:16).

The combination of transparency and honesty with other believers with faith-filled prayer and encouragement will allow heaven to get involved in helping you to do what you cannot do on your own. Your willingness to become vulnerable with others will be increased the more passionate you become about your goal.

Conversation with God:

I thank you, Father, for Jesus, who demonstrated the power of humility. Help me not to be fearful of sharing my weakness because I know by drawing on the help of others through my honesty you will make me strong.

Gear 4: RESOURCE your plan: rebuild your schedule, budget and energy around your plan

Once we have immersed ourselves in the plan and increased our desire to see the goal achieved, we then can manage our resources better. We are more likely to say 'no' to options in our lives that will take resource, time or energy away from the goal that we are passionately pursuing. Our winning purpose requires razor sharp focus which means we are able to discern what is distracting us from where we are headed.

In Luke 14 Jesus helps us to see the importance of planning in His kingdom. He points to the everyday natural tasks that require diligent planning in order to succeed and helps us to see that the same is true of Kingdom assignments. The key point Jesus makes is that when we take on a Kingdom assignment we have to put EVERYTHING behind it or not take it on.

Kingdom Key: *Suppose one of you wants to build a tower. Won't you first sit down and estimate the cost to see if you have enough money to complete it? For if you lay the foundation and are not able to finish it, everyone who sees it will ridicule you, saying, 'This person began to build and wasn't able to finish.'*

Or suppose a king is about to go to war against another king. Won't he first sit down and consider whether he is able with ten thousand men to oppose the one coming against him with twenty thousand? If he is not able, he will send a delegation while the other is still a long way off and will ask for terms of peace. In the same way, those of you who do not give up everything you have cannot be my disciples (Luke 14:28-33).

Kingdom planning it not driven by a desire to accumulate but by stewarding what we have so we can measure and stay aware of the cost.

Conversation with God:

I thank you Father that you have entrusted me with health, energy and finances. They all belong to you and I know that I am simply managing them. Help me to use them to build your Kingdom and increase my capacity to handle more so that I can increase my effectiveness.

Gear 5: COACH and TEACH others: Learn through teaching others. Start with those close to you.

When we use the most valuable skill we have (coaching) on the most valuable people in our lives then we will not need convincing of the need to carry on through all our relationships.

For those of us with children, the coaching has to start at home. Remember, one of the important aspects of coaching is that by doing it we are making ourselves accountable to what we are teaching. Our teaching is part of that immersive experience and who better to make ourselves accountable to than those who see us the most. Our family and friends get to see the real me. We will find that when we start with our family we will create an awareness of how we can coach and teach almost anyone in the various contexts that we find ourselves in.

Kingdom Key: *Start children off on the way they should go, and even when they are old they will not turn from it* (Proverbs 22:6).

Coaching moments have different guises, some are organised and others are organic.

As people who follow Jesus we need to involve ourselves in both.

Kingdom Key: *Jesus, undeterred, went right ahead and gave His charge: "God authorised and commanded me to commission you: <u>Go out and train everyone you meet</u>, far and near, in this way of life, marking them by baptism in the threefold name: Father, Son, and Holy Spirit. Then instruct them in the practice of all I have commanded you* (Matthew 28:18-20, The Message).

Jesus makes it clear that we are commanded and commissioned to go and train others. This is a priority for all who follow Jesus. Very often Christians have struggled to see how they can train and disciple when they are working the best hours of their week in secular jobs. However, as we have seen throughout this book, training and coaching can be done in any context and does not require an 'official' ministry title. Whilst we need to take care when it comes to sharing our faith through our work, we can add value to people, thus demonstrating the Kingdom through behaviour.

You are a coach for Christ so it's time to start coaching! Why not think about holding a small group discussion based on The Winning Conversation book in your work place? Help to add value to people and show them you care about unlocking the MORE that is in them!

Who knows what conversations will follow?

Some of you who are reading this book will go on to coach for a living and through your coaching will be able to demonstrate what an authentic Christ follower looks like.

Conversation with God:

Father, I thank you for those who have trained and discipled me. Help me to be aware of the urgency to coach and train others for your Kingdom starting with those closest to me. I also ask that you direct me through your Holy Spirit to the people you want me to coach on a more organised/intentional level.

Gear 6: BUILD a life that seeks to help others unlock what is in them through your PURPOSE.

By regularly asking the question 'what difference can I make?' we create an awareness of the world around us.

Ultimately our *life map* is about helping others in Jesus' name. The way we avoid getting caught up in self-analysis and introspection is to constantly seek out serving opportunities. After all, your USP as a person is your **Unique Serving Prospect**.

Our *life map* is about creating focus while at the same time realising that the journey is going to be full of surprises about how we are used and who we serve. We are after all working in partnership with God the Holy Spirit (2 Corinthians 6:1) who will guide us and make us aware of the steps we need to take in our service of others.

Kingdom Key: *Above all, love each other deeply, because love covers over a multitude of sins. Offer hospitality to one another without grumbling. Each of you should use whatever gift you have received to serve others, as faithful stewards of God's grace in its various forms. If anyone speaks, they should do so as one who speaks the very words of God. If anyone serves, they should do so with the strength God provides, so that in all things God may be praised through Jesus Christ. To Him be the glory and the power forever and ever. Amen* (1 Peter 4:8-11).

In short we hold the rope and create the tension for immersing ourselves in our life map and in an ongoing conversation with God the Holy Spirit, willing to go anywhere and do anything He leads us to.

Our course = life map planning

Our steps = Spirit-led serving

Kingdom Key: *In their hearts humans plan their course, but the Lord establishes their steps* (Proverbs 16:9).

Conversation with God:

Father, I am aware that your ways are higher than my ways and your thoughts greater than my thoughts. I bring all that I have prepared and lay it on the altar and give you full permission to do what you want with it. I thank you that you know what is best for me and I walk into today listening to that still small voice that is guiding me.

Day 63: The Winning Awareness 1

Living by faith is about allowing the unseen reality of God and His Kingdom to influence the visible reality of our lives (2 Corinthians 5:7). We are naturally drawn to what can be seen visibly and our choices will often be driven by this bias. However, the winning conversation is about maintaining awareness that the God who lives in me is my starting point for my choices and decisions.

i) Soul hunger

Our life-giving source is God who created us (Gen 1:26). We carry the same natural temptation of Adam and Eve to fulfil our desires from the outside-in, through that which looks good and feels good (Gen 3:6). Cultivating the winning conversation driven by God's principles will unlock the supply of heaven to fill our souls with love, joy, peace and hope (Phil 4:19).

Our source comes from His power not from our striving.

Kingdom Key: *His divine power has given us everything we need for a godly life through our knowledge of Him who called us by His own glory and goodness* (2 Peter 1:3).

The resource that supplies a godly life comes from me building my life around my knowledge of Christ which creates my experience of Him through obedient living. When I build around His consistent commands in my life, that consistency makes me compatible for the plans and purposes that He has for me. While my winning goal may highlight my lack of current capability, I know that I will be made capable if I keep building my internal conversation on the unchanging truths of who Christ is and who I am in Him.

Producer verses consumer

Paul helps us to see that our consumption of the love, joy, peace and hope of God is so that we can overflow into the lives of others. God wants WHO He is to cascade through his creation and you and I are part of His 'pipeline.'

Kingdom Key: *May the God of hope fill you with all joy and peace as you trust in Him, so that you may overflow with hope by the power of the Holy Spirit* (Romans 15:13).

The flow of heaven is available to run through your life so you do not have to settle for a spiritual drought in the 'desert' of your circumstances.

The prophet Jeremiah helps us to see that when our souls feed on what man has to offer, we end up in lack.

Kingdom Key: *This is what the Lord says: "Cursed is the one who trusts in man, who draws strength from mere flesh and whose heart turns away from the Lord. That person will be like a bush in the wastelands; they will not see prosperity when it comes. They will dwell in the parched places of the desert, in a salt land where no one lives"* (Jeremiah 17:5-7).

However, when we draw on the resource of a consistent God (Heb 13:8) we can flourish in order to help others flourish.

Kingdom Key: *Blessed is the one who trusts in the Lord, whose confidence is in Him. They will be like a tree planted by the water that sends out its roots by the stream. It does not fear when heat comes; its leaves are always green. It has no worries in a year of drought and never fails to bear fruit* (Jeremiah 17:7-8).

ii) Conversation clashes

Any frustration in my life right now will be due to the distance between my expectations and my reality. This is the result of us carrying an inconsistent internal conversation. When my internal conversation does not line up with God then my heavenly assignment to make a difference in this world leads to striving and ultimately failing in my own strength. This can and will only end up one way -a burnout or, worse still, crashing out of the race.

When the consistency of God's Word leads our lives it produces a consistency in our soul. When I look at the life of Joseph (Gen 37-50) I see a man whose extremely inconsistent circumstances were navigated from a consistency that flowed from his commitment to keeping his assignment and the God of the assignment as his focus. His circumstances could easily have caused him to draw conclusions about God and himself that would have ultimately robbed him of his dream. However, whether he was in the pit, Potiphar's house, the prison or the palace, he lived a life that was driven by the consistency of God leading him.

This consistent living produced the realisation of his dream.

Kingdom Key: *There should be a consistency that runs through us all. For Jesus doesn't change—yesterday, today, tomorrow, he's always totally himself* (Heb 13:8 , The Message).

Conversation with God:

Father, I thank you for your consistent nature. As I build my life around the commands of your Word, may it unlock a consistency in my inner conversation. I am sorry for the words that I speak to myself that are incompatible with who you have made me. I choose to speak words of life that make me capable of carrying out the assignment that you have for me.

Day 64: The Winning Awareness 2

iii) Convincing conmen

Our internal conversation is a battle of competing voices. We all have strong defaults that will cause us to gravitate toward a self-centred losing conversation.

Kingdom Key: *The heart is deceitful above all things and beyond cure. Who can understand it? "I the Lord search the heart and examine the mind, to reward each person according to their conduct, according to what their deeds deserve"* (Jeremiah 17:9-10).

It is essential that we take enough time to stop and allow a divine appraisal to take place led by the Holy Spirit (John 16:13) and God's Word (Heb 4:12). Jeremiah reminds us that left to its own devices our heart will hijack our conversation and ultimately our Kingdom assignment.

When I read God's Word I should be looking for the question God is asking me. 'What is Jesus saying to me through what I am reading?' This reveals the true state of my heart. When I do this, and involve other people to whom I make myself accountable, I also stay on top of my 'conversation clash.'

It is dangerous to believe that my motivation will always stay on track without a daily MOT with the Holy Spirit. We can use the Bible to fool ourselves and reinforce incorrect scripting. That is not the approach we should take. We approach the Bible to have a revelation of Jesus. When we see Him in a new light it reveals more about who we are in Him. This helps us to kill off the old conversation attached to my old identity and to embrace the winning conversation attached to my new identity in Him. The more I see myself in Him, the more His consistency becomes my consistency which helps me avoid conversation clash.

iv) Fear of feedback

If the fear of the Lord is the beginning of knowledge (Proverbs 1:7) then a fear of feedback, because of how it will possibly make us feel, reveals true ignorance.

I have often struggled in this area over the years. My determination to do well meant that I would avoid conversations or situations that would highlight my lack. Looking back I can see this was ignorant behaviour and counterproductive to my development. If my motive was to grow in order to serve other people then I would learn to see past my feelings because of the burning passion I had to achieve my goal. I can see that at times my goal was simply to look good.

If you fear feedback like I did then be aware that we need what I call 'motivation salvation.' Our motivation needs to be reborn from being self-centred to Christ-centred.

Kingdom Key: *You are the ones chosen by God, chosen for the high calling of priestly work, chosen to be a holy people, God's instruments to do His work and speak out for Him, to tell others of the night-and-day difference He made for you—from nothing to something, from rejected to accepted* (2 Peter 1:9-10, The Message).

Peter reveals that my value has already been set and no level of performance by me can either subtract or even add to it.

One way that we can avoid the fear of feedback is to focus on WHY we need it. If our goal is to be reflectors of His glory then we need to identify what could be deflecting that glory (2 Corinthians 3:8).

It's time to get your eyes off yourself and fully focused on Him and the people you are here to serve. Fight the fear and go find feedback!

v) Fruitless fights

Fruitless fights are when we allow outside voices to interfere with our internal conversation. The greater the provocation to react the more potential we have to instil a deeper conviction through blessing rather than cursing in our response.

Kingdom Key: *But to you who are listening I say: Love your enemies, do good to those who hate you, bless those who curse you, pray for those who mistreat you. If someone slaps you on one cheek, turn to them the other also. If someone takes your coat, do not withhold your shirt from them. Give to everyone who asks you, and if anyone takes what belongs to you, do not demand it back. Do to others as you would have them do to you* (Luke 6:27-31).

Jesus calls on His followers to use the element of surprise when someone places an unfair demand on us - to respond from a heart that seeks to bless the offender as opposed to reacting to the offence.

Whenever we seek to deal with the symptoms of a person's poor choices we actually waste our time and energy. However, when we love someone by dealing with the root, we turn what could have been fruitless into something fruitful.

Why walk one mile with someone who demands that from you when you could take the second mile causing them to move from feeling a false sense of power as a persecutor to being rendered powerless through an act of mercy? (Matt 5:41)

When offended we can choose to either own the offence or own the responsibility to use it as a unique serving prospect (USP). Any offence offered to you is a fight that does not belong to you. Don't be like the person in Proverbs 26:17 who rushes headlong into a pointless and energy-draining encounter.

Kingdom Key: *Like one who grabs a stray dog by the ears is someone who rushes into a quarrel not their own* (Proverbs 26:17).

Conversation with God:

Father God, I invite you to examine my heart and to silence the competing voices of selfishness and sin. I choose to allow your voice to call the shots in my life. Help me to actively fight the fear of feedback and find trusted voices that will speak the truth to me in love (Eph 4:15). I want to get better, to show myself as a trusted servant.

Day 65: Momentum killers and builders

Momentum Killers

Losing sight of the goal

It is easy to lose sight of our overarching goal when life gets busy. We can learn about the power of focus from Peter, the disciple who walked on water. When Peter realised that Jesus was walking on the water he was inspired by a goal. This goal caused his faith to rise.

Kingdom Key: *Jesus immediately said to them: "Take courage! It is I. Don't be afraid." "Lord, if it's you," Peter replied, "tell me to come to you on the water." "Come," he said. Then Peter got down out of the boat, walked on the water and came toward Jesus* (Matthew 14:27-29).

The moment Peter took his eyes off Christ he lost the momentum of his miracle.

But when he saw the wind, he was afraid and, beginning to sink, cried out, "Lord, save me!" Immediately Jesus reached out His hand and caught him. "You of little faith," he said, "why did you doubt?" (Matthew 14:30-31).

I have not found a better catalyst for momentum than spending time with Jesus, downloading a picture of a better future for the people that I serve. Likewise, I have never found a bigger killer of momentum than spending time focusing on what is not happening or what I do not have.

Deciding not to decide

Life is full of decisions and sometimes the purposes of God can feel out of reach. We feel like we do not have the clarity to make solid and confident decisions.

Faith creates a tension. When we have clarity on what we desire we can often lack clarity on how we get there. This lack of clarity creates increased dependence on God's ability to orchestrate all things for our good (Rom 8:28). It also creates an interdependence between believers because we realise that the pieces of the jigsaw that make up the picture of what we want to see happen lie inside relationships.

Desperation for clarity causes us to go deeper in relationships with people. As we make ourselves vulnerable with others we make ourselves relatable and people connect to our purpose as we inspire them to go for theirs! Remember, God is an interconnected God and so the edges of our lives and plans will always appear incomplete. Our completeness comes through Him and the Body of Christ (one another).

While focusing on WHO we are in Christ and crystallising the WHY of our lives, God will cause clarity on the HOW and WHAT to come through connections with other people.

Kingdom Key: *If you don't know what you're doing, pray to the Father. He loves to help. You'll get his help, and won't be condescended to when you ask for it. Ask boldly, believingly, without a second thought. People who "worry their prayers" are like wind-whipped waves. Don't think you're going to get anything from the Master that way, adrift at sea, keeping all your options open* (James 1:5-8, The Message).

There is one thing you can be sure of - the moment you are in indecision you need to make a decision.

I would rather make the wrong decision in faith than wait for a right decision without faith. God can move me in the right direction toward the right outcomes but only if I am creating movement. Indecision is a lack of faith and without faith I cannot please God. Pray to God with certainty about what you are believing for and do not 'worry through your prayers.'

Contradictions left unchallenged

We all carry internal contradictions and when left unchallenged we become unproductive and ineffective. Paul's Letter to the Romans (chapters 7-8) helps us to see that we are walking contradictions. We desire to do one thing but end up doing something else that we were determined not to do.

Why do we leave our contradictions unchallenged? Like many of the 'non-urgent' but important activities in life, we live in blissful ignorance that they are having an underlying negative impact. In fact we spend a lot of time and energy dealing with the symptoms of these contradictions.

Many people see getting their car serviced as a waste of money. Others regard physical exercise as a waste of time. However, these activities help maintain or even improve efficiency. By not dealing with these things, the loss in efficiency actually means that we are wasting time and energy. Our investment in the non-urgent but important activities of life protects us against ineffectiveness. The same is true when it comes to the 'non-urgent' and yet highly essential process of prayer and reading the Bible.

Kingdom Key: *If the axe is dull and its edge unsharpened, more strength is needed, but skill will bring success* (Ecclesiastes 10:10).

The light of God's Word, the power of His presence, the observation of a leader or friend, can all help sharpen us, challenge us and remove the bluntness of our internal contradictions.

Comfortable Goals

It is the stretch of a goal that causes the potential of an individual or group of people to be unlocked. Revelation of a bigger future creates an immediate gap between our ability and what is required to see the goal met. For the believer this causes us to dig for a deeper revelation of who we are in Christ, and to increase trust and reliance on Him which creates momentum. A comfortable goal can be achieved in our own strength and does not require untapped potential.

Kingdom Key: *Trust in the Lord with all your heart and lean not on your own understanding; in all your ways submit to Him, and He will make your paths straight* (Proverbs 3:5-6).

Our goal has to cause us to lean into God, to trust Him entirely with the result. The moment we have it all figured out is the moment we know the goal is not big enough.

Uncomfortable goals + Total dependence on God = Unlocked Kingdom potential

Momentum Builders

Momentum builders often come in the form of problems. It is important that as people of faith we are able to see the raw potential that exists inside the moment of stress, struggle, uncertainty, crisis and failure. In faith we can view these moments from the inside-out in the following way:

From Mayhem to Momentum

There is a great example of how David suddenly found himself in crisis and how he used it to build the momentum of victory from his defeated situation.

Upon returning to Ziklag after being out at battle David's world was suddenly turned upside down. He experienced the mayhem of a personal crisis, leadership challenge and mutiny. However, he demonstrated how the power to change any situation is not to turn inward in fear, but to go to God in faith.

Kingdom Key: *David and his men reached Ziklag on the third day. Now the Amalekites had raided the Negev and Ziklag. They had attacked Ziklag and burned it, and had taken captive the women and everyone else in it, both young and old. They killed none of them, but carried them off as they went on their way.*

When David and his men reached Ziklag, they found it destroyed by fire and their wives and sons and daughters taken captive. So David and his men wept aloud until they had no strength left to weep. David's two wives had been captured—Ahinoam of Jezreel and Abigail, the widow of Nabal of Carmel. David was greatly distressed because the men were talking of stoning him; each one was bitter in spirit because of his sons and daughters (1 Samuel 30:1-6).

From Stress to Strength

Stress is when that which is external to us exerts force upon us. It is when these forces feel stronger than us, crushing any strength we carry inside, bringing the risk of implosion.

David had extreme pressure placed on him all at once. Not only did he have to deal with the personal crisis of not knowing where his family was or even if they were alive, he lost the support of his men who were disorientated in their grief. David's life was in danger because they were venting their anger on him and in the midst of all this he had to lead.

With his back against the wall David had the key - his relationship with God: But David found strength in the Lord his God (1 Samuel 30:6b).

The reason we can turn stress to strength is because as Christ followers we know we have a supply of strength that can overcome any external force. The prophet Isaiah reminds us of this and how we can renew that strength so that we can grow through the challenges we face.

Kingdom Key: *The Lord is the everlasting God, the Creator of the ends of the earth. He will not grow tired or weary, and His understanding no one can fathom. He gives strength to the weary and increases the power of the weak. Even youths grow tired and weary, and young men stumble and fall; but those who hope in the Lord will renew their strength. They will soar on wings like eagles; they will run and not grow weary, they will walk and not be faint* (Isaiah 40:28b-31).

It is when we start to believe that our stressful situations cannot change that we cross the borders into the dangerous territory of hopelessness. It is then that we must remember that hope is not a circumstance or even a plan, it is a person and His name is Jesus. He is ready to supply our need when we call. Our demand for more strength will never outweigh God's supply of strength for our lives. Your refill is only a prayer away!

If we want to create momentum, step 1 is about stopping and waiting. Practically you need to make sure you regain your physical strength, eat and sleep well and spend some time with God. Very often we do not feel we can afford to do this but the truth is that we cannot afford not to do this. This is where we have to draw on the strength of relationships that we have, being unafraid to ask for help in order to create this necessary space.

From Struggle to Strategy

Step 2 of creating momentum from mayhem is to take our struggle into God's presence and download heaven's strategy.

1 Samuel 30:7-8: *Then David said to Abiathar the priest, the son of Ahimelek, "Bring me the ephod." Abiathar brought it to him and David inquired of the Lord, "Shall I pursue this raiding party? Will I overtake them?"*

I do not think that David's decision to seek God was an

emotional impulse but more a case of having to tell himself what to do in this situation. He led himself by taking the disciplined steps to respond and not react in the heat of the situation. Out of his conversation with God came his strategy.

"Pursue them," he answered. "You will certainly overtake them and succeed in the rescue."

We may not hear the audible voice of God but when we take our struggle into God's presence, our motivation is weighed before God and our desires are aligned to His. This creates the right soil for great choices to be birthed in our thinking.

I believe our plans will please God when we work them from the inside-out. When our spirit is aligned and in charge we can then align the desires of our soul and find ourselves ready to unlock the potential that He has already placed inside us.

I recommend setting some time aside to take a big sheet of paper and a pen and whilst in God's presence make the struggle plain on paper and start to allow your desires to be shaped by God. Allow the Holy Spirit to unlock your imagination and get a vision for the next steps.

From Uncertainty to Certainty

David left that place certain what he needed to do and while not every step was made clear, he knew that when you act in faith on what you do know, God works with that faith and it unlocks the activity of heaven in a situation.

1 Samuel 30:9-10: *David and the six hundred men with him came to the Besor Valley, where some stayed behind. Two hundred of them were too exhausted to cross the valley, but David and the other four hundred continued the pursuit.*

While we don't have all the details of what happened in this situation, I believe it was David's strength of conviction and sense of certainty that caused the men to regain their confidence and hope and to follow David despite each man having their own personal crisis of not knowing where their loved ones were. David was selective with the men he took forward with him because he knew he needed those who could fully engage with the plan.

Step 3 for creating momentum from your mayhem is to clarify what you do have certainty about and to stop focusing on what you are uncertain about. What you focus on you feed and what you feed grows. David chose to focus on what he could do in this situation and by doing so inspired his men to do the same.

A leader's job is to create focus on a shared outcome and to keep everyone moving in the same direction towards that single goal.

Galvanise everything that is in your power behind what you do know.

From Crisis to Compassion

The last thing you feel you want when you are facing your own crisis is to get involved in someone else's crisis. Whilst in pursuit of the raiding party who were responsible for the destruction at Ziklag, David and his men see a man in need. Rather than ignoring him with the 'valid' excuse of their own crisis, they decide to stop and offer help.

1 Samuel 30:11-12: *They found an Egyptian in a field and brought him to David. They gave him water to drink and food to eat— part of a cake of pressed figs and two cakes of raisins. He ate and was revived, for he had not eaten any food or drunk any water for three days and three nights.*

Our crisis is often a wakeup call to get compassionate about other people in crisis. Crises soften hearts and cause us to become increasingly aware of other people in need.

Step 4 is to ask yourself, who is God making you aware of through your crisis? When you serve someone else's crisis, God gets involved in yours (Proverbs 19:17).

David's compassion unlocked God's provision. This was no ordinary man in need. He was the key to unlock their situation.

1 Samuel 30:13-15: *David asked him, "Who do you belong to?*

Where do you come from?"

He said, "I am an Egyptian, the slave of an Amalekite. My master abandoned me when I became ill three days ago. We raided the Negev of the Kerethites, some territory belonging to Judah and the Negev of Caleb. And we burned Ziklag."

David asked him, "Can you lead me down to this raiding party?"

He answered, "Swear to me before God that you will not kill me or hand me over to my master, and I will take you down to them."

The keys to unlock your situation lie in unlikely places with unlikely people so be ready to experience the 'unlikely' provision of God as you are obedient.

From Failure to Future

At the start of this crisis David could have called it a failure of leadership and withdrawn from the men. It is so easy to draw conclusions far too early. We are often tempted to make permanent decisions in temporary situations. However, this story and many others in the Bible teach us to hold our nerve and trust in God.

Kingdom Key: *Keep vigilant watch over your heart; that's where life starts. Don't talk out of both sides of your mouth; avoid careless banter, white lies, and gossip. Keep your eyes straight ahead; ignore all sideshow distractions. Watch your step, and the road will stretch out smooth before you. Look neither right nor left; leave evil in the dust* (Proverbs 4:25-27).

When we focus on God and where our heart is we put ourselves in a proactive state ready to work with heaven on our Kingdom assignment. In the remaining part of 1 Samuel 30 (verses 21-31) we see that this situation established some key convictions in David that became the foundation for his reign as King. Not only that, David shared the plunder from this victory with other nations and through this act of generosity he built a platform with people who would become allies in the future years. Little did he know that Saul was about to die and he was going to take the throne.

Your mayhem is ready to create momentum if you are willing to follow these steps.

Conversation with God:

Father God, help me to remember these steps in moments of mayhem. I thank you that you are my all-sufficient one and you never leave my side. I choose to be in faith when it feels easier to give in to fear. I thank you that you are committed to the development of my character.

Day 66: The Enjoyment of Winning

Winning from a place of rest

Why would an almighty and all-powerful God need to rest? It always amazes me that God chose to rest on the seventh day after creating the earth. I do not think this is so much about God needing to take 'a breather' as a revelation of the nature of God and the rhythms of heaven.

As we have established throughout this book, the rhythms of the Kingdom work counter to the rhythms of the world. The Kingdom of God can appear upside-down whereas in fact once we live in the Kingdom we realise that they are the right way up for our design.

Jesus modelled the rhythms of heaven whilst outworking his three years of ministry on earth. Jesus exhibited that effective Kingdom DOING comes out of effective Kingdom investment in our BEING. To try and fulfil the Kingdom assignment using the rhythms of the world is to create an unmanageable and incompatible combination. Trust me, I've tried! Many people have crashed out of pursuing their Kingdom assignment because they discovered the harsh reality of this incompatibility.

Kingdom Key: *Jesus resumed talking to the people, but now tenderly. "The Father has given me all these things to do and say. This is a unique Father-Son operation, coming out of Father and Son intimacies and knowledge. No one knows the Son the way the Father does, nor the Father the way the Son does. But I'm not keeping it to myself; I'm ready to go over it line by line with anyone willing to listen.*

Are you tired? Worn out? Burned out on religion? Come to me. Get away with me and you'll recover your life. I'll show you how to **take a real rest. Walk with me and work with me—watch how I do it.** *Learn the u**nforced rhythms of grace.** I won't lay anything heavy or ill-fitting on you. Keep company with me and you'll learn to live freely and lightly"* (Matthew 11:27-30, The Message).

Let's pick up on three phrases from this passage:

Take a 'real rest'

While the rest that Jesus is referring to does incorporate time given to recreation and relaxation, Jesus is referring to a rest that undergirds everything that we do. The 'real rest' Jesus embodies in the Gospels is that intimacy with the Father that builds a strong sense of WHO I am (Matthew 14:23). In addition to this He built Himself up through declaring Scripture (Luke 4:4, 8,10) which crystallized WHY He came to earth (His assignment). Jesus also incorporated the disciplines of prayer, meditative study and fasting to maintain rest.

Rest is not about ticking a box on our to-do list. It's a posture, a disposition of allowing our conversation with God to be intertwined in all that we do.

Jesus helped those people who were becoming burned out with religion. Religion overemphasises the HOW and the WHAT, causing the WHO and WHY to die. This is of course a victory for Satan who knows that it is the WHO and WHY that unlocks Kingdom potential. He is undeterred by Christians who are focused on the HOW and WHAT because these are the 'seen' things of this life which ultimately do not have any bearing on eternal matters.

Walk, Work and Watch

We know that Jesus is not compromising on the Kingdom results he is looking for when He advocates a life lived from a position of rest. In fact it is the key to fruitfulness. Remember that growth ultimately is in God's hands (1 Corinthians 3:6); our job is to create an environment conducive to growth.

As we walk with Christ, work with Him and watch for what He is blessing, we move from 'getting' God to make stuff happen to 'letting' God do what He wants to do.

Learn the Unforced Rhythms of Grace

The Psalmist helps us see that the manifestation of God's presence never comes from a place of human striving - as if we can make God manifest - but from a place of rest.

Kingdom Key: *He says, "Be still, and know that I am God; I will be exalted among the nations, I will be exalted in the earth"* (Psalm 46:10).

When we create an internal state of stillness and rest and live from this place, His Kingdom will flow through us. As I have reiterated throughout this book, this is about order.

Every one of us is expected to produce results. We live in a results-driven world. The constant challenge is that the world expects instant results and often gives little room or time for natural rhythms through process to take place. What an amazing opportunity for people of God's Kingdom to show how things should work. We are to be walking examples of how a correct order can unlock the potential inside of us.

Results in the Kingdom are not forced; they are a bi-product of prizing God's process in our lives. The results of the Kingdom are not separate from the results that are demanded by your job. Just as any branch connected to a tree is fruitful if the tree is rooted into good ground, so anything connected to you will bear fruit if you focus on being planted in the right conditions of WHO you are and WHY you are alive.

Build a Winning Future for Others

Whatever our current job or role in life, we are all called to help unlock the potential in the lives of other people. Dare I say that we will live lives of quiet or public dissatisfaction until we realise that this is the goal for which we have been designed. My hope is that you get a taste of how you can become effective for the Kingdom of

God in **ANY** context if you live according to the principles of the Kingdom and cultivate a winning conversation.

Be Part of a Winning Movement

Why not let me know if you are interested in joining our coaching movement. I believe that Christians have a great opportunity to serve their communities and sectors through their winning purpose. I believe that every Christian should be a coach in their working environment. This may or not be a recognised part of your official role, but I hope you can now see that every conversation has the potential to be a coaching conversation to unlock the MORE that lies inside every human being. My belief is that ultimately the potential inside a person is unlocked when they become connected to Father God through a relationship with Jesus Christ.

If you do not have a faith in Jesus Christ then before you start this book again why not join me in a moment of prayer where you can start the one conversation that shapes all other conversations.

First Conversation with God:

Father God I thank you that sent Jesus to this world to re-establish the connection between mankind and yourself.

I am thankful you loved me enough to allow Jesus to be crucified to pay the price for my sin.

I believe that He rose again and now I can come to you through my faith in the Lord Jesus Christ.

I choose today to start my conversation with you.

I want to see the Kingdom of God transform my life and serve God by seeing the lives of others transformed in this world.

Thank you that I now have the assurance of a place in heaven and I commit my life to following you.

Amen.'

SECTION 10: THE WINNING MOMENTUM

Made in the USA
Columbia, SC
04 December 2018